Abraham Lincoln
The Man & His Faith

G. FREDERICK OWEN

Tyndale House Publishers, Inc.
Wheaton, Illinois

Originally published under the title
A Heart That Yearned for God,
by Third Century Publishers, Inc.,
who have granted permission for this
Tyndale House Publishers. Inc. edition.

Sixth printing, March 1989
Library of Congress Catalog Card Number 81-52112
ISBN 0-8423-0000-7
Copyright © 1976 by G. Frederick Owen.
Printed in the United States of America

In the dome of the
Library of Congress at Washington
is the inscription from the Prophet Micah:
"What doth the Lord require of thee,
but to do justly, and to love mercy,
and to walk humbly with thy God."
No man in American history—
no man in the history of the world—
ever more completely filled this measure
of a man of God than did
Abraham Lincoln.

—Dr. John Wesley Hill

In this marble temple, as in the hearts of the people for whom he saved the union, the memory of Abraham Lincoln is enshrined forever.

CONTENTS

Introduction

In this book we have a wonderfully fine full length story of the life and faith of Abraham Lincoln. In graphic, absorbing style the author takes Lincoln's own words, and the accounts of those who knew him, and weaves an authentic and unforgettable narrative of the life, religion, and statesmanship of the greatest American of the past two hundred years — in fact some think the greatest life lived since Jesus Christ.

Running like a scarlet thread throughout his life is the wholesome instruction and sacred influence of his Christian mother. Her life, her parting words, and the Scriptures which she read to him and his sister Sarah put iron in his soul and a hunger for God and righteousness which often surfaced in the many changing scenes of his great and eventful life. His rise to fame and usefulness, and his poise is unparalleled in modern times.

Dr. Owen has so vividly portrayed for us the life and faith of this great American that I have been profoundly moved, and I believe thousands of other lives will gather inspiration, wisdom, and lasting good as they follow Abe Lincoln from his birth in that Kentucky log cabin to his final burial in the finest tomb ever erected on the American continent.

Mrs. Dawson Trotman

Foreword

Abraham Lincoln, like Moses, and Paul, and Luther, was one of those rare spiritual giants that emerged in history towering above and beyond his own time and his own country. As Americans we select him as a pattern of true Americanism. And certainly no man ever pondered more deeply his own way of life as it related to God, the welfare of his fellowman and his country. No other American has been so greatly loved, so largely quoted, and so indelibly stamped on the memories of our people. From the awesome Lincoln Monument in Washington to the penny in our pockets we are bidden to think about this strange and mystical figure who haunts us and bids us to better ways of life.

What is the secret of his hold upon the thinking of so many different people from all over the world? Many of us are convinced that Lincoln cannot be explained apart from his faith in God and his growing love for Christ and the Bible. On March 4th, 1861 Lincoln places his hand on an open Bible and became the 16th president of the United States. Four years later on March 4th, 1865 on a rainy day, he placed his hand on the Bible again to assume the oath of office for the second time, but the Bible was a different book for him now. The events of four years in the White House had driven him to God in prayer and into a search of the Scriptures and a spiritual pilgrimage such as no other president has ever known. His second inaugural address sounds like a sermon on the will of God in the life of a nation. Its citations of Scripture are so frequent that the second inaugural address must factually be regarded as the most official religious document in American history.

Lincoln's faith caused him to see that law and constitutional government are a great gift from God. His sense of justice made him know that no man was wise enough or good enough to be the master and owner of another. The conviction that the union must be preserved and that slaves must be freed laid upon him a simple but terrible responsibility. He believed that the task of saving freedom under God was the purpose for which God had made him an instrument in His "Almighty hand for His almost chosen people."

This book with its clear prose, new insights and common sense regarding Lincoln should be a blessing and inspiration to all people of all ages in life who pray and look for leadership in this momentous generation.

Billy and Ruth Graham

ix

A Heart That Yearned for God

Some years ago, while in company with friends, we were approaching Westminster Abbey in London. There in the park facing that national shrine was a large, fine statue of Abraham Lincoln.

Being somewhat surprised, I said, "So you have Lincoln here, too."

"Oh, yes," said my English banker friend, "We admire him as one of the great men of all times — perhaps the greatest aside from Jesus Christ."

As we continued our travels in other countries, we found that the life, character, and achievements of Abraham Lincoln had in a very profound manner gripped the hearts and deeply impressed the minds of men in almost every land. Even in the remotest corners of the earth he had become to many the very embodiment of all that is good. His very name had been dwelt upon with reverence and hope.

Being only an average American with no teaching in Lincolnism, other than that gained in the schools, I was hardly prepared to hear such praise of him as had fallen from the lips of the London banker, or to fully understand the estimates of so many in other lands. Not until I had lived in Washington and Springfield—the two cities where Lincoln wrought so heroically—and had made a special study of Lincoln, did I know that the Hon. John Hay, who was Lincoln's private secretary, and himself a statesman of sterling worth, had called Lincoln "the greatest man since Jesus Christ" *or that Tolstoy had even gone so far as to picture Lincoln as* "a minature Christ."

With Lincoln's life a matter of record, and with so many great men's estimates of Lincoln's character in print, I then came to wonder how so many Americans—even professors in high schools, colleges and universities—could question Lincoln's Christianity, or even go so far as to style him "an unbeliever", "a religious skeptic", "a deist", "an agnostic", "an infidel", or even "an atheist". I now understand—they did not know Lincoln, nor his deepest heart yearnings after God.

1

CHAPTER 1
Parentage and Early Training

Near Elizabethtown, Kentucky, a certain camp meeting had been in progress for several days when a strangely divine religious fervor settled over the congregation. The people waited with an awed intensity, when suddenly the camp was spiritually stirred. The kneeling multitude sprang to their feet and broke into a chorus of shouts which rang through the woods of the campground.

A young man, who had been absorbed in earnest prayer, arose and began leaping and shouting praise to God. Simultaneously, a young woman sprang forward, her eyes fixed heavenwards and her lips vocal with a sweet heavenly song. Her joy increased until, grasping the hand of the young man, they blended their voices in ecstatic melody.[1]

A week leter, on June 12, 1806, these two-Thomas Lincoln and Nancy Hanks-were married by the Rev. Jesse Head, "according to the laws of the Methodist Church, and the State of Kentucky." Friends and neighbors from far and wide came to the wedding supper. They were served "bear meat, venison, wild turkey and ducks, eggs wild and tame . . . maple sugar swung on a string, syrup in big gourds, peach and honey, and a sheep that the two families

2

barbecued whole over coals of wood burned in a pit. . ."[2]

After marriage the couple occupied the new log house Thomas had built for them on two residence lots which he owned in Elizabethtown. He was a carpenter and road surveyor, widely known for his honesty and good sense. What a home it must have been, for Nancy was highly intelligent, cheerful, devout, competent, industrious-skilled in spinning, weaving, and all the household arts of the day.[3]

Above all she possessed a deep religious strain which characterized both her appearance and conduct. The following year the Lincoln's first child was born; they named her Sarah. Soon after this they moved to a farm which Thomas had purchased on the Big South fork of Nolin Creek, three miles from Hodgensville, and about fourteen miles from Elizabethtown. Here they lived in a large one-roomed log cabin with a "huge" outside chimney, a single window, and a home-made door. Their domestic happiness was increased when just at sunrise, on the Sabbath morning of February 12, 1809, a boy was born to Thomas and Nancy Hanks Lincoln.

They named the boy "Abraham" after his grandfather. When Nancy was stronger she patted little Abe and vowed to rear him for God and humanity. She dreamed, as all mothers do, of a great future for her son. But she could not have dreamed anything so wonderful as the future would be.[4] Another child, a boy, came to the Lincoln home a year later, but lived only a few days.

In May, 1811, Thomas Lincoln purchased a 230 acre farm on Knob Creek about eight miles from Hodgenville. It was good farm land, yet on it were tall trees and bluffs and gorges which made it a place of beauty. The creek and its tributaries teamed with fish, and the surrounding hills were full of game. It was here in this serene and restful environment that Abraham Lincoln lived from the beginning of his third year to the end of his seventh year. It was here he received his formative and lasting impressions of Kentucky and of life.

Abe and Sarah went to school a few months out of two years. Nancy Hanks Lincoln helped them with their lessons and taught them constantly at home. Thomas Lincoln told them pioneer stories and Abe remembered especially the one about his grandfather who was at work near his cabin with his sons, Mordecai, Josiah, and Thomas, when a shot from the bushes brought him down.

Mordecai ran to the house and seized a gun, and looking through a window, saw an Indian in war paint stooping to pick up Thomas. Mordecai fired and killed the savage, then fired at the others in the bushes and frightened them away.

The Bible was one of the few books in the home of Thomas and Nancy Hanks Lincoln. And it was from his mother's lips that little Abe first heard the sublime Bible stories and verses. And, with her encouragement, he began to commit to memory short Bible verses, and to become familiar with the simpler aspects of the moral code laid down in the Bible. Later he could repeat from memory whole Psalms and other chapters.

Thomas and Nancy Lincoln were active members of the Little Mount Baptist Church and church-going was a regular part of the Lincoln family life. From the pastor, and from Methodist circuit riders and evangelists of rare eloquence, Abe received lasting impressions. These men of God not only cooperated with his parents in teaching him "a healthy code of morals," but from them he received "his first notion of public speaking." For years afterwards one of Abe's chief delights was to gather his playmates about him and preach until his young auditors were moved—sometimes to tears. [5]

In the autumn of 1816 the instinct to move westward came over Thomas Lincoln, "partly on the account of slavery, but chiefly on the account of the difficulty in land titles in Kentucky." He sold his farm, and bidding his wife be ready to go into the wilderness on his return, he loaded their meager household goods upon a small flatboat of his own construction and floated down Knob Creek, Salt River, and the Ohio to a point on the north banks of the river where the household goods were left in storage. Sixteen miles away in Spencer County, Indiana, he staked out an eighty acre tract by piling up brush at the four corners, and erecting a hunter's half-face camp. He then returned to Kentucky for his family.

Nancy Lincoln took Sarah and Abe to the tiny grave of her youngest child and the three said good-by to the little one whom the children had scarcely known, but "for whom the mother's grief was so keen that the boy never forgot the scene." [6]

The journey of almost a hundred miles was one of long delight and wonder. Abe "saw forests greater than he had ever dreamed of, peopled by strange birds and beasts, and he crossed a river (the Ohio) so wide that it must have seemed to him like a sea." [7]

When the family arrived where their household goods had been left, a wagon was hired, and Thomas Lincoln, with Nancy and the two children and all his worldly possessions, moved to the wilderness land on Pigeon Creek in southwestern Indiana-near the present town of Gentryville. Here with the help of neighbors, Thomas built an eighteen foot square log house with a large fireplace and an overhead loft which served as Abe's bedroom. Wild turkey, deer, bear, and an abundance of smaller game such as duck, squirrel, rabbit, quail, and wild pigeons, were plentiful here. Abe shot a wild turkey with a rifle when he was only nine years of age. There was beauty in the woods, along with many kinds of nuts, and a great variety of berries and wild fruits. An ax was put into Abe's hands and he began to take his part in felling trees and clearing land.

Pigeon Creek community had organized a Baptist Church just before the Lincoln family moved there but there was no church building yet, and no minister to preach the Word, perform marriage ceremonies, or to bury the dead. The nearest doctor was thirty miles away.

When Abe was nine a mysterious malady called "milk sickness" fell upon the community and took a heavy toll. Nancy Hanks was a faithful nurse in caring for others. Finally she sickened, and in those days of illness Abe spent many hours reading to her from the Sacred Book. When he was almost ten she passed away and he treasured all through his life her last words:

I am going away from you, Abraham, and I shall not return. I know that you will be a good boy; and that you will be kind to Sarah and your father. I want you to live as I have taught you, to love your Heavenly Father and keep His commandments.[8]

Stunned by the blow which had fallen upon him, Thomas Lincoln, aided by Dennis Hanks, sawed and planed planks and made a coffin, fastening it together with wooden pegs which Abe had whittled. At sunset on the autumn day of October 5, 1818, they laid away their loved one in a clearing on the summit of a hill within sight of the cabin "she had made to bloom into a Christian home." No minister was available, therefore the grief-bowed father prayed a simple prayer "attended by the reading of a Bible passage as he knew that Nancy Hanks would have desired."[9]

That there was no complete religious service held by a minister weighed heavy on little Abe's heart. When spring came he secured his father's consent, and wrote to Rev. David Elkins, whom he had often heard preach at the Little Mount church near their home in Kentucky. He asked Rev. Elkins to come and preach the funeral sermon at his mother's grave.[10] The minister replied that he would be there to conduct the service on a certain Sunday. Parson Elkins journeyed on horseback and arrived on Wednesday. Word was sent to all neighbors for a score of miles around, and by Sunday there came together the greatest multitude that had ever gathered in the region.

As the hour drew near for service, they grew quiet and meditative. Wherever there was room they found rude seats on logs and stumps and even on the ground. The preacher offered prayer. With one accord the people sang a solemn funeral hymn. As next he eulogized the saintly woman, recollection mingled with respect and love, and honest grief was freely poured out for her whom they all recognized instinctively as the worthiest in that whole region to be a Christian wife and Christian mother to the ones who loved her best.

With the service ended, Parson Elkin flung himself into the saddle and headed South again. The settlers scattered on their homeward way. The family in quiet stole back to the cabin. Then when all were gone Abe turned toward the grave, flung himself upon the cold dead earth, wept as he had wept when first the clods fell on the coffin, and prayed and prayed to God to give him strength to live the life his mother would approve.[11]

Tom Lincoln and the children went often to visit Nancy's grave but they were never able to put up more than a simple uncut red sandstone marker to designate the grave of their noble pioneer mother. However, after sixty years had passed Mr. P. E. Studebaker, of South Bend, Indiana, raised a suitable memorial on which was inscribed:

NANCY HANKS LINCOLN
Mother of President Lincoln
Died Oct. 5, A.D. 1818
Aged thirty-five years

Lincoln never forgot his mother, or the influence of her Christian teaching upon his life. The resemblance between Abe and his mother, and a certain secret sympathy between them, intensified both his mind and his emotions.

"All that I am," he used to say, "my angel-mother made me." The memory that lingered longest was the thought of her as she sat in the old log cabin teaching him the *Ten Commandments*.

6

Many a time afterwards when he was asked how he had found courage to decline some tempting bribe, or resist some wrong suggestion, he said that in the critical hour he heard his mother's voice once more repeating the old old words: *"I am the Lord thy God; thou shalt have no other gods before me."* 12

CHAPTER II
Abe Grows to Manhood

A difficult year was in store for the Lincoln family after the passing of such a wonderful wife and mother who was the guiding spirit of the home. Twelve year old Sarah became housekeeper and cook while Abe helped his father clear more land and make things go on the farm. But in the lonely months after their mother's death, the Bible she had read and taught them to read was the greatest comfort he and his sister had.[1]

That winter a school was started in an unhewn log cabin about two miles from the Lincoln home. Andrew Crawford, the teacher, had been justice of the peace, and was fairly proficient in the three R's and "in the use of the birch rod." He not only taught the regular courses in reading, writing, and arithmetic, but cherished lofty notions of the importance of dignified manners. Therefore he offered an extra course in good manners, in which he taught his "scholars" some of the best usages of polite society—"showing how they were to enter a room, how to make and receive instructions, how a gentleman should salute a lady, how the lady should bow and curtsy." And, "it was noted that from this time Abe always removed his coon-skin cap in the presence of ladies."

Sometime afterwards James Swaney taught school in the community for a time, and Abe further "improved his learning."

While visiting a family, some twenty miles from their home, Thomas Lincoln observed an old, soiled copy of Bunyan's *Pilgrim's Progress*. Realizing its worth, he borrowed the book, and on returning home placed it in Abe's hands. The boy was so delighted his eyes sparkled; that day he could not eat, that night he was so deeply interested in the story that he could not sleep. So thrilled was Abe in following Christian to the Eternal City that he eagerly read the book from beginning to end, then was half way through it the second time when a lady heard of his love for reading and presented him a copy of *Aesop's Fables*. He read and reread the fables until he was so familiar with them he never forgot them or the lessons they were designed to teach.

From Josiah Crawford, a distant neighbor, he borrowed Weem's *Life of Washington*. A storm came, and the cover of the book was damaged. Young Abe pulled corn for three days to pay the neighbor for the book, and it became his very own. Thus, four great books entered his life: The *Bible* to teach him of God and moral responsibility; *Pilgrim's Progress* to stimulate his motives to one day reach Heaven; the *Life of Washington* to teach him love for and loyalty to his country; and *Aesop's Fables* from which he learned shrewdness and humor and the value of a story; which caused him, in after years, to frequently say, "That reminds me of a story."

After 13 months in a motherless home, Thomas Lincoln went away, promising Sarah and Abe that he would come back. He made his way to Elizabethtown, Kentucky, and presented himself at the home of Sarah Bush Johnson. In childhood, they had been playmates; now, she was a widow. Mr. Lincoln talked straight to the point, "I have no wife and you no husband. I come a purpose to marry you. I knowed you from a gal, and you knowed me from a boy. I've no time to lose; and if you're willing let it be done straight off." They were married the following day, December 2, 1819, by Rev. George L. Rogers, a Methodist minister, and soon started back for southern Indiana.

Abe and Sarah had a nice surprise some days later when four horses and a wagon came into their clearing and their father said,

"Here, children, is your new mommy."

The new mother came well provided with household furniture–"one fine bureau, one table, one set of chairs, one large clothes-chest, cooking utensils, knives, forks, bedding, and other articles." And tucked among the furniture, in the wagon, were three books: *Webster's Speller, Robinson Crusoe,* and *The Arabian Nights.* Abe seized upon these and read them over and over until their contents were his own. The new Mrs. Lincoln was a woman of energy, thrift, and gentleness, and at once made the cabin more homelike and helped the children with habits of cleanliness and comfort. Her presence and her smiles of motherly love radiated sunshine throughout the Lincoln home.

Sarah Bush Lincoln was a kind stepmother to Abe and Sarah. Abe became strongly attached to her, and she to him. She saw the depth of his mind and soul and provided quiet time for him while he read by the firelight "till he quit of his own accord"–which was often after the midnight hour. He secured a copy of *The Life of Benjamin Franklin,* and a *History of the United States,* and as he afterward told a friend that he "read through every book he had ever heard of in that county, for a circuit of fifty miles."

The second winter after his stepmother came, a school was started about four miles away by Azel W. Dorsey. He taught reading, spelling, and arithmetic. Abe learned to read more fluently and became a master speller. Abe's mother and his previous teachers had taught him to write, but Mr. Dorsey gave him special attention, and he practiced often until he became so proficient that he was soon known as the best penman in the community. This was considered such an accomplishment that some of the neighbors had him write letters and special documents for them.

Abe learned all kinds of farm work—to drive a team, to milk cows, to handle the old shovel-plow, to wield the sickle, to thresh wheat with a flail, to go to mill and have the grist turned into flour. His father taught him carpentry and cabinet-making, and in this capacity he often served as his father's assistant. He excelled as a woodsman. As he grew older he earned the reputation of being able to "strike with a maul heavier blows, and to sink an axe deeper into the wood" than anyone in that section of the country.

For twenty-five cents a day—paid to his father—he worked for the neighbors as "hostler, ploughman, wood-chopper, and carpenter, besides helping with the chores, and entertaining during the evening hour." He knew so many stories and fables, and was so entertaining, that no gathering he attended ever went without wholesome life. Little wonder that he never lacked for a job.

Many other families, much on the same social level with the Lincolns, settled in the Pigeon Creek Community. For the most part the traditions of old fashioned religion were in vogue, yet there were no camp meetings in this immediate area. A Baptist church was organized the first year the Lincolns came. Four years later a church building was erected with hewn logs, a fireplace, and brick chimney. Thomas Lincoln was the head carpenter, and Abe helped construct the building, then became the sexton.[2] The Lincoln family attended the church, and Thomas and Sarah later became members. Abe read the Bible, and frequently quoted from the Scriptures, yet he never made a profession of religion.

However, Abe Lincoln was far from being passive to the character forming forces which were in vogue about him. As Carl Sandburg has written, "At the Pigeon Creek settlement, while the structure of his (Abe's) bones, the build and hang of his torso, and limbs took shape, other elements, invisible yet permanent, traced their lines in the tissues of his head and heart." The plain, inspired preaching at the church; the Sabbath day, Christmas and Easter, along with the "clean burning fire" which he saw in the lives of certain Christian families who "said grace at meals" and had prayers "in the morning on rising, and evening prayers at bed-time;" left a sacred residue with him for life. Contemplation of time and death, the partners who have to be reckoned with in the scheme of life, caused Lincoln to copy and carry with him a certain rhyme:

Time! what an empty vapor 'tis!
    And days how swift they are:
Swift as an Indian arrow—
    Fly on like a shooting star,
The present moment just is here,
    Then slides away in haste,
That we can never say they're ours,
    But only say they're past.[3]

In the community gatherings there were games, story-telling and sometimes drinking. Abe usually excelled in the games, and was good at telling stories, but he took no part whatever in drinking.[4]

When Abe was sixteen years of age, a great revival meeting was conducted at the village of Rockford, four miles from the Lincoln home. The speaker in those services was Rev. James Smith, who

11

at that time was a traveling Cumberland Presbyterian minister. Years later, Rev. Smith became pastor of the First Presbyterian Church of Springfield, Illinois. Abe attended the revival, and heard the evangelist speak on "Is there no balm in Gilead. Is there no physician there." He was not only deeply impressed, but was to remember the text and the sermon for many years to come.

At the age of seventeen Abe had the physique of a man. He hired out for thirty-seven cents a day to James Taylor, who operated a ferry twelve miles away at Troy, Indiana, where Anderson Creek joined the Ohio River. In his leisure moments Abe built a small scow. One day two travelers rushed down to the river bank calling for transportation to a steamboat lying off the creek mouth. Young Lincoln put them in his scow and brought them alongside the steamer just as it took off. As the two men jumped aboard he pitched their carpet bags after them. Leaning over the rail, each man tossed a silver half-dollar into his boat, much to the astonishment of Abe, who "could scarcely credit that I, a poor boy, had earned a dollar in less than a day."[5]

On other occasions he carried passengers to midstream so they could board passing steamers. This led him into his first experience with the law. He was brought before Samuel Pate, a Kentucky justice of the peace, on complaint of the Dill Brothers, ferrymen from the Kentucky side. The Dills claimed to have exclusive right under a Kentucky license to ferry across the stream from Kentucky, whereas Lincoln had no right to ferry across from the Indiana side. Abraham pleaded his own case. He said he did not take passengers entirely across the river, but only carried them to midstream in order that they might board the steamers when there was no other way for them to get there. Thus he had not "set them over the river" and therefore had not violated the Kentucky statute which required a license for such service. Judge Pate sustained Abraham's defense and released him. This experience gave him a keen interest in law and the courts, and he frequently visited this little Kentucky court to hear cases tried and decided.[6]

In his seventeenth year, Abe wrote an essay on temperance which so impressed Aaron Farmer, a Baptist preacher of local renown, that he sent it to an Ohio newspaper for publication. About this time Lincoln also prepared an essay on the American government, calling attention to the necessity of preserving the Constitution and the perpetuation of the Union. John Pitcher, a lawyer, who afterwards became a judge declared this composition "a world beater." [7]

When young Lincoln was nineteen, James Gentry, the merchant at Gentryville, employed him to assist his son Allen in taking a cargo boat loaded with produce down the Ohio and the Mississippi rivers to New Orleans. At night they tied up alongside the river bank and slept upon the deck, during the day the craft floated down the stream under the direction of its helmsmen. Abe and Allen were pleased with their work and never for a moment regretted their acceptance of the positions they occupied. Nothing occurred to mar the success of the trip, nor the excitement of a flatboat expedition of some eighteen hundred miles.

However, one night they were attacked by seven negros who were intent on killing and robbing them. They succeeded in driving the negros from the boat, then 'cut cable', 'weighed anchor' and left. On arriving in New Orleans the two young merchants sold their goods at a handsome profit, saw many things in the strange, glamorous city, then returned to Indiana by river boat.

CHAPTER III
Lincoln On His Own At New Salem

In the spring of 1830, soon after Abe came of age, the Lincoln family sold their Indiana home, put all their possessions into two wagons drawn by ox teams and started for Illinois. Abe drove one of the teams. At Vincennes they stopped for several days to gather supplies and repair wagons. Abe visited the shop which produced the *Western Sun,* and for the first time in his life he saw a printing press. The family then crossed the rain-swollen Wabash River near a point where Lincoln Memorial Bridge now spans that historic stream. Facing north westward, they traveled onward over prairie lands where wild grass waved and bowed before the breeze like the tide of a summer sea, and across streams where beavers built dams and wild pigeons came in clouds that shadowed the sun.

One day, after fording a river, the Lincoln family discovered that they had left Abe's dog on the other side. The banks were fringed with broken ice and the dog was whining piteously and afraid to make the plunge. Had Abe followed the counsel of the family, he would have left the frightened animal; but he couldn't

14

endure the thought of abandoning the dog. So the family waited while he waded the icy stream and returned with his quivering pet under his arm. Lincoln afterwards declared that the dog's frantic leaps of joy, and other demonstrations of gratitude were sufficient reward for his efforts.[1]

About ten miles west of Decatur, Illinois, the Lincoln family settled a new place on the north side of the Sangamon River. Abraham stayed with his father long enough to help build a log cabin, clear some ground, and split sufficient rails to fence ten acres of ground. This was the last regular work he ever did for his father.

During part of the winter of 1830, Abe split rails for Major Warnick, who was sheriff of Macon County. For two weeks he was laid up with frozen feet, but occupied this time in reading and studying a set of the laws of Illinois which Major Warnick had in his home.

Before the winter was over Abraham, together with his stepmother's sons, John D. Johnston, and John Hanks, hired themselves to Denton Offutt, a speculating businessman of Springfield. They agreed to take a flatboat loaded with merchandise from Beardstown, Illinois, to New Orleans. In March they purchased a large canoe and came down the Sangamon River where they met Mr. Offutt at Springfield, only to learn that he had failed in getting a flatboat at Beardstown. This led to their hiring themselves to him for twelve dollars per month each, and in a reasonably short time the three men cut the timber from government land above the mouth of Spring Creek, floated it down to a mill on the Sangamon River, seven miles northwest of Springfield, and had it sawn into planks.

About the middle of April the boat was finished and loaded with provisions, and started down the Sangamon. In going over the mill dam at New Salem the heavy flatboat stuck, and the bow of the boat began to fill with water. Abe and his assistants unloaded the cargo, consisting mostly of barrels of pork. Lincoln then went ashore, borrowed an augur at Onstot's Copper Shop, bored a hole in the hull at the bow, tipped the boat forward with the bow suspended over the dam and the water drained out. When the hole was plugged, the boat was eased over the dam into the water below. The cargo was reloaded and the boys were soon on their way. The villagers who had watched the large ungainly young man direct operations in the flatboat episode formed the opinion that "the

15

big fellow knew his business."

Since this was Abe's second trip to New Orleans, he maneuvered the flatboat onto the waters of the Mississippi River. After floating downriver for more than a thousand miles, he finally arrived in the great Southern port where he disposed of the cargo to good advantage. For nearly four weeks Lincoln stayed in New Orleans getting what knowledge he could of the place, the people, and their customs.

He, along with the young men with him, "saw negroes chained, maltreated, whipped and scourged." In their rambles, they came upon a slave auction where a fine mulatto girl was being pinched and prodded and trotted up and down the room like a horse to show how she moved, that 'bidders might satisfy themselves,' as the auctioneer said, 'of the soundness of the article he sold.' He saw a mother sold to one bidder and her child to another. Lincoln left the auction with a bleeding heart, with iron in his soul, and a resolution that "If I ever get a chance to hit that thing, I'll hit it hard."

To work his way home Abe helped fire a boiler on a Mississippi steamer to St. Louis. From there he walked back to visit his parents and helped them move to a new home at Goose Next Prairie. Then he headed for New Salem to await the arrival of Denton Offutt, with the goods for a new store in which Lincoln was to be his assistant.

Soon after his arrival in New Salem, the townspeople gathered in a store building to conduct an election. One Mentor Graham was officiating as election clerk. The other election clerk, a young merchant by the name of John McNamar, was ill. Graham, learning that Lincoln could write, asked him to take McNamar's place. Lincoln did so and thus, from the very beginning, took part in the politics of New Salem and Sangamon County.

Mentor Graham, the election clerk and schoolmaster, was a man of stalwart character and unusual worth in the community. He lived in a brick house about a mile west of town, and taught the community school, for which he received a tuition of five cents per day for each pupil.

Denton Offutt's stock of merchandise finally arrived and Abe Lincoln began his career as a merchant. The store was located on the bluff above the river near Bill Clary's grocery which was a hangout for the Clary's Grove boys when they came to town "to trade, gossip, drink or play." They were a rough crowd — reckless and fearless but known to be as loyal to a friend as they were implacable to a foe. Jack Armstrong was their leader, and in "free for all" fights they had settled the question of supremacy with the boys of their own and other near-by settlements.

Offutt was an enthusiastic friend and supporter of his new clerk. He bragged continually of Lincoln's mental and physical might. He claimed that Abe was exceedingly smart, and that he could outrun, throw or whip any man in the community. The Clary's Grove boys sized up the situation and were willing to concede his intellectual superiority, but the physical honors had "to be won before they were worn."

Jack Armstrong challenged Lincoln to a wrestling match. All arrangements were made, and the crowd gathered in a square near Offutt's store. Armstrong was a "formidable opponent, experienced, hard, and heavy set." Lincoln stood six feet four inches and weighed 185 pounds. He had a frame that was gaunt but sinewy, and he possessed the self confidence of one who had been a recognized champion in his former home. At the beginning of the wrestling match the two men circled warily, grappled and twisted, neither able to throw the other. Then, after a long while, Armstrong began to get the worst of it. By a studied move, Lincoln was in the act of placing both of Jack's shoulders to the grass, when Armstrong's friends rushed in to aid him. Lincoln left Armstrong, backed against Offutt's store, denounced them for their unfairness and offered to fight any or all of them individually. None accepted. Then, to the astonishment of everyone concerned, the tense moments were broken by Jack Armstrong who hurried over and shook Lincoln's hand. They agreed to call the match a draw.[2]

The wrestling match gave Lincoln a reputation for courage, strength, and fairness with onlookers, and it convinced the Clary Grove boys that he "belonged." They admired his physical prowess and his own honesty and truthfulness soon won their confidence. During his remaining years in New Salem they followed and supported him in most everything he did. The boys made him judge of many of their contests. He once refereed a cock fight in which one of the roosters belonged to Babb McNabb. Babb had bragged about the fighting qualities of his bird but when it was matched with a seasoned veteran of the New Salem pit, Babb's rooster turned tail and ran. At a safe distance he mounted a fence, proudly spread his feathers and crowed lustly. Babb paid over his wager to the owner of the victor, then turning to his own bird he said, "Yes, you little cuss, you are great on dress parade, but not worth anything in a fight." Years later, when General McClellan was exhausting the patience of Lincoln and the country by continually drilling and reviewing the Army of the Potomac, but persistently refusing to fight, Lincoln remembered this incident and likened McClellan to Babb McNabb's rooster.[3]

To many, Lincoln soon came to be an authority to be respected somewhat on a level with a sheriff or constable. One day a man came into the store and began swearing in the presence of women. Lincoln asked the man to stop; but he persisted, fondly boasting that nobody should prevent his saying what he wanted to. When the women were gone, the man began abusing Lincoln so hotly that Abe said: "Well, if you must be whipped, I suppose I might as well whip you as any other man." Going outdoors with the fellow, Lincoln threw him on the ground and rubbed smart-weed in his eyes until he pleaded for mercy.

Abe's total honesty excited no less admiration. Two incidents seem to have particularly impressed the community. Having discovered on one occasion that he had taken six and one-quarter cents too much from a customer, he walked three miles that evening, after his store was closed, to return the money. Again, he weighed out a half-pound of tea, as he supposed. It was the last thing he had done before closing up at night. On entering in the morning he discovered a four-ounce weight in the scales. As soon as he saw his mistake, he closed shop and hurried to deliver the remainder of the tea. This unusual regard for the rights of others soon won him the title of "Honest Abe."[4]

During the autumn of 1831 the New Salem Debating Society was organized, largely under the influence of Dr. John Allen, Mentor Graham, and the more intellectual members of the village. Graham invited young Lincoln to the meetings. He came, paid rapt attention, and joined the society. When it came his time to debate "he arose to speak, his tall form towered above the little assembly. Both hands were thrust down deep into the pockets of his pantaloons. A perceptible smile at once lit up the faces of the audience, for all anticipated the relation of some humorous story. But he opened the discussion in splendid style, to the infinite astonishment of his friends. As he warmed to his subject, his hands would for-

18

sake his pockets, and enforce his thought by awkward gestures; but would very soon again seek their resting place. He pursued the question with reason and argument so pithy and forcible that all were amazed. The president, at his fireside after the meeting, remarked to his wife that there was more than wit and fun in Abe's head; that he was already a fine speaker; that all he lacked was culture to enable him to reach the high destiny that he knew was in store for him."[5]

Having considerable leisure time on his hands, Lincoln suggested to Mentor Graham that he "had a notion to study English grammar." Graham advised, "If you are going before the public you ought to do it." He then told him that he might borrow Kirkham's *English Grammar* from John C. Vance, who lived in a neighboring settlement six miles north. Without waiting to finish his meal, Abe set out on foot and in due time returned with the book. He studied it on every possible occasion — at times while lying full length on the counter with his head on a parcel of calico. When a passage was obscure he went to Graham for help. He had Bill Green ask questions from the book, while he recited answers and definitions. How well he mastered the subject is evidenced in all his after speaking and writing.

He read history, and his interest in literature was stimulated by Jack Kelso, the village philosopher, who did little labor and a lot of loafing. Kelso came often to the store and "opened to young Lincoln the magic pages of Shakespeare and Burns." Kelso's wife took in boarders to supplement his scant earnings. Lincoln boarded with them for a while and listened eagerly while Kelso read or quoted from Shakespeare and Burns. Other intellectuals lived in New Salem and contributed towards Lincoln's education: James Rutledge, whose library consisted of twenty-five or thirty volumes; Dr. Allen, a graduate of Dartmouth Medical College, who organized a Sunday School and a Temperance Society; Dr. Regnier, a capable colleague of Allen's; David Rutledge who organized the debating society; Rev. John M. Berry, a Presbyterian minister who pastored at Rock Creek and occasionally preached in New Salem; Bowling Green, Justice of the Peace; and Harvey Ross who carried the mail and attended Illinois College at Jacksonville. But Lincoln owed most to Mentor Graham; his ever readiness to help was a constant stimulus. David Rutledge said: "I know of my own knowledge that Graham did more than all others to educate Lincoln."[6]

Despite his friendship with the rather wild young men of Clary's Grove, Lincoln did not drink. Bill Green, Lincoln's helper at the store, came the nearest to getting Lincoln in question about liquor when he bet a man a good fur hat that Lincoln could lift a barrel of whiskey from the floor and hold it while he took a drink. The crowd gathered, and Lincoln sat on the floor, lifted the barrel off the floor, rolled it on his knees till the bunghole reached his mouth, took a mouthful, let the barrel down—stood up and spat out the whiskey. A year or two after this, he spoke on temperance at the nearby Presbyterian Church, yet pleaded for tolerance and sympathy for "the unfortunate class of fellow creatures" who had fallen victims to intemperance.

Lincoln was well-exposed to religion while at New Salem. He boarded at the home of John M. Cameron, who was not only the owner of the mill, but was an ordained minister in the Cumberland Presbyterian Church and part time preacher. His home was religious, and he had eleven daughters, some of whom teased Lincoln about his long legs and arms. His quaint reply was, "I'm not much to look at."

At the eating table or during candlelight Abe not only heard about how the village of New Salem was started, but he heard the Bible read, and at times was present at family prayers. All of this must have reminded him of the wonderful days when his mother lived.

The Rutledges were a deeply religious family. Onstot, Allen, Berry and Cameron were Presbyterians, while Mentor Graham and Joshua Miller were leading members of the Baptist Church. Various ministers preached in the school house at New Salem, and at Sand Creek, some seven miles southwest was "Walter's Camp" where a well known Methodist camp meeting was conducted annually.

Ten miles away, at Pleasant Plains, lived Rev. Peter Cartwright, the famous circuit rider and evangelist, who preached extensively in this section of the country. In those days young Lincoln knew of Cartwright and must have heard him at least a few times during his years at New Salem.

Lincoln grew in favor with his friends and neighbors until there was rekindled in him the longstanding desire to get into some kind of public service. On talking the matter over with his close friends, he decided to place himself in line for election as a member of the State Legislature.

Mentor Graham helped him, and on March 9, 1832, he announced his candidacy in a circular addressed directly to the voters of the county. On March Sixteenth it appeared in the *Sangamon Journal,* and opened with the splendid words:

> *FELLOW CITIZENS: Having become a candidate for the honorable office of one of your representatives in the next general assembly of this state, in accordance with an established custom and the principles of true republicanism, it becomes my duty to make known to you, the people whom I propose to represent, my sentiments with regard to local affairs.*[7]

Then there followed very thorough and thoughtful statements concerning internal improvements such as: a practical plan whereby the Sangamon River could be made navigable "to vessels of from twenty-five to thirty tons burden for at least one half of all common years, and to vessels of much greater burden a part of the year;" a law against usury; and amendments to the existing estray and road laws. Then came his remarkable pronouncement on education, as follows:

> *Upon the subject of education, not presuming to dictate any plan or system respecting it, I can only say that I view it as the most important subject which we as a people can be engaged in. That every man may receive at least a moderate education, and thereby be enabled to read the histories of his own and other countries, by which he may duly appreciate the value of our free institutions, appears to be an object of vital importance, even on this account alone, to say nothing of the advantages and satisfaction to be derived from all being able to read the Scriptures, and other works both of religious and moral nature, for themselves.*
>
> *For my part, I desire to see the time when education—and by its means, morality, sobriety, enterprise, and industry—shall become much more general than at present, and should be gratified to have it in my power to contribute something to the advancement of any measure which might have a tendency to accelerate that happy period.*[8]

The closing paragraph of this first declaration of Lincoln's was most remarkable in that it frankly revealed his very self and soul, as would be his custom in coming years. Note its directness:

> *But, fellow citizens, I shall conclude. Considering the great degree of modesty which should always attend youth, it is probable I have already been more presuming than becomes me. However, upon the subjects of which I have treated, I have spoken as I have thought. I may be wrong in regard to any or all of them; but, holding it a sound maxim that it is better only sometimes to be right than at all times to be wrong, so soon as I discover my opinions to be erroneous, I shall be ready to renounce them.*
>
> *Every man is said to have his peculiar ambition. Whether it be true or not, I can say, for one, that I have no other so great as that of being truly esteemed of my fellow men by rendering myself worthy of their esteem. How far I shall succeed in gratifying this ambition is yet to be developed. I am young, and unknown to many of you. I was born, and have ever remained, in the most humble walks of life. I have no wealthy or popular relations or friends to recommend me. My case is thrown exclusively upon the independent voters of the country; and, if elected, they will have conferred a favor upon me for which I shall be unremitting in my labors to compensate. But, if the good people in their wisdom shall see fit to keep me in the background, I have been too familiar with disappointments to be very much chagrined.* [9]

Thus it was that in March of 1832, less than two years after coming to Illinois, twenty-three year old Abraham Lincoln started on his public career.

Lincoln's advocacy of navigating the Sangamon River seemed a very timely one, for before the month was out a small, light-draft steamboat, the *Talisman* with merchandise cargo from Cincinnati arrived at Beardstown on the Illinois River. It was ready, when the ice jams cleared, to make the trip upstream to New Salem and Springfield.

The shipmaster asked for help and a boatload of men, including Lincoln, worked with long-handled poleaxes and crowbars, clearing the channel of snags and overhanging branches. Amidst cheers, laughter, and clapping of hands, the *Talisman* puffed and whistled her way up the Sangamon to New Salem, tied up at Portland Landing, seven miles north of Springfield. The city, then a place of some five hundred population, went wild in excitement and celebration. Springfield, they supposed, would become a great trading center. Their rejoicing was short-lived, however, for the *Talisman* lay only about a week at the landing when the receding water forced her to start the return trip. Rowan Herndon, an experienced boatman, was engaged to pilot her to Beardstown, and Lincoln was employed as his assistant. They made only four miles a day, and the boat barely kept afloat as the river fell. At New Salem, part of the dam had to be torn down to let her pass. Herndon and Lincoln finally got the boat to Beardstown, received forty dollars apiece for their work, and walked back to New Salem. [10]

When Lincoln arrived back in New Salem the people were all aroused by a new cause for excitement. Trouble had been brewing in northwestern Illinois between white settlers and Indians. In April, 1832, Chief Black Hawk recrossed the Rock River with five hundred braves and Governor Reynolds had called for volunteers from the state militia to help repel the Indians. All male white inhabitants between the ages of eighteen and forty-five were required to enroll in the militia.

Both Denton Offutt and Abe had been giving less and less attention to the store, and the business there was about to "wink out." Offutt salvaged what he could of his assets and went east. Abe closed up the business with the creditors, and volunteered for thirty days service in the state militia. The Clary's Grove boys and others joined him.

One morning soon after their signing up, an army officer rode his mud-spattered horse into New Salem. He brought notice of Governor Reynolds' desire for 400 volunteers from the Sangamon County militia to report at Beardstown by April 24. Lincoln borrowed a horse and rode to Richland Creek, nine miles southwest, to join a company of friends and neighbors who formed themselves into a company. The first order of business was to elect a captain, or company commander. In voting each man stepped out and stood by either Lincoln or one William Kirkpatrick. Three-fourths of the men at once went to Lincoln—then one by one those standing by Kirkpatrick left him until he was almost alone. Years later Lincoln was to write that he was "surprised at this election, and had not since had any success in life which gave him so much satisfaction." He at once appointed Jack Armstrong his first sergeant, William F. Berry and Alexander Trent as corporals, and had his other many friends in the ranks. Nine days later he promoted from the ranks his rival William Kirkpatrick. They marched to Beardstown and went into camp as part of an army of 1,600 mobilizing there.[11]

Captain Lincoln's company was a rough pioneer group that knew little or nothing of military discipline. The captain was as raw as the company. All his resourcefulness and adaptability were required to supplement his scanty knowledge of military science. On one occasion he was marching his company in two platoons of twenty men abreast when they came to a narrow gate. Unable to think of the proper command for the soldiers to form in single file so the company could go "endwise", Lincoln shouted: "Halt! This company will break ranks for two minutes and form again on the other side of that gate!" The men leaped over the fence or ran through the gate as they pleased and were soon marching regularly on their way.[12]

Although this particular company did not have to fight any Indians, they did a great deal of fighting and wrestling among themselves and with the soldiers of other companies. Lincoln was at his best in these campfire sports. He took an active hand in these games, and demonstrated again and again his superiority as a wrestler. Only once was he beaten. He also had opportunity to indulge his love of story-telling to the utmost, and from these experiences he got the materials for many excellent stories which he used later in life. He won the good will and admiration of his men; learned something of soldiers and the soldier's life; the value and difficulties of leadership; and met such men as John T. Stuart, John H. Hardin, Joseph Gillespie, Edward D. Baker and others whose acquaintance was later to be helpful to him. Just before disbanding, the men of his company agreed to support his candidacy for the State Legislature.[13]

Lincoln was mustered out of the service at Black River, Wisconsin, on July 16. His horse and that of his mess-mate, George Harrison, were stolen the night before. On the way back to Peoria they walked and rode part way on the horses of comrades. They also bought a canoe and steered their way to Havana where they sold the canoe and walked the rest of the way to New Salem.

August 6, Election Day, was eighteen days off and Lincoln resumed his campaign. He went from house to house, farm to farm, and village to village; talking, making friends, telling anecdotes. As he talked to a farmer he helped him pitch his hay, cradle his wheat, or pull his corn. He made a few speeches, of which one was reported as follows:

"Fellow Citizens," said he, "I presume you all know who I am — I am humble Abraham Lincoln. I have been solicited by many friends to become a candidate for the Legislature. My politics are short and sweet, like the old woman's dance. I am in favor of a national bank. I am in favor of the internal improvement system and a high protective tariff. These are my sentiments and political principles. If elected I shall be thankful; if not, it will be all the same." [14]

Lincoln was not elected to the Legislature. Sangamon County was entitled to four representatives and there were thirteen candidates. Lincoln ran eighth with 657 votes. The highest vote received by any candidate was 1,127. The lowest of the four successful candidates was the Reverend Peter Cartwright, who received 815. Lincoln was not discouraged for in his own New Salem precinct he received 177 of the 300 votes cast. His defeat was due to his being relatively unknown outside the New Salem community. But from the campaign he had derived valuable experience in public speaking, an increased confidence in himself, and an extensive acquaintance with the people. With considerable zest, he looked forward to the strong possibilities of a successful race two years hence.

Desiring to become a merchant in a store where he could meet the people, exchange views with strangers, discuss politics, narrate anecdotes, and do some reading in slack times, Lincoln bought out the partner of William F. Berry and formed the partnership company of Berry and Lincoln. Berry was already deeply in debt, and Lincoln borrowed the money with which to purchase his interest in the store. His creditor said, "I believed he was thoroughly honest and that impression was so strong in me I accepted his note in payment of the whole. He had no money, but I would have advanced him still more had he asked for it." [15]

The partnership was not a happy one, neither did it prove profitable. Berry, a son of Rev. John M. Berry, was a wild young man who indulged in drinking, gambling, and carousing. Lincoln spent much of his time talking, joking, and reading books. A turning point in his career occurred when, as he said:

One day a man who was migrating to the West drove up in front of my store with a wagon which contained his family and household plunder. He asked me if I would buy an old barrel for which he had no room in his wagon, and which he said contained nothing of special value. I did not want it, but to oblige him I bought it, and paid him, I think, half a dollar for it. Without further examination I put it away in the store, and forgot all about it. Some time after, in overhauling things, I came upon the barrel, and emptying it upon the floor to see what it contained, I found at the bottom of the rubbish a complete edition of Blackstone's Commentaries. I began to read those famous works, and I had plenty of time; for during the long summer days, when the farmers were busy with their crops, my customers were few and far between.

The more I read, the more intensely interested I became. Never in my whole life was my mind so thoroughly absorbed. I read until I devoured them.[16]

This was the beginning of Lincoln's serious study of law — an enormous contribution toward his future way of life. But it added nothing to the declining business of the store. By early spring it was evident that something must be done to stimulate grocery sales. Berry advocated selling liquor in small quantities — even by the drink — to the regular customers and to the Stage Passengers. A license was taken out by Berry and the bond required in connection with its issuance signed with Lincoln's as well as Berry's name; but neither signature was in Lincoln's handwriting.

It is not altogether clear what took place in this "conscience crises," but Lincoln did not drink, nor did he like the liquor business. It is probable that this was one of those "critical hours" to which he later referred, when in the face of "temptation and wrong suggestion" he heard his mother's voice once more repeating the old, old words, *"I am the Lord thy God; thou shalt have no other gods before me."*

It is certain that Dr. John Allen, Mentor Graham, and other worthy community leaders supported him. In describing this crisis in Lincoln's life, Carl Sandburg put it this way: "Selling pork, salt, powder, guns, trading calico prints and bonnets for eggs and furs had only a mild interest for Lincoln, but taking the cash of men and boys for hard liquor didn't come easy — and a few weeks after the firm got its license, Lincoln, in a deal of some kind, turned his interest in the store over to Berry."[17]

Berry had no money of his own, consequently the two sold out to William and Alexander Trent. But as it turned out, neither of the Trents had any money, so they bought the store just as Lincoln and

Berry had originally bought it—their notes were accepted for the purchase price. Before the notes became due the Trent brothers disappeared. The few groceries which they had in the store were seized by creditors, and the doors closed. Berry soon died in the midst of his wild career, and the debt of $1,100 was left entirely on the shoulders of Abe Lincoln. To Abe, in those days, that was an appalling load—especially under the circumstances he assumed it. However, speaking later, he said:

> That debt was the greatest obstacle I have ever met in life; I had no way of speculating, and could not earn except by labor, and to earn by labor eleven hundred dollars, besides my living, seemed the work of a lifetime. There was, however, but one way. I went to the creditors and told them that if they would let me alone I would give them all I could earn over my living, as fast as I could earn it. [18]

Nearly all his creditors were "trustful and lenient" with him and allowed him to take his time, yet the burden of the debt bore heavily upon him. He always spoke of it as the "national debt" and made payments from time to time as he was able. The last dollar of the debt was finally made seventeen years later—in 1849, just after he returned from serving a term in Congress.

On May 7, 1833, soon after the store failed Lincoln was appointed Postmaster of New Salem. One report was that the appointment came as a result of a petition circulated and sent to President Andrew Jackson by the New Salem women. Be that as it may, the appointment pleased him very much. As postmaster he was exempt from militia and jury duties, could send and receive personal letters free, could read the out-of-state newspapers which came to New Salem, and was enabled to become acquainted with almost every settler in that part of the country. Lincoln conducted the office in a highly satisfactory manner and was always anxious to please and accommodate, even when he had to walk several miles to deliver a special letter.

The mails came only twice a week, and Lincoln had considerable leisure time. In the autumn when new settlers crowded into the community, the demand arose on all sides for section lines to be run, boundary lines to be established, roads located, corners to be pegged, and surveys made for new towns. John Calhoun, County Surveyor who had heard good things of Lincoln; sent a messenger to New Salem to ask him to become assistant County Surveyor.

Abe was found in the woods splitting rails between mail deliveries. He and the messenger sat down together on a log and talked it over, and Abe was persuaded to go to Springfield to see Calhoun. He accepted the post with the understanding that he could continue to express his political opinions as he chose, and that he would be given time to learn.

Lincoln knew very little about surveying, yet his father had been a surveyor and so had George Washington. Now he would have his turn at the profession. He borrowed books from Calhoun, enlisted the help of Mentor Graham, and went to work on Robert Gibson's *Theory and Practice of Surveying,* and Flint's *Treatise on Geometry, Trigonometry, and Rectangular Surveying.* He studied day and night as his post office duties would permit. In fact he had so many long sieges of night study that his friends became uneasy about his health. But he mastered the books within six weeks, obtained a fifty-dollar horse on credit, procured a compass and chain and reported to Calhoun for duty in January of 1834. [19]

Abe was assigned the northern part of the county, which lay adjacent to his home community. He worked between mails, and his pay was $2.50 for "establishing" a quarter section of land, $2.00 for half a quarter, and 25 cents to 37½ cents for town lots. He averaged about $3.00 a day plus traveling expenses, which up to that time was about the best pay he had received. His surveys became known for their care and accuracy. This is evidenced by the fact that many who had disputes over land boundaries submitted their controversies to him, confident that his honesty and competence was such that when he made a survey his verdict would end the matter. He made friends wherever he worked. "Not only did his wit, kindliness, and knowledge attract people," observed Coleman Smoot, "but his strange clothes and uncouth awkwardness advertised him, the shortness of his trousers causing particular remark and amusement. More and more the name 'Abe Lincoln' became a household word." [20] He surveyed roads, farm lands, school sections, and town sites such as Bath, New Boston, Albany, Huron, and Petersburg. Some of the old corners located by him are still in existence, and the people of Petersburg remember with pride that they live in a town which was laid out by Lincoln during the summer of 1836.

As he surveyed, he paid on his "national debt." One creditor grew impatient, however, and sued him and got judgment. When

Abe was unable to pay, the sheriff levied upon his personal possessions, including his horse, saddle, bridle and surveying instruments. Deprived of these chief means of making a living, Lincoln's immediate future looked somewhat gloomy. Fortunately, Uncle Jimmie Short, a friend who "liked Abe Lincoln" bought the horse, saddle, and surveying instruments at the sheriff's sale and returned them to their owner. Lincoln never forgot his benefactor. He repaid the money from his subsequent earnings as a lawyer, and years later, as President of the United States, appointed his friend "Uncle Jimmie" as an Indian agent in California. [21]

On April 19, 1834, Lincoln's named appeared again in the *Sangamon Journal* as a candidate for the State Legislature. By that time he was not only better known, but was backed by John T. Stuart, a Springfield lawyer and County Whig leader, by Bowling Green, a local Democrat leader, and by many others who believed in Lincoln and "loved him for his own sake."

During the campaign period Lincoln issued no formal declaration of his principles and made only a few speeches. He campaigned quietly, talking to farmers whom he met on surveying trips, and solicited votes as he delivered mail. Rowan Herndon, who had moved to a large farm at Island Grove, says: "Lincoln came to my home during harvest. There were some thirty men in the field. He got his dinner and went out in the field where the men were at work. I gave him an introduction, and the boys said they could not vote for a man less he could make a hand. 'Well, boys,' said he, 'if that is all, I am sure of your votes.' He took hold of the haying cradle, and led the way all round with perfect ease. The boys were satisfied, and I don't think he lost a vote in the crowd."

On seeing Lincoln, Dr. R.F. Barrett inquired, "Can't the party raise any better material than that?" But after hearing him speak he declared that Lincoln amazed him, that "he knew more than all the other candidates put together." In the election on August 4, 1834, Lincoln ran second among thirteen Sangamon County candidates. John Dawson ran first with 1,390 votes, Lincoln 1,376, and his friend John T. Stuart ran fourth, with 1,164 votes.

After the election, Lincoln continued distributing mail, surveying, doing odd jobs and mingling with the people as he awaited the opening of the Illinois Legislature some four months away. Added to all this was the study of law. During the summer campaigning, in their more intimate moments together, Lincoln had intimated to Major John T. Stuart something of his interest in law, and how he had been fascinated with *Blackstone's Commentaries*. Stuart suggested that Lincoln study law for a profession. Abe was highly pleased, and Stuart loaned him law books which he avidley studied. At spare times he studied in the post office or in his room, at other times out in the woods where he went over and over legal statutes until they were fixed in his mind.

Realizing that as a representative of the people he should be better dressed, Lincoln accepted a loan of $200 from Coleman Smoot, a well-to-do farmer, with which he paid a couple of small pressing debts and purchased a new sixty-dollar tailor made suit, along with a few other articles of wearing apparel.

In late November, twenty-five year old Abe Lincoln dropped his books, put away his surveying instruments, turned his post-master duties over to an assistant and joined Major John T. Stuart and other elected legislators on a seventy-five mile stage-coach trip from Springfield to Vandalia, the state capital. Lincoln roomed with Stuart, "whose leadership made their room a Whig center."

In the legislature he received a few committee assignments, drafted and introduced two or three bills, and met many influential young men, some of whom would become bankers, lawyers, mayors, governors, Congressmen, and U.S. Senators. Among these was Stephen A. Douglas, a young lawyer, with whom Lincoln's life was destined to come into frequent and momentous contact. Small wonder that when the session ended on February 13, 1835, he returned to New Salem with his ambition fired to resume his legal studies, along with his duties as postmaster and deputy surveyor.

In the same spring, soon after Lincoln's return from the legislature, he fell in love.

On first coming to New Salem in 1831, he boarded for a time in the home of James Rutledge who had been born in South Carolina, lived many years in Kentucky, then came to Illinois and was one of the founders of New Salem. Rutledge was a "high-minded man of a warm and generous nature and had the universal respect of the community." One of his ancestors signed the Declaration of Independence; one was Chief Justice of the United States Supreme Court, and another was a prominent leader in the American Congress.

Ann May Rutledge was the third of nine children. She was a bright, beautiful and gentle person, with blue eyes and auburn hair;

cheerful and a good conversationalist. Abe and Ann had studied together when they were special students of Mentor Graham, and her name was preserved upon the title page of their *Kirkham's Grammar*. Then she had gone away to be a resident student at the Female Academy at Jacksonville. In the meantime she had met John McNamar who had come to New Salem from New York. He purchased property in the vicinity and he and Ann became engaged. After a while, McNamar returned to the East with a promise of coming back for marriage. However, his letters became farther and farther apart, and finally ceased. Waiting for letters from her departed suitor, Ann often went to the New Salem Post Office where Lincoln was postmaster. When she had waited long after the last letter came, she confided in Abe.

Ann Rutledge was now twenty-two and Abe was twenty-six and in many ways the idol of the New Salem community. The rare intelligence and spiritual apprehension, common to both, brought vast enjoyment when they were together. Abe gallantly pressed his suit, and in the early summer of 1835 Ann promised to become his bride. Neither of them had money, therefore they decided that she should go with her brother to Jacksonville and spend the winter there in the Academy. Lincoln was to continue his law studies; then the next spring when she had returned from school and he had been admitted to the bar, they would be married.

The summer was a pleasant one for Ann and Abe, although the Rutledge family had moved to Sand Ridge, seven miles away. Lincoln often rode horseback across country to see her. At times they walked in the woods together, and talked of their future. A few times Abe stayed all night in the neighboring farm home of his friend "Uncle Jimmy" Short.

During the late summer Abe and Ann were both stricken with a strange sickness, thought by some to be typhoid fever. Lincoln recovered but Ann grew steadily worse. When it was seen that there was no hope, James Rutledge came galloping in to New Salem saying, "Ann's calling for you, Abe, hurry!" Lincoln was privileged to visit Ann for an hour. That visit was significantly historic, yet none but the two ever knew, for the depth of their love for each other could be measured only by the depth of their characters.

Ann passed away on August 25, 1835. The following day they buried her in the Concord Cemetery, seven miles northwest of New Salem. At the head of her grave was placed a large boulder on which was written ANN RUTLEDGE.

The blow was almost too much for Abe. In his dejection he said, "There is nothing to live for now." Graham's reply was, "God is bringing about a higher purpose, Lincoln. Surely he is, Lincoln." With quivering lips and weeping eyes, he said, "Maybe you're right, Graham." But he continued to visit the grave saying, "My heart is buried there."

Squire Bowling Green took Lincoln to his home for a time, and here under the loving care of Green and his good wife Nancy, Lincoln regained considerable self-control. Afterward Lincoln was forever different. He came into possession of a patience, a strange power of insight into the transience of life, and a sympathy which only the unseen force of sacred sorrow can produce. Mr. Whitney, a fellow lawyer, expressed it thus: "The life and death of Ann Rutledge was not a misadventure, or in vain, for when the veil is withdrawn from the things that are now hidden, the existence and being of this modest and unobstrusive girl of an obscure hamlet, will be hailed as one of the agents of destiny in the salvation and regeneration of the nation."

In later years, Ann's body was taken from the Concord Cemetery and reentered in Oakland Cemetery at Petersburg which was nearer the sight of New Salem. Edgar Lee Masters embodied the deep meaning of Ann's life and mission in the lines of the poem which are engraved on her granite gravestone:

> Out of me unworthy and unknown
> The vibrations of deathless music!
> "With malice toward none,
>   with charity for all."
> Out of me forgiveness of millions
>   toward millions,
> And the beneficent face of a nation
> Shining with justice and truth.
> I am Ann Rutledge
> Who sleeps beneath these weeds.
> Beloved of Abraham Lincoln,
> Wedded to him, not through union,
> But through separation.
> Bloom forever, O Republic,
> From the dust of my bosom!
> January 7th, 1813—August 25th, 1835

Also, about this time a poem called "Mortality" appeared in a newspaper. Ten of its fourteen verses read:

Oh, why should the spirit of mortal be proud?
Like a fast-flitting meteor, a fast-flying cloud,
A flash of the lightning, a break of the wave,
He passeth from life to his rest in the grave.

The leaves of the oak and the willow shall fade,
Be scatter'd around and together be laid;
And the young and the old, and the low and the high,
Shall molder to dust and together shall lie.

The maid on whose cheek, on whose brow, in whose eye,
Shone beauty and pleasure,—her triumphs are by;
And the memory of those who have loved her and praised,
Are alike from the minds of the living erased.

The hand of the king that the scepter hath borne,
The brow of the priest that the miter hath worn,
The eye of the sage, and the heart of the brave,
Are hidden and lost in the depths of the grave.

The peasant whose lot was to sow and to reap,
The herdsman who climb'd with his goats to the steep,
The beggar who wander'd in search of his bread,
Have faded away like the grass that we tread.

The saint who enjoy'd the communion of heaven,
The sinner who dared to remain unforgiven,
The wise and the foolish, the guilty and just,
Have quietly mingled their bones in the dust.

So the multitude goes, like the flower and the weed,
That wither away to let others succeed;
So the multitude comes, even those we behold,
To repeat every tale that hath often been told.

For we are the same things our fathers have been,
We see the same sights that our fathers have seen,
We drink the same stream, and we feel the same sun,
And run the same course that our fathers have run.

The thoughts we are thinking our fathers would think;
From the death we are shrinking from, they too would shrink;
To the life we are clinging to, they too would cling;
But it speeds from the earth like a bird on the wing.

'Tis the twink of an eye, 'tis the draught of a breath,
From the blossom of health to the paleness of death,
From the gilded saloon, to the bier and the shroud,—
Oh, why should the spirit of mortal be proud?

Abe read it and liked it so well that he memorized it, sent hand written copies to several friends, and recited it aloud in whole or in part numberless times in the remaining years of his life. When asked if he had written the poem, his reply was "I would give all I am worth, and go in debt to be able to write so fine a piece as I think this is." Many supposed the poem merely conveyed a sense of the melancholy. But Lincoln — a keen lover of humor — was very sure that it mirrored a "sense of the unimportance of trifles" and contributed to life that "sense of proportion" which he so heartily craved.

Early the next December, Representative Lincoln was again in Vandalia for the special session of the Legislature. With re-election ever in mind, he carefully watched the interests of Sangamon County and its citizens — his chief thought being to initiate plans for the removal of the state capital from Vandalia to Springfield. In January, 1836, the legislative session was over, and he returned to the study of law and the duties as postmaster and surveyor.

During the summer of 1836, Lincoln pressed his campaign for re-election to the Legislature. In announcing his views in the *Sangamon Journal*, he added these significant words:

> *If elected, I shall consider the whole people of Sangamon my constituents, as well those that oppose me as those that support me. While acting as their representative, I shall be governed by their will on all subjects upon which I have the means of knowing what their will is; and upon all others, I shall do what my own judgment teaches me will best advance their interests. Whether elected or not, I go for distributing the proceeds of the sales of the public lands to the several States, to enable our State, in common with others, to dig canals and construct railroads without borrowing money and paying the interest on it.*[22]

In this campaign Abe made numerous speeches, engaged in debates, and at times was directly attacked by opponents, yet he gave ample proof of his ability to take good care of himself. Once in Springfield, after making a very impressive speech in which, as Joshua Speed says, "he carried the crowd with him and swayed them as he pleased," he was attacked by George Forquer. Forquer, a prominent lawyer, had recently left the Whig party and become a Democrat and had immediately been appointed Register of the

Land Office at a salary of $3,000. Shortly after receiving the appointment he had also built a new frame house, upon which he had erected a lightning rod—the first one in town. Forquer rose, and with some show of superiority, made a slashing speech in which he said, "this young man Lincoln will have to be taken down, and I am sorry that the task devolves upon me."

Lincoln stood near him, with arms folded, never interrupting him. When Forquer was done, Lincoln walked to the speaker's stand and said:

> *The gentleman commenced his speech by saying that this young man would have to be taken down, and he was sorry the task devolved upon him. I am not so young in years as I am in the tricks and trade of a politician; but live long or die young, I would rather die now than, like the gentleman, change my politics and simultaneous with the change receive an office worth three thousand dollars a year, and then have to erect a lightning rod over my house to protect a guilty conscience from an offended God.* [23]

Some who were there said that friends carried Lincoln from the courthouse on their shoulders. And Forquer's lightning rod was long spoken of in derision.

His campaign for re-election in 1836 was so well conducted and his record so good that he received the highest vote cast for any candidate. Each of the other six representatives, and the two senators elected from Sangamon County were members of the Whig Party, and each of them stood six feet or over, and in the coming Legislature they were to be dubbed "The Long Nine."

The Tenth Legislature met December 1, and Lincoln, the longest of the "Long Nine" was the acknowledged strategy director and Floor Leader of the Whig party.

There was a general desire that the capital be moved from its early seat at Vandalia, and the rivalry among other towns was keen. Sangamon County was bent on winning the prize for its own Springfield. Lincoln spearheaded the drive, but in the course of the contest certain measures came to be associated with the issue to which Lincoln on moral grounds was unalterably opposed. In the midst of the contest, a night caucus was called for the purpose of dissuading Lincoln from his stand. Lincoln stood firm. Then, past the hour of midnight, he arose in the caucus and delivered a speech of extraordinary earnestness, which he closed with these words:

> *You may burn my body to ashes and scatter them to the winds of Heaven: you may drag my soul down to the regions of darkness and despair to be tormented forever; but you will never get me to support a measure which I believe to be wrong, although by doing so I may accomplish that which I believe to be right.* [24]

The objectionable clauses were deleted from the measure, and when the vote was taken Springfield received 35 votes on the first ballot, and a majority of votes on the fourth ballot. In two years Springfield was to be the capital of the state of Illinois. Many official dinners were given the "Long Nine," and there was prolonged jubilee and rejoicing in the new capital-to-be. Lincoln received a lion's share of the praise. One toast ran: "Abraham Lincoln: he has fulfilled the expectations of his friends, and disappointed the hopes of his enemies."

CHAPTER IV
Lincoln as Lawyer and Politician

Soon after Lincoln's sweeping election to the Legislature in 1836, he appeared before two justices of the Supreme Court, took his bar examinations, and on September 9 was certified of good character and given a temporary license. Some months later, after the successful session of the Tenth Assembly was over, he presented himself to the clerk and took the oath to support the Constitution of the United States and of Illinois. On March 1, 1837, the license, with the oath endorsed thereon, was placed on file and the name of Abraham Lincoln was formally enrolled as an attorney or counsellor, licensed to practice law in all the courts of the state of Illinois.

Changes in his life were now imminent! Springfield had extended to him an urgent invitation to launch his new career in their city. Everything seemed auspicious for such a move.

Six years before, he had come to the village of New Salem like "a piece of floating driftwood," as he said. He had been received with kindness, had made valuable friendships, and had worked his way up to a position of leadership not only in New Salem but in the county and state as well. He now enjoyed a measure of skill as a politician and had fair prospects to become a statesman of some value. He owed much to New Salem—especially to such good, high-minded men as Mentor Graham, Bowling Green, [1] and Dr. John Allen—but many families were moving away, and the village was now rapidly "dying on the vine."

Four weeks after he became a full-fledged lawyer, Lincoln decided to accept Springfield's invitation. Therefore, he resigned his postmastership; sold his compass, chain, marking pins, and Jacob's staff; delivered the last mail to be given out at the post office; packed his few belongings in his saddle bags; borrowed a horse from Bowling Green and, on April 15, 1837, rode away from this small village which had been a haven of refuge to him for these critical years of his life. Often in later years he would illustrate his remarks with rural analogies drawn from his New Salem experiences.

Arriving in Springfield with only $7.00 in his pocket, Lincoln went to the only cabinet-maker in the town and ordered a single bedstead. He then went to the store of Joshua F. Speed—whose friendship he had previously formed, set his saddle-bags on the counter and inquired what the furnishings for a single bedstead would cost.

Speed says: "I took slate and pencil, made a calculation and found the sum for furnishings complete would amount to seventeen dollars in all. Said he: 'It is probably cheap enough, but I want to say that, cheap as it is, I have not the money to pay; but if you will credit me until Christmas, and my experiment here as a lawyer is a success, I will pay you then. If I fail in that I will probably never pay you at all.' The tone of his voice was so melancholy that I felt for him. I looked up at him and I thought then as I think now that I never saw so gloomy and melancholy a face in my life. I said to him: 'So small a debt seems to affect you so deeply, I think I can suggest a plan by which you will be able to attain your end without incurring any debt. I have a very large room and a very large bed in it, which you are perfectly welcome to share with me if you choose.' 'Where is your room?' he asked. 'Upstairs,' said I, pointing to the stairs leading from the store to my room. Without saying a word, he took his saddle-bags on his arm, went up stairs, set them down on the floor, came down again, and with a face beaming with pleasure and smiles exclaimed, 'Well, Speed, I'm moved.' " This was the beginning of one of Lincoln's finest friendships.

Another friend, William Butler, with whom Lincoln had become intimate at Vandalia, and who was clerk of the Sangamon Circuit Court, told Lincoln he could take his meals at the Butler home and there would be no mention of board bills.

Attorney John T. Stuart, who had suggested that Lincoln study law, had loaned him law books, roomed with him in Vandalia, and had observed his politics and leadership through two sessions of state legislature, had just recently offered Lincoln a partnership in his established law practice. Lincoln had accepted and on the very day of his arrival (April 15, 1837) the *Sangamon Journal* carried the notice:

John T. Stuart and A. Lincoln
Attorneys and Counsellors at Law
will practice cojointly
in the courts of this judicial circuit
Office, No. 4 Hoffman Row, upstairs.

Stuart was a man of dignified and commanding presence — handsome, polished, and courtly — one of the ablest and most prominent lawyers of Illinois. To be associated with him was no less than providential, and certainly a proud moment in life, for the twenty-eight-year-old Lincoln. After arranging for room and board, he could ascend the stairs to Major Stuart's office and for the next four years be at home professionally. What a comfortable sensation Lincoln must have had when that evening he wrote on the fly-leaf of his Websters Dictionary, "A. Lincoln, Esq. Attorney and Counsellor at Law."

Lincoln's knowledge of the fundamental principles of law as taught by Blackstone and Chitty, "together with a fine intellect, ability to marshal facts, power of reasoning, common sense, force of character, tenacity of purpose, ready wit, gift of gab" and oratorical ability were quite sufficient to make him a worthy assistant to Stuart. The mutual admiration that existed between the two was all that could be desired. Each complimented the other, but in different directions. Yet Lincoln was the inexperienced junior partner — in many respects little more than a lawyer's clerk.

At first he managed the partnership business, copied documents, prepared briefs and pleadings, made entries in the firm's account book, and read. He read in the fields of politics, literature, philosophy, and science. But most of all he "read law." In the course of that "law-reading," he says:

> *I constantly came upon the word 'demonstrate.' I thought at first that I understood its meaning, but soon became satisfied that I did not. I said to myself, 'What do I mean when I demonstrate more than when I reason or prove?' I consulted Webster's Dictionary. That told of 'certain proof,' 'proof beyond the possibility of doubt'; but I could form no idea what sort of proof that was. I thought a great many things were proved beyond a possibility of doubt, without recourse to any such extraordinary process of reasoning as I understood 'demonstration' to be. I consulted all the dictionaries and books of reference I could find, but with no better results. You might as well have defined 'blue' to a blind man. At last I said, 'Lincoln, you can never make a lawyer if you do not understand what "demonstrate" means'; and I left my situation in Springfield, went home to my father's house, and stayed there till I could give any proposition in the six books of Euclid at sight. I then found out what 'demonstrate' means, and went back to my law-studies.*[2]

Lincoln joined a group of young men who organized a society "to encourage public speaking, debating, and literary efforts." They held their meetings at Joshua Speed's store. Also, he joined the Young Men's Lyceum which held public meetings. He never missed an opportunity to make a public address or to learn more about the art of public speech.

His first court case came when Stuart was busy with his campaign for congress and turned the case over to Lincoln to try "as he deemed best." The case was *Hawthorne vs. Woolbridge,* involving the use of two oxen for breaking up some prairie-sod, assault and battery, claims and counter claims. Lincoln brought about conciliation and the case never came to trial.

But soon there were other cases which did come before the court, and the junior member of the firm gave good account of himself. His procedure was to champion the cause of the party whom he thought to be in the right, and try his cases on principle rather than on precedent. He based his arguments on the solid foundation of right and justice, and appealed to the faculty by whicn jury members distinguished truth from falsehood and right from wrong. He used the language of the people as he demonstrated. He grew eloquent as he pled, and his popularity as a young jury pleader spread. His practice in Springfield, as well as on the circuit, increased until Stuart and Lincoln enjoyed one of the best law practices in the Circuit Court of Sangamon County.

Serious considerations of love and marriage again engaged Abe's attention.

In the autumn of 1836, Mrs. Abel of New Salem, when going to Kentucky on a visit, laughingly proposed to bring back her sister, Miss Mary Owens, on condition that Lincoln marry her. Lincoln accepted the proposal in the spirit it was made, and, as he said, was "most confoundedly well pleased" with the prospect. For he had seen the said sister three years before, and thought her "intelligent, and agreeable, and saw no good objection to plodding life through hand in hand with her."

The lady took her journey and in due time returned with her sister, Miss Owens. When Lincoln met her, she appeared to have changed somewhat, especially to have grown stoutish (she then actually weighed 150 pounds) and as he thought lost some of her beauty. Nevertheless, as he says, "I determined to consider her my wife" and set about "in search of perfections in her which might be fairly set off against her defects. I tried to imagine her handsome, which, but for her unfortunate corpulency was actually true. Exclusive of this, no woman that I have seen has a finer face. I also tried to convince myself that the mind was much more to be valued than the person, and that she was not inferior, as I could discover, to any with whom I had been acquainted."[3]

For many months Miss Owens and Lincoln were in a "half-engaged condition." And it was expected that when in Springfield he would arrange for their future home there, but instead he fell to brooding over the fact that he had never been in any bondage, "either real or imaginary," and that his resources were unfit to support a wife in Springfield. Therefore, in some of his weaker moments he wrote her:

Friend Mary. I am often thinking of what we said of your coming to live at Springfield. I am afraid you would not be satisfied. There is a great deal of flourishing about in carriages here, which it would be your doom to see without sharing in it. You would have to be poor without the means of hiding your poverty. Do you believe you could bear that patiently? Whatever woman may cast her lot with mine, should any ever do so, it is my intention to do all in my power to make her happy and contented; and there is nothing I can imagine, that would make me more unhappy than to fail in the effort. I know I should be much happier with you than the way I am, provided I saw no signs of discontent in you. What you have said to me may have been in jest, or I may have misunderstood it. If so, then let it be forgotten; if otherwise, I much wish you would think seriously before you decide. For my part I have already decided. What I have said I will most positively abide by, provided you wish it. My opinion is that you had better not do it. You have not been accustomed to hardship, and it may be more severe than you now imagine. I know you are capable of thinking correctly on any subject; and if you deliberate maturely upon this, before you decide, then I am willing to abide your decision.[4]

This strange, dispassionate view of their relations seems to have brought no decision. Some three months later Lincoln wrote that he could not think of her "with entire indifference" and that he wanted "in all cases to do right, and most particularly so. . .to do right with you."

I now say, that you can now drop the subject, dismiss your thoughts (if you ever had any) from me forever, and leave this letter unanswered, without calling forth one accusing murmur from me. And I will even go further, and say, that if it will add any thing to your comfort, or peace of mind, to do so, it is my sincere wish that you should. Do not understand by this, that I wish to cut your acquaintance. I mean no such thing. What I do wish is, that our further acquaintance shall depend upon yourself. If such further acquaintance would contribute nothing to your happiness, I am sure it would not to mine. If you feel yourself in any degree bound to me, I am now willing to release you, provided you wish it; while on the other hand, I am willing, and even anxious to bind you faster, if I can be convinced that it will, in any considerable degree, add to your happiness. This, indeed, is the whole question with me. Nothing would make me more miserable than to be-

lieve you miserable — nothing more happy, than to know you were so. [5]

Miss Owens had sufficient discernment to recognize the "disinterestness" of such "love-making." She refused Mr. Lincoln's offer. Later she explained that she found him "deficient in those little links which make up the chain of a woman's happiness." Lincoln says, "I was mortified. . .my vanity was deeply wounded." He returned to the study and practice of law with a singular devotion.

In August, 1837, Mr. Lincoln, with six other lawyers and two doctors, went in a band wagon from Springfield to attend a camp-meeting held six miles west of Springfield at the "Salem Church." On the way Lincoln cracked jokes about the horses, wagon, the lawyers, the doctors — indeed about nearly everything. At the camp-meeting Rev. Dr. Peter Akers, a great and strangely gifted Bible preacher then in the fullness of his powers, preached a sermon on "The Dominion of Jesus Christ." The object of the sermon was to show that the dominion of Christ could not come in America until American slavery would at last be destroyed by civil war. For more than two hours the preacher unrolled his argument and even gave graphic pictures of the war that was to come. "I am not a prophet nor the son of a prophet," said he, "but a student of the prophets. As I read prophecy, American salvery will come to an end in some near decade, I think in the sixties. . . ."

At the climax of his sermon he cried at the top of his voice: *"who can tell but that the man who shall lead us through the strife may be standing in this presence!"* Only thirty feet away stood Lincoln drinking in his every word.

That night, on the return trip to Springfield, Lincoln was silent. After some time one of the doctors, an intimate friend, asked: "Lincoln, what do you think of that sermon?" After a moment Lincoln replied: "It was the most instructive sermon, and he is the most impressive preacher, I have ever heard. I never thought such power could be given to mortal man. Those words were from beyond the speaker. The Doctor has persuaded me that American slavery will go down with the crash of a civil war." Then for a few moments he was silent. Finally the solemn words came slowly forth: "Gentlemen: you may be surprised and think it strange, but when the Doctor was describing the Civil War, I distinctly

43

saw myself as in second sight, bearing an important part in that strife." Some were there who believed that, even then, he caught a glimpse of his part in the bloody drama more than a score or year distant, and the fearful tragedy in which it was to end.

The next morning, when Mr. Lincoln came late to his office his partner, without looking up, said: "Lincoln you have been wanted," then glancing up at Lincoln's haggard face he exclaimed: "Why, Lincoln, what's the matter with you?" Lincoln replied by telling him about the sermon, and said: *I am utterly unable to shake from myself the conviction that I shall be involved in that tragedy.*[6]

After this experience Lincoln's return to the study and practice of law was characterized by a marked change in his habits. He gave much more attention to study, and his colleagues in Springfield and on the circuit noticed the change. After court closed in the town on the circuit, the lawyers usually gathered on the veranda of the tavern, telling stories and chaffing one another. Lincoln often joined them long enough to tell a story, then while they laughed he slipped away to his room to study. Frequently he worked on far into the night. "Placing a candle on a chair at the head of the bed," says Mr. Herndon, "he would study for hours. I have known him to study in this position until two o'clock in the morning."[7]

The movement to abolish slavery was not only accompanied by ordinary opposition but by many mob outrages in which there were cases of burnings, murder, and extreme violence.

Especially notable was the tragic incident which happened at Alton, only sixty miles from Springfield. Elijah P. Lovejoy, a Presbyterian minister, editor of a paper in St. Louis, moved to Alton where announcements were made that he would edit the abolitionist paper there. His printing press arrived on a Sunday and that night was dumped into the Mississippi River by unknown persons. Friends bought him another printing press which a mob took and threw into the river. They did it once more, with a third press, after he had helped organize an antislavery society.

Word arrived that Ohio abolitionists were sending him another press. It arrived and was moved into a warehouse. Mr. Gilman, the owner of the warehouse, declared his intentions to stand guard all night. Nineteen friends, including Editor Lovejoy, joined him. About ten o'clock a pro-slavery mob stormed the warehouse and demanded the surrender of the press. When it was not forthcoming they threatened to set the building on fire. A ladder was placed against the building and a man began to ascend it to carry out the threat. Volunteers were called for from the defenders to go out and stop the attempt at arson. When Elijah Lovejoy and two others responded, the mob shot five bullets into his body and he had only enough strength to run upstairs into the office room where he expired. Owen Lovejoy, a Congregational minister, knelt at the grave and vowed "never to forsake the cause that had been sprinkled with my brother's blood."

Lincoln heard and was stirred to prepare a carefully written oration, "The Perpetuation of Our Political Institutions," which eleven weeks after the Alton outrage he delivered before a large audience at the Young Men's Lyceum of Springfield. Taking as his theme the danger and wickedness of mobs and the value and necessity of law and order, he pointed to our forefathers of the Revolution who, at a cost of death and mutilation, had won the liberties of men now being violated, saying:

"Whenever the vicious portions of population shall be permitted to gather. . .and burn churches, ravage and rob provision stores, throw printing presses into rivers, shoot editors, and hang and burn obnoxious persons at pleasure, and with impunity; depend on it, this Government cannot last."

He dealt with "momentous sacred ideas, based in love of the American Dream, of personal liberty and individual responsibility." He spoke of a toleration of free discussion, that even abolitionists could have their say, but that the interposition of mob law was neither necessary, justifiable, or excusable. *"There is no grievance that is a fit object of redress by mob law."* His plea for law and order made so great an impression on his audience that it was ordered printed in the *Sangamon Journal*.

Thus, Abraham Lincoln began to mold public opinion, and direct the thinking and activities of both those who were for, and those who were against, slavery which was so soon to loom large on the American horizon.

CHAPTER V
Lincoln Marries Mary Todd

Ninian W. Edwards, the brilliant son of the former governor of Illinois, was Lincoln's close friend and fellow representative. His wife was the daughter of Robert Smith Todd, president of the Bank of Kentucky in Lexington. Their two story brick home was one of the largest and finest in Springfield—a place to which the best in society was invited on special occasions. To this home came Miss Mary Todd, a younger sister of Mrs. Edwards and a cousin to John Todd Stuart, Lincoln's law partner. Two years before she had come on a visit; now she was twenty-one years of age and after differences with her stepmother in Kentucky, she had come to Springfield to stay.

Lincoln had doubtless heard of her through Edwards and Stuart. She had heard of the strange and most unusual character of Abe Lincoln.

They first met at a rather elaborate entertainment given at the American House in Springfield in December of 1839. Many ladies who "spun blithly in Springfield's social whirl" were there, also many honorable men such as Stephen A. Douglas, James Shields and other younger notables of the capital. But for some reason, not plain to others, Mary and Abe were strangely drawn to each other. They were to be often in each other's company during the coming months.

Being of a distinguished heritage, and having been brought up in the cultured atmosphere of Lexington, Mary Todd had been educated at a private academy, and at the exclusive school of Madame Mentelle, where she learned French, music, dancing, drama, and all the other genteel social graces. She was a pretty young lady with light brown hair, sparkling blue eyes, fair skin, and possessed a pleasingly plump figure. She was stylish in dress, intelligent, witty, well-read, and attuned to the affairs of the day. It was said of her that she had as much beauty as Ann Rutledge and as good a mind as Mary Owens. Her laughter "could dimple in wreaths running to the core of her" but she was born to impulses and given to occasional excesses of temper. To Lincoln, she was the "first aggressively brilliant, feminine creature who had crossed his path." He readily took to her.[1]

Mary apparently was drawn to Lincoln because of his character, his political sagacity, and his prospects of becoming a great man. A clue to her thinking along this line was revealed one evening at a fireside party when a young woman who was married to a rich man along in years was asked, "Why did you marry such a withered-up old buck?" and she answered, "He had lots of houses and gold." In surprise, quick tongued Mary Todd said, "Is that true? I would rather marry a good man, a man of mind, with a hope and bright prospects ahead for position, fame, and power than to marry all the houses, and gold in the world."[2]

Sometime during the year of 1840 Lincoln and Mary Todd were engaged to be married.

To the suggestion that they had come from different classes in society, and were not a match, she said she knew her own mind; that Lincoln had a future, and was her man more than any other she had met. Lincoln was fascinated with Mary, and evidently truly loved her, yet the love affair was not always to go smoothly. Lincoln was away much of the time, traveling by horseback, pleading cases in various towns located on the Eighth Judicial Circuit, and could not go to all the parties, concerts, and gatherings Mary was going to. She grew lonely, flared with jealousy, and failed to be as congenial as she might have been when they were together. Lincoln's old spirit of indecision about entering the state of matrimony returned, he grew melancholy, and finally wrote a letter to her begging off. Then he showed the letter to his friend Speed, and Speed threw the letter in the fire, saying in effect that such feelings of the heart shouldn't be put on paper and made a record that could be brought up later.[3] Lincoln went to the Edward's home and told Mary all that was in the letter. Mary broke into tears, Lincoln took her into his arms, kissed her, and the engagement was on again.

The wedding was set for New Year's Day, 1841. But Lincoln soon grew wretched—felt that he had yielded to tears and "sacrificed a reasoned resolve because he couldn't resist the appeal of a woman's grief." Mary Todd saw he was not himself, and perceived that nothing between them could be normal until he should recover. The date for the wedding came, but the wedding was only a dream, for Lincoln did not appear. Over Springfield the gossip spread that Mary Todd had jilted Lincoln. Both let the affair go without explanation.

Two weeks later Lincoln took to his bed—miserably sick. Only Speed and Dr. Henry saw him. After a week he was up and around. But he was emaciated in appearance and feeble in tone—certainly not the old-time Lincoln. His doctor, A. G. Henry, advised a change of scene, a complete break from his present surroundings.

To his law partner, Congressman John T. Stuart at Washington, D. C., he wrote of his inability to attend to any business in their office. He asked Stuart to see Daniel Webster, the new Secretary of State, and request that Lincoln be appointed U.S. Consul at Bogota, Columbia. Stuart failed to land the consulate.

Early in 1841 Joshua Speed sold his store in Springfield and returned to his folks in Kentucky. In August Lincoln went to visit him and rest for three weeks in the large Speed home near Louisville. There he enjoyed the presence and counsel of his best friend, met Fanny Henning, the young woman Speed was later to marry, and perhaps best of all, Speed's mother, a sweet and serene Christian lady, Mrs. Speed talked with him, gave him a mother's care, and made him a present of an Oxford Bible.[4]

On returning to Springfield Lincoln attended the sessions of the state legislature, pled a few cases in court, and during the coming year nearly became entangled in a duel. From this, the most unfortunate experience in his life, he learned one of life's most valuable lessons—to never write an anonymous letter, to always be scrupulously careful, and never to inflict a personal wound by anything he said or wrote.

Excerpts from various letters to friends revealed the fact that the final chapter had not been written in the tangled love affair of Lincoln and Mary Todd.

When Speed married Fanny Henning and a month later wrote Lincoln that he was far happier than he had expected to be, Lincoln wrote in reply:

> It cannot be told how it now thrills me with joy to hear you say you are 'far happier than you ever expected to be.' That much I know is enough. I know you too well to suppose your expectations were not, at least, sometimes extravagant, and if the reality exceeds them all, I say: Enough, dear Lord. I am not going beyond the truth when I tell you that the short space it took me to read your last letter gave me more pleasure than the total sum of all I have enjoyed since the fatal first of January, 1841. Since then it seems to me I should have been entirely happy, but for the never-absent idea there is one still unhappy whom I have contributed to make so. That still kills my soul. I cannot but reproach myself for even wishing to be happy while she is otherwise. She accompanied a large party on the railroad cars to Jacksonville last Monday, and on her return spoke, so that I heard of it, of having enjoyed the trip exceedingly. God be praised for that. [5]

In June of 1841, Mary wrote a letter to her friend Mercy Levering in which she revealed the fact that she did not desire anything to be over and the past sealed so far as she and Lincoln were concerned:

> The last three months have been of interminable length. After my gay companions of last winter departed, I was left much to the solitude of my own thoughts, and some lingering regrets over the past, which time can alone overshadow with its healing balm. Thus has my spring time passed. Summer in all its beauty has come again. The prairie land looks as beautiful as it did in the olden time, when we strolled together and derived so much of happiness from each other's society. [6]

49

Mutual friends endeavored to bring about the reconciliation of Abraham and Mary. During the late summer, Mrs. Simeon Francis, wife of the editor of the *Sangamon Journal,* invited Lincoln to a party in her parlor. Mary Todd was purposely among the guests. That evening Mrs. Francis brought the two together and said, "Be friends again." Whatever hesitations went on in Lincoln's heart, they both were glad to be friends again. Other meetings, followed in the Francis home, and Miss Todd made it clear to him that if another date should be fixed for a wedding, it should not be set so far in the future as it was the time before. Lincoln agreed.

Early in October Lincoln wrote Speed, "I want to ask you a close question. 'Are you now in *feeling,* as well as *judgment,* glad you are married as you are?' From anybody but me this would be an impudent question, not to be tolerated, but I know you will pardon it in me. Please answer it quickly, as I am impatient to know." Speed's answer to Lincoln was yes, he was glad both in feeling and judgment that he had married as he did.

A few weeks later, on the morning of November 4, 1842, a rather agitated Lincoln climbed the steps of the home of the Reverend Charles Dresser, at the corner of Eighth and Jackson Streets. Dr. Dresser admitted him, and listened while the thirty-three year old lawyer made a profound announcement:

"I want to get hitched tonight."

The couple had planned to be married in a quiet wedding at the parsonage, but on the street Lincoln met Ninian W. Edwards and told Edwards that he and Mary were to be married that evening. Edwards gave notice, "Mary is my ward and she must be married at my house." When Edwards asked Mary Todd if what he had heard was true, she told him it was true, and they made the Edward's big house ready.

Notwithstanding the brief notice, the wedding was made a genuine social affair. Abraham Lincoln and Mary Todd stood together in the Edwards' parlor, and the Reverend Charles Dresser in canonical robes performed the ceremony as the two spoke the marriage vows. There were two bridesmaids, forty guests, and a bountiful wedding supper. Five days later Lincoln ended a letter to Sam Marshall, a Shawneetown lawyer, with the words: "Nothing new here, except my marrying, which to me, is a matter of profound wonder."

Abe was at that time thirty-three years of age, and Mary was twenty-three. Their first home was at the Globe Tavern, which was a modest boarding house "very well kept by a widow lady by the name of Beck." Their room was the same as that formerly occupied by Dr. William S. Wallace, and the price for their room and board was $4.00 per week each. Here they lived until their first son, Robert, was born August 1, 1843. Then, five months later, with $1,500 earned from his improved law practice, Lincoln purchased Dr. Dresser's story-and-a-half house—the one where he had announced his intentions to "get hitched." The house was painted a light brown, and was quite complete with a cistern, a well, a pump, a barn, and a carriage house on the back lot. Abe purchased a horse, hired the village blacksmith to construct a buggy, procured a cow, and with his own hands built a stable in the barn. At last Lincoln and Mary had a home of their own.

The young couple was quite contented, only that Mary insisted that the house should be built up into a full two-story home. She said that "everybody who was quality" in Kentucky lived in a two-story house. Abe agreed to the improvement, but deferred the matter longer than Mary thought he should. Therefore, on one occasion when he was away on the circuit for several weeks, Mary conspired with their next door neighbor, a skilled carpenter, to raise the roof and add the other story; which was done. When Abe returned, he looked the two-story house over with great surprise, and walking on past, inquired of a passer-by where Abraham Lincoln lived. His house was pointed out to him, and Abe slowly walked back and knocked at the door. Mary had observed the performance through the window, so when she opened the door and Abe asked if this was the home of Abraham Lincoln, she required him to introduce himself before he was admitted. This home would remain their residence for seventeen years, until February 1861, when he went to Washington as President. It was the birthplace of all the four children, except Robert.

CHAPTER VI
Years of Development

When Abraham Lincoln had married and moved into the only house that he should ever own, he then settled into a most interesting professional career, and into a deeper study and better understanding of life, of law, of religion, and of statesmanship.

The marriage of Lincoln and Mary Todd was termed by many "a policy union" from which he derived social prestige and she, public prominence. This, of course, was an over simplification. They certainly did supplement each other to a reasonable degree, and there were special contributions, particularly to his life. The fact that Lincoln had a home, a family, and domestic responsibilities were vital factors which were to add stature to his life.

"The house on Eighth Street in Springfield," says Mrs. Ruth Randal, "was a typically happy American home with a husband and wife deeply devoted to each other and to their children. The family had its ups and downs, as all families do. Mrs. Lincoln was subject to migraine headaches and was at times emotionally unstable. Robert as a little fellow had one crossed eye, Tad had a lisp, and there were childhood illnesses. But when Lincoln walked home from his law office after the day's work, Willie and Tad would usually be watching for him. They would run down the street to meet him and swing on his long coattails as he approached the house. After supper they would climb all over him as he sat telling them a story, or perhaps they all had a game of blindman's bluff. The days fell into the pleasant pattern of small-town life. The Lincolns were surrounded by helpful friends and were themselves good neighbors."[1]

Lincoln would take his boys for walks in the country, explaining to them such things as animal tracks, small stones, or anything else they happened to see. Sometimes he would put his own and the neighbor's children in his buggy and go out to the Sangamon River for fishing and a picnic. When a circus came to town he would take the children to see it. Mrs. Lincoln gave birthday parties for the boys, and after the house was enlarged there were big entertainments. Lincoln's home life helped him develop patience, longsuffering, and to think of people as the "family of man."[2]

In both law and politics Lincoln had excelled while in partnership with John Todd Stuart. In Springfield and elsewhere he was known as "one of nature's noblemen." Yet he was only a junior partner in law, and in politics the favorable impression he had made reached only a little way beyond his county and district. There was yet a long way to go—even in the fundamentals of his professions.

Stuart had been one of the ablest trial lawyers in the state, and Lincoln had learned much from him during their partnership from 1837 to 1841. Yet Stuart's long absence from Springfield—especially after his election to Congress for a second term—made the continuance of the partnership impractical; therefore, they reached an agreeable parting of the ways, and the *Sangamon Journal* printed a professional notice of the dissolution of the Stuart and Lincoln partnership.

Stephen T. Logan, one of the greatest lawyers of his day and one of the most talented technicians of the science and philosophy of law, had observed Lincoln's ability at simplification, at convincingness, and his scrupulous honesty, and had made him an offer of a junior partnership. Feeling keenly the deficiencies of his own legal education and deeply desiring the advice and guidance of just such an older and more experienced man as Logan, Lincoln gladly accepted the offer. The professional title of *Logan and Lincoln* pleased the people when it was announced, and wherever it was heard. It was a great combination: Logan was no orator, yet he was methodical, industrious, painstaking, precise, and possessed the true qualities of a great advocate. He had also served for two years as judge of the Fifth Circuit. He liked Lincoln and caused him to adopt a habit of a closer application and deeper study of the principles underlying a lawsuit, to study the authorities, and to more carefully prepare each case in advance. He taught Lincoln to give greater attention to details, to thoroughness, and exactitude; he trained him to logically and tersely state his points to the court, and to emphasize the main point of his case as he argued to the jury.

Logan was without doubt one of the most constructive influences in molding Lincoln's professional life. Lincoln complimented Logan by learning well the lessons he taught, and by contributing oratory, true eloquence, wit, wisdom, and the elements of a successful politician. He had access to the Library of the State Supreme Court, only a short distance from the Logan and Lincoln office. He did specific reading, and availed himself of the necessary materials which qualified him to appear in court with his case well prepared.[3]

Logan and Lincoln soon rose to the top among Illinois law firms, owing to Logan's ability, Lincoln's skill in reasoning to juries, and the fact that they were located in the state capital where the Sangamon County Circuit Court, the Supreme Court and the United States District Court were located. Legal cases of various kinds came from all over Illinois, and for some time the firm handled most of the cases brought before the Supreme Court. At the Court's December, 1841 term — just one year and one month after Lincoln's marriage to Mary Todd — Lincoln argued fourteen appeals, losing only four. The Logan and Lincoln firm argued twenty-four cases during the 1842-43 terms, and was successful in all but seven.

Logan and Lincoln participated in almost every manner of court case over the state from theft to murder. Between February 1842 to March 1843 they handled seventy-seven bankruptcy cases. In these he learned much about money and the intricate problems connected with business and Commerce. A few Supreme Court cases in which Lincoln was involved as counsel became landmarks in Illinois jurisprudence; notably the seduction case, *Grable vs Margrave*. In the Gallatin County Circuit Court, Thomas Margrave sued William G. Grable to recover damages because Grable had allegedly seduced his daughter. The County Court awarded Margrave $300 for the "loss of his daughter's services, disgrace inflicted on the Margrave family, and the loss of the society and comfort of his daughter." Grable, the alleged seducer, appealed to the State Supreme Court.

Lincoln was employed by Samuel D. Marshall, Margrave's Shawneetown lawyer, to defend Margrave in the State's Supreme Court in September 1841. In his argument, Lincoln pictured the low, vile, selfish seducer on the one hand, and the disgrace inflicted on the Margrave family on the other. He pled for material compensation as the least to be expected. The Supreme Court upheld the Gallatin County verdict, and decreed: "The father may not only recover the damages he has sustained by the loss of service, and the payment of necessary expenses, but the jury may award him compensation for the disgrace cast upon the family, and the loss of the society and comfort of his daughter."[4]

The Supreme Court's ruling in this case, which followed the pleadings of Lincoln, became a guide in the assessments of damages in a large number of future seduction cases. In another monumental court case, Miss Eliza Cabot, a Menard County schoolteacher, sued for slander. Lincoln acted as her counsel and not only won a verdict of $1,600 in her favor, but established a widespread fear in the minds of would-be slanderers.

The firm of Logan and Lincoln enjoyed a large and commendable practice—considered by many to be about the best in the state. And although Lincoln received only one-third of the firms earnings, yet there was invaluable education, training, and discipline, along with an income considerably above a bare living. However, during the summer of 1844, when three years of his wonderfully fine association had passed, Judge Logan advised Lincoln that he wished to take into practice his son David. Lincoln was by that time ready to begin on his own account. So after talking the matter over, they dissolved the partnership amicably and in friendship. Lincoln left Logan with an established reputation as one of the outstanding leaders of the Illinois bar.[5]

Lincoln needed a junior partner—someone to remain in the office, keep records, and do the many tasks which would save his time. His reputation was such that most any younger lawyer in the state would have welcomed a partnership with him. He passed them all by and chose William H. Herndon, a young man twenty-six years of age and licensed to practice law. Many considered this a strange thing for Lincoln to do—to ally himself with an "inexperienced novice" who, though admittedly shrewd, lacked so many of the commendable traits of character so apparent in Lincoln. Yet he knew young Herndon, for he had clerked in the Speed store, slept upstairs in the large room with Speed and Lincoln, had attended classes for a time at Illinois College, and studied law in the office of Logan and Lincoln. His particularly redeeming features were that he idolized Lincoln, and "had already become uncommonly strong and influential in molding the political opinions of the young men of Springfield."

Herndon says he was surprised when Lincoln invited him to become his partner, "but when he remarked in his earnest honest way, 'Billy, I can trust you, and you can trust me,' I felt relieved and accepted his generous proposal." A sign soon went up in front of the office: *Lincoln and Herndon, Attorneys and Counsellers at Law.* It remained there until after Lincoln's. assassination.

It was a curious alliance. Lincoln always called his junior "Billy," while the latter addressed him as "Mr. Lincoln." Lincoln was a conservative, while Herndon was a militant radical. Lincoln was a total abstainer, while Herndon all through his career was a victim of the drinking habit. Lincoln believed firmly in the controlling influences of his "Heavenly Father," while Herndon was an agnostic and held many rationalistic concepts which he tried so hard, and so vainly to foist on Lincoln. Yet"despite the dissimilarities in their thoughts, habits, and temperaments, they were mutually helpful" and formed a fairly good combination from a business and political standpoint. "Billy" almost worshipped his friend and hero, and was more ambitious politically for Lincoln than Lincoln himself. Lincoln exerted a "silent, steady, masterful" influence over his law partner who performed the more routine jobs, handled correspondence, and dug up authorities and precedent cases while Abraham Lincoln prepared briefs and went out on the circuit to plead cases, or took them through the State Supreme Court.

Business began somewhat slowly for the new firm of Lincoln

and Herndon. But in a short time Lincoln's name and political associations, along with his natural following, brought all the business they could accommodate. Lincoln handled scores of cases in the sessions of the Eighth Judicial Circuit during the year, and argued twenty-four cases at the December, 1845, term of the State Supreme Court. The fees paid them for their work in these cases usually varied from $5 to $50; never more than $100. Lincoln often collected when on the circuit, and would bring the money back to the office and withdraw from his pocket Herndon's one-half wrapped in a paper with slip attached. When Herndon was absent he would write his name on the package, indicating from where it came and place it in a drawer where Billy would be sure to find it. One day Herndon asked him why he was so prompt and particular in the matter and he replied:

"Well Billy, there are three reasons: first, unless I did so I might forget I had collected the money; secondly, I explain to you how and from whom I received the money, so that you will not be required to dun the man who paid it; thirdly, if I were to die you would have no evidence that I had your money. By marking the money it automatically becomes yours and I have no right in law or morals to retain or use it. I make it a practice never to use another man's money without his consent."[6]

While Lincoln rode the circuit pleading law cases during 1846, he also made personal calls on all the Whig leaders — most of whom were fellow lawyers — requesting them to use their influence to get him elected as party candidate for the U.S. Congress. He wrote letters, and electioneered. And, then, at the Whig convention in Petersburg, May 1, 1846, Mr. Lincoln was nominated.

The Democrats, at their convention, nominated Peter Cartwright, the famous rugged, old fashioned circuit-riding, Methodist evangelist, as their candidate for Congress. Thus the circuit-riding Whig lawyer faced the circuit-riding Democratic evangelist.

There was never a more stalwart or uncompromising minister of the Christian faith than Peter Cartwright. As a "Boy Preacher" he had carried his Bible and rifle and conducted great revivals in Kentucky during the time the Lincolns lived there. He had continued in Kentucky for years and wherever he went a revival visited the community. In 1824 Bishop Roberts had appointed him to travel the Sangamon Circuit. In 1826 he had become Presiding Elder

57

of the district which included two-thirds of the state. The great preacher had held revival meetings and conducted camp-meetings in all that section of the country. He was admired for his eloquence, strong common sense, his stand for temperance and against slavery. Lincoln had seen him and heard much of his ways. The two great men seeking the same office where both were so well known might have offered a lively contest, only that as a politician Cartwright was out of his element — as he later admitted.

When the campaign was well under way, the Cartwright promoters indulged in dirty politics by circulating the idea that Lincoln was "an atheist, aristocrat, and duelist." The charge of aristocracy arose from the social connections of Mrs. Lincoln; the duelist charge arose from his near conflict with Shields (of which he was so ashamed that he always remained silent); but the charge of atheism he answered with a handbill and a statement which appeared in the *Illinois Gazette* of Lacon, August 15, 1846, in which he gave specific statements regarding his religion. It read:

> *A charge having got into circulation in some of the neighborhoods of this District, in substance that I am an open scoffer at Christianity, I have by the advice of some friends concluded to notice the subject in this form. That I am not a member of any Christian Church, is true; but I have never denied the truth of the Scriptures; and I have never spoken with intentional disrespect of religion in general, or of any denomination of Christians in particular. It is true that in early life I was inclined to believe in what I understand is called the "Doctrine of Necessity" — that is, that the human mind is impelled to action, or held in rest by some power, over which the mind itself has no control; and I have sometimes (with one, two, or three, but never publicly) tried to maintain this opinion in argument. The habit of arguing thus however, I have, entirely left off for more than five years. And I add here, I have always understood this same opinion to be held by several of the Christian denominations. The foregoing, is the whole truth, briefly stated, in relation to myself, upon this subject.*

> *I do not think I could myself, be brought to support a man for office, whom I knew to be an open enemy of, and scoffer at, religion. Leaving the higher matter of eternal consequences, between him and his Maker, I still do not think any*

man has the right thus to insult the feelings, and injure the morals, of the community in which he may live. If, then, I was guilty of such conduct, I should blame no man who should condemn me for it; but I do blame those, whoever, they may be, who falsely put such a charge in circulation against me. [7]

Lincoln's supporters advised him not to attend any meetings where Cartwright was speaking, especially religious meetings where he was to preach. Yet, it is said that he did attend one evening at a revival meeting. At the close.of the service the evangelist called upon all those who wished to give their hearts to God and go to heaven to stand up. A number of men, women, and young people stood. Then the preacher invited all who did not wish to go to hell to stand up. All stood up—except Lincoln. Then observing that Mr. Lincoln had not responded to either invitation and had refused to indicate a desire either to go to heaven or not to go to hell, Cartwright broke all propriety of his profession, and addressing him directly, said, "May I inquire of you, Mr. Lincoln, where are you going?" Lincoln drew himself up gradually to his full height and said very slowly and very distinctly:

I came here as a respectful listener. I did not know that I was to be singled out by Brother Cartwright. I believe in treating religious matters with due solemnity. I admit that the questions propounded by Brother Cartwright are of great importance. I did not feel called upon to answer as the rest did. Brother Cartwright asks me directly where I am going. I desire to reply with equal directness: 'I am going to Congress.' [8]

Three months later the count of ballots gave Lincoln 6,340 votes, Cartwright 4,829, and Walcott (Abolitionist) 249. Mr. Lincoln was the only Whig congressman elected in the state of Illinois.

No one had given him more aid in the campaign than faithful Billy Herndon, and he was very happy over his partner's success. Of the $200 which Lincoln's friends gave him for campaign expenses, he returned all but 75 cents. "I made the canvass on my own horse," he said, "my entertainment, being at the houses of friends, cost me nothing; my only outlay was 75 cents for a barrel of cider, which some farmhands insisted I should treat to."

He wrote his friend Joshua Speed, "Being elected to Congress, though I am very grateful to our friends for having done it, has not pleased me as much as I expected." But Mary Todd Lincoln

59

was highly pleased. She would now be the wife of Congressman Abraham Lincoln.

During the months intervening before he could take his seat in Congress, Lincoln carried out the routine of writing his pleadings, attending court, and riding the circuit. As usual, his cases varied greatly. There was one, however, which was quite unusual, especially in the way he handled it. An old negro woman named Polly came into the law office of Lincoln and Herndon and sobbed out her story. She and her children had been born in slavery in Kentucky, but her owner, a man named Hinkle, had brought the family to Illinois.

"Later, unable to hold them in bondage in a free State, he had set them free. Shortly thereafter her son found work as a waiter and deckhand on a steamboat and sailed down the Mississippi. While the boat was docked at New Orleans, the young negro foolishly went ashore. That night he was seized by a policeman and thrown into jail for the violation of a law which prohibited any colored person from being at large after dark without a pass from his owner. By the time he was brought to trial and ordered to pay a fine, his boat had sailed and he was left stranded. Of course he was unable to pay his fine. Under the law there was but one fate in store for the negro—to be sold to the highest bidder in satisfaction of the sentence. It was then that the old negro mother learned of her son's plight. In her misfortune she came to Lincoln and his partner and begged for aid.

"Lincoln was incensed over what he regarded as an outrage against the rights of a free person. He besought Herndon to visit Governor Bissell to urge him to use his official influence for obtaining the immediate release of the youth. Herndon returned from the State House with a report that the governor regretted that he had no legal or constitutional right to act in the premises, and therefore could do nothing at all.

"'By the Almighty!' exclaimed Lincoln excitedly, when he heard what the governor had said, 'I'll have the negro back here or I'll have a twenty years agitation in Illinois until the governor does have a legal and constitutional right to do something in the premises.'"

"But in the meanwhile immediate action had to be taken to save the young negro from being sold. So while the 'twenty years agitation' was still in the formative stage, Lincoln and Herndon, after appealing in vain to the Governor of Louisiana, engaged Colonel A. P. Fields as their correspondent in New Orleans, and from their own meager purses and contributions from a few friends, sent him sufficient money to pay the fine and other expenses of the case. In due time the youth was returned to his home in Illinois, and the two lawyers were content with only the heartfelt gratitude of the old negro mother as their fee."[9]

In July of 1847, Lincoln went on a four-day stage trip to Chicago where he was one of hundreds of delegates to the River and Harbor Convention aimed to promote internal improvements and to stimulate action of the Polk administration. The convention met in a big tent, and Lincoln met famous men from all over the country. A noted New York lawyer, David Dudley Field, spoke against certain internal improvements as unconstitutional. Horace Greeley wrote to his New York *Tribune* that "Hon. Abraham Lincoln, a tall specimen of an Illinoisan. . .was called out, and spoke briefly and happily in reply to Mr. Field."[10]

One day during this stage coach trip Lincoln was riding in company with a Kentucky colonel. After they had ridden a number of miles together, the colonel took a bottle of whiskey out of his pocket and said, "Mr. Lincoln, won't you take a drink with me?"

Mr. Lincoln replied, "No, Colonel, thank you, I never drink whiskey."

They rode along together for a number of miles more, visiting very pleasantly, when the gentlemen from Kentucky reached into his pocket and brought out some cigars, saying: "Now, Mr. Lincoln, if you won't take a drink with me, won't you take a smoke with me? For here are some of Kentucky's finest cigars."

And Mr. Lincoln said: "Now, Colonel, you are such a fine, agreeable man to travel with, maybe I ought to take a smoke with you. But before I do so, let me tell you a little story, an experience I had when a small boy.

"My mother called me to her bed one day when I was about nine years old. She was sick — very sick — and she said to me. 'Abey, the doctor tells me I am not going to get well. I want you to promise me before I go that you will never use whiskey nor tobacco as long as you live.' And I promised my mother I never would. And up to this hour, Colonel, I have kept that promise.

Now would you advise me to break that promise to my mother and take a smoke with you?"

The colonel put his hand gently on Mr. Lincoln's shoulder and, with a voice trembling with emotion, replied: "No, Mr. Lincoln, I wouldn't have you do it for the world. It was one of the best promises you ever made. And I would give a thousand dollars today if I had made my mother a promise like that and kept it as you have done."

On October 23, 1847, Lincoln leased his house on Eighth Street for ninety dollars for one year—"the north-up-stairs room" reserved for furniture storage. Two days later, with Mrs. Lincoln and their sons Robert and Eddie, he set out for Lexington, Kentucky, where they visited for three weeks. For the first time, Lincoln met his in-laws, Mrs. Lincoln's father and stepmother, State Senator and Mrs. Robert S. Todd, and Levi Todd, assistant manager of the cotton mills of Oldham, Todd and Company.

While there he sensed the steadily growing anti-slavery movement in Kentucky. He saw slaves auctioned, saw them chained in gangs heading south to cotton fields, and heard of the auction sale in Lexington of Eliza "a beautiful girl with dark lustrous eyes, straight black hair, rich olive complexion, only one sixty-fourth African, white yet a slave."

Calvin Fairbanks, a young Methodist minister, bid higher and higher against a thick-necked Frenchman from New Orleans. Reaching $1,200 the Frenchman asked, "How high are you going?" Fairbanks replied, "Higher than you, Monsieur."

The bids rose to where Fairbanks said slowly, "One thousand, four hundred and fifty dollars." Seeing the Frenchman hesitating, the sweating auctioneer pulled Eliza's dress back from her shoulders, showing her neck and breasts, and cried, "Who is going to lose a chance like this?" To the Frenchman's bid of $1,465, the minister bid $1,475. Hearing no more bids, the auctioneer shocked the crowd by "lifting her skirts" to bare her body to waist, and slapping her thigh he called "Who is going to be the winner of this prize?" Over the mutter and tumult of the crowd came the Frenchman's slow bid of "one thousand, five hundred and eighty dollars."

The auctioneer lifted his gavel and called, "one—two—three." Eliza turned a pained and piteous face toward Fairbanks, who now bid, "One thousand, five hundred and eighty-five." Then the auctioneer said, "I am going to sell this girl. Are you going to bid?" The Frenchman shook his head. Eliza fell in a faint, and the auctioneer said to Fairbanks, "You have bought her cheap, sir. What are you going to do with her?" Fairbanks cried, "Free her!" Most of the crowd shouted and yelled in glee. Many wept for joy. [11]

Lincoln saw Negro house servants in the Todd home, read books in the big library of Robert Todd and heard Henry Clay on November 13, 1847, before an immense audience say, among other things;

"Autumn has come, and the season of flowers has passed away. . . .I too am in the autumn of life, and feel the frost of age. . . .I have ever regarded slavery as a great evil." [12]

CHAPTER VII
From Congress To Circuit Lawyer

By stage and rail the Lincoln family traveled seven days to arrive in Washington December 2, 1847, and found temporary lodging at Brown's Hotel. After a few days Lincoln moved his family to Mrs. Sprigg's boardinghouse located where the Library of Congress now stands. Several other Whig legislators roomed or boarded at Mrs. Spriggs and Lincoln soon became a general favorite "because of his simple manners and fund of jokes."

The well-planned city had wide intersecting streets, many squares and parks, but few of the fine buildings we now see. Even the capitol had only a wooden dome and neither of the wings were yet built. The White House was there, the front of the Treasury had been completed, and the foundation of the Smithsonian Institute had just been laid. The city had thirty-seven churches of eight denominations. Its population totalled 40,000, of whom 8,000 were free Negroes and 2,000 slaves.

On December 4, Lincoln attended a caucus of Whig congressmen, and was present and took the oath of office when the Thirtieth Congress convened on December 6. He drew a seat in the back row of the Whig side, and was surrounded by nationally known men with whom he would have much to do in the coming years. He seemed somewhat overanxious to distinguish himself, or, at least, he wrote Herndon in this vein: "As you are all so anxious for me to distinguish myself, I have concluded to do so before long." A few days later he made his first speech, the improvement of our postal system, and did well. Or, as he put it in a letter to Herndon: "I find speaking here and elsewhere about the same thing. I was about as badly scared, and no more, as I am when I speak in court." Herndon spread the news, and replied that the people were delighted and were already planning for his re-election.

However, when the controversial issue of the Mexican War came up it was different. The war had grown out of the annexation of Texas in 1845. Texas claimed the Rio Grande as her South West frontier, while Mexico insisted the Nueces River was the boundary. War broke out over the issue. President Polk, as the representative of our government, supported the position taken by Texas, and sent troops. Public opinion in general backed the policies of President Polk. The Whigs—Lincoln's political party, and just at this juncture a dwindling party—took the position that the war had been instigated by slaveholders for the extension of slave territory and therefore was unnecessarily and unconstitutionally commenced by the President.

Lincoln made somewhat of a study of events leading up to the conflict and unfortunately joined the Whig attack on the Administration. He made some forceful speeches, but they were taken as being unpatriotic and certainly they were disrespectful to President Polk. The Congress was unmoved by them, the President ignored the speeches, and Lincoln's constituency back in Illinois could not understand his attitude.

Lincoln made other speeches in which he displayed his wide knowledge of constitutional law and history, yet he made no serious impression upon either the nation or his party. However, he learned much from congressional colleagues. Alexander H. Stephens of Georgia—brilliant, small of stature, and tubercular in health—earned his deepest admiration. To Herndon back home, he wrote in 1848: "I just take up my pen to say, that Mr. Stephens of Georgia, a slim, pale-faced, consumptive man, with a voice like

65

Logan's has just concluded the very best speech, of an hour's length, I ever heard. My old, withered, dry eyes are full of tears yet. If he writes it out anything like he delivered it, our people shall see a good many copies of it."

Conspicuous by reason of his age, talents, and former service to the country was former President John Quincy Adams, eighty-one years old, "honest, experienced, shrewd and fearlessly uncompromising on moral issues."[1] Lincoln was on the floor of the house on that morning of February when Adams stood up to speak, suddenly he clutched his desk with groping fingers, then slumped to his chair, and was carried out to linger and die, saying, "This is the last of earth, but I am content." In the final hour Henry Clay in tears held his hand, and Lincoln served with a committee on arrangements. Mr. Adams was given a state funeral, and many said he "could have no fear of the recording angel."[2]

During his two year sojourn in Washington, Congressman Lincoln gained an understanding of Washington, and, a contact with national affairs that he could not have received in any other way. He attended sessions of the Supreme Court where he heard "such giants of the bar as Rufus Choate, Reverdy Johnson, and Daniel Webster arguing, pleading, and building the fabric of American law." He also met Chief Justice Roger B. Taney, and three days after the termination of the Thirtieth Congress, he was admitted to the practice of law before the United States Supreme Court, and on the same day he argued his first case before this high tribunal.[3]

When Abraham Lincoln returned home from Congress he was less popular than at any other period of his entire political career. In many ways things looked rather gloomy for Abe. He was out of office and out of money. He tried to get the appointment of Commissioner of the General Land Office at Washington at a salary of $3,000 a year, but failed. Then in August of 1849, Secretary of State John M. Clayton notified Lincoln of his appointment to the office of either Secretary or Governor of the new state of Oregon. He replied, "I respectfully decline the office." Mainly, it would seem, because Mary would not let him accept. She did not want to leave the society of Springfield for a frontier post, and she believed there was something better for him.

Lincoln was a natural born lawyer. He liked law and in Illinois his high reputation as a lawyer was unique. Grant Goodrich, a prominent member of the Chicago bar with an extensive law practice urged Lincoln to become his partner, but Lincoln refused the offer on the grounds that his health might not be good in Chicago. Therefore, he re-entered the practice with Herndon, and from 1849 to 1854 practiced law "more assiduously than ever." Herndon was now a fairly good lawyer within his own right, and was a source of considerable strength and encouragement to Lincoln. Yet as the junior partner he remained in charge of the office at Springfield, while Lincoln went out again to travel the Eighth Circuit which, until 1853, consisted of fourteen counties covering virtually one fifth of the state of Illinois. Court was usually held in the county seat, and to visit the fourteen county seats meant a journey of approximately five hundred miles. Half the year was taken with sessions on this circuit—three months at the spring session and three months at the fall term of court.

On "an indifferent, rawboned specimen" of a horse, Lincoln would set out from home with his saddle-bags stuffed with documents, a law book, and some changes of underclothing. Strapped to his saddle was a "slicker coat" and a cotton umbrella to shelter him when the elements were rough. Early in the 1850s, when the roads were somewhat improved, he hitched the horse to his buggy and rode in greater comfort. He was not usually alone, for itinerant lawyers were his circuit-riding companions, along with Judge Davis who presided over the courts. Thus it was usually a jovial and carefree company that rode along, judge and lawyers, "forgetful for the time being of their legal difficulties, and entertaining each other with jokes and good humor." On arriving at the county seat where the court was scheduled to hold session for from two days to a week, the judge and lawyers often stayed at the same crowded inn where the lawyers usually slept two in a bed. Judge Davis weighed three hundred pounds and required a bed alone.

Court day was a holiday in the average county seat. From the entire countryside came men, women, and children on horseback, in wagons, and afoot to assemble indiscriminately in and around the county court building. The courthouses were sometimes only makeshift buildings, but more often they were an attractive wood or brick structure whose graceful verandas with large columns or pillars often adorned the front. Inside were a few office rooms and a large courtroom with knotty pine floors, wooden benches and a slightly raised platform for the judge and jury.

When court was officially opened by the sheriff's announcement, and the summoning of the jury by the clerk, the courtroom was always crowded with people intent on hearing all that went on. They were especially interested in hearing the lawyers plead their cases. Lincoln, because of his eloquence, his many human interest stories, and his ease in quoting from the Scriptures, was usually their hero. His stories always illustrated some point. For example, one day in a trial atmosphere of great excitement, wild confused statements, few facts, and considerable blustering on the part of the opposing attorney, Lincoln observed:

"That reminds me of a farmer who lost his way on the Western frontier. Night came on, and the embarrassments of his position were increased by a furious tempest which suddenly burst upon him. To add to his discomfort, his horse had given out, leaving him exposed to all the dangers of the pitiless storm.

"The peals of thunder were terrific, the frequent flashes of lightning affording the only guide on the road as he resolutely trudged onward, leading his jaded steed. The earth seemed fairly to tremble beneath him in the war of elements. One bolt threw him suddenly upon his knees.

"Our traveler was not a prayerful man, but finding himself involuntarily brought to an attitude of devotion, he addressed himself to the Throne of Grace in the following prayer for his deliverance:

" 'O God! hear my prayer this time, for Thou Knowest it is not often that I call upon Thee. And, O Lord! if it is all the same to Thee, give us a little more light and a little less noise.' "

The judge and Lincoln were the only members of the entire bar who regularly made the rounds of all the fourteen county seats — the judge because his duties required it, and Lincoln because he loved the court life, and the unusual attachment which came to exist between him and Judge Davis, who had few if any equals in the state.

Lincoln could accomodate himself to any surroundings and circumstances, was content with the food and lodging, and was friendly, cordial and frank. There was "something about his kind and amiable expression and sad, quizzical eyes which gave everyone the impression that here was a man of truthfulness and integrity who could be trusted implicitly." He experienced brief spells when he was gloomy and dejected, and stared absentmindedly at the walls. Yet his lovable traits, his effective pleadings at court, and his character made folks forget his idiosyncrasies. They loved him for what he was and acclaimed him the most popular lawyer on the circuit.

In May of 1849, Dennis Hanks had written Lincoln of the illness of his father: "He Craves to See you all the time & he wonts you to Come if you ar able to git hure, for you are his only Child that is of his own flush & blood. . .he wonts you to prepare to meet him in the unknown world, or in heven, for he think that ower Savour has a Crown of glory, prepared for him I wright this with a bursting hart. . . ." A few days later another letter came saying his father was better, and would be well in a short time. 4

Eddie, the second child of Mr. and Mrs. Lincoln, died on February 1, 1850, after an illness of fifty-two days. Death came just before his fourth birthday and the grief stricken parents being unable to locate the Episcopal clergyman who had married them, turned to Dr. James Smith, Pastor of the First Presbyterian Church, to officiate at the funeral. This led to an intimate acquaintance, wherein Dr. Smith was to mean much to the family.

In the loss of Eddie, the unseen force of sacred sorrow again plowed Lincoln's soul and turned his thoughts towards the great question of life after death. Instinctively he quoted over and over the lines of his favorite poem, *Oh Why Should the Spirit of Mortal Be Proud.* Following the funeral there appeared in the *Illinois Journal* these unsigned lines entitled "Little Eddie":·

The angel death was hovering nigh,
And the lovely boy was called to die.
Bright is the home to him now given,
For 'of such is the kingdom of heaven.'

No one knew for certain who wrote the verse, but it was generally supposed to have been written by Abe and Mary, since they had the phrase "Of such is the Kingdom of Heaven" engraved on little Eddie's white marble stone.

Dr. Smith gave Lincoln a copy of his book, *The Christian Defense,* and he took the family and withdrew to Kentucky for a week's rest in the Todd house. On their return the family rented a pew at $50 per year and became constant attendants at the First Presbyterian Church. The children attended Sunday school.

Shortly thereafter there was revival in the church, and Mr. and Mrs. Lincoln attended not only the regular meetings, but the inquiry meetings also. When the candidates were examined at the close of the meetings Mr. Lincoln was in Detroit prosecuting a patent right case. Mrs. Lincoln stated that she was confirmed in the Episcopal church when she was twelve years of age but did not wish to join the church by letter, but on profession of faith, as she was never converted until in this series of meetings. She was admitted.

When Mr. Lincoln returned he made no move to join, as he had reached no satisfactory experience of spiritual conversion. He continued to be interested, however, as evidenced by the following experience as related by Rev. James F. Jacquess, pastor of the First Methodist Church, Springfield. He said:

"I was standing at the parsonage door one Sunday morning, a beautiful morning in May, when a little boy came up to me and said: 'Mr. Lincoln sent me around to see if you was going to preach today.' Now, I had met Mr. Lincoln, but I never thought any more of Abe Lincoln than I did of any one else. I said to the boy: 'You go back and tell Mr. Lincoln that if he will come to church he will see whether I am going to preach or not!' The little fellow stood working his fingers and finally said: 'Mr. Lincoln told me he would give me a quarter if I would find out whether you are going to preach!' I did not want to rob the little fellow of his income, so I told him to tell Mr. Lincoln that I was going to preach. . . .

"The church was filled that morning. It was a good-sized church, but on that day all the seats were taken. Mr. Lincoln came into the church after the services had commenced, and there being no vacant seats, chairs were put in the altar in front of the pulpit, and Mr. Lincoln and Governor French and wife sat in the altar area during the entire services, Mr. Lincoln on my left and Governor French on my right. I had chosen for my text the words: 'Ye must be born again,' and during the course of my sermon I laid particular stress on the word *must*. I noticed that Mr. Lincoln appeared to be deeply interested. A few days after that Sunday Mr. Lincoln called on me and informed me that he had been greatly impressed with my remarks on Sunday and that he had come to talk with me further on the matter. I invited him in, and my wife and I talked and prayed with him for hours. Now, I have seen many persons converted; I have seen hundreds brought to Christ, and if ever a person was converted, Abraham Lincoln was converted that night in my house. His wife was a Presbyterian, but from remarks he made to me he could not accept Calvinism. He never joined my church, but I will always believe that since that night Abraham Lincoln lived and died a Christian gentleman."[5]

Some months later the session of the Presbyterian church invited Mr. Lincoln to deliver a lecture on the Bible. On the evening of the lecture the church was full, and he gave such a powerful message that many divines and others pronounced it "the ablest defense of the Bible ever uttered in that pulpit." In his address Mr. Lincoln advocated placing the Bible in every house in the state and drew a striking contrast between the Ten Commandments and the law codes of the most eminent lawgivers of antiquity. In closing he used these words:

> It seems to me that nothing short of infinite wisdom could by any possibility have devised and given to man this excellent and perfect moral code. It is suited to man in all conditions of life, and includes all the duties they owe to their Creator, to themselves and to their fellow-man. [6]

In January of 1851 word came of his father's last illness, and Lincoln could not go to the bedside because of sickness in his own family but wrote his step-brother, John D. Johnston:

> I feel sure you have not failed to use my name, if necessary, to procure a doctor, or any thing else for Father in his present sickness. My business is such that I could hardly leave home now, if it were not, as it is, that my own wife is sick-abed. (It is a case of baby-sickness, and I suppose is not dangerous.) I sincerely hope Father may yet recover his health; but at all events, tell him to remember to call upon, and confide in, our great, and good, and merciful Maker; who will not turn away from him in any extremity. He notes the fall of a sparrow, and numbers the hairs of our heads; and He will not forget the dying man, who puts his trust in Him. Say to him that if it be his lot to go now, he will soon have a joyous meeting with many loved ones gone before; and where the rest of us, through the help of God, hope ere-long to join them. [7]

When death came to Thomas Lincoln on January 17, 1851, his only son could not go because of a crowded court calendar. Yet, Lincoln felt confident for his father was to the last a church-going, consistent Christian man, whose invariable closing words of grace at meals Abe remembered as, "Fit and prepare us for

71

humble service, we beg for Christ's sake. Amen."

Lincoln had helped his family get started with their 120-acre Coles County farm home and had sent them money from time to time, therefore the farm had been willed to him as the sole heir. The following summer after the father's death, Abe had deeded the west 80 acres to John D. Johnston, subject to Sarah Bush Lincoln's dower right. But the stepbrother was a kind of a dude and dandy who idled about until he was in serious debt. He appealed to Lincoln for a loan of $80, writing that he needed the money so badly that he "would almost give his place in heaven for the loan." Lincoln refused to send money, but gave the young man some sharp advice: "You are not lazy, and still you are an idler. I doubt whether since I saw you, you have done a good whole day's work, in any one day....This habit of uselessly wasting time, is the whole difficulty." Lincoln promised that for every dollar Johnston would earn he would give him another dollar. Then said, "You say you would almost give your place in Heaven for $70 or $80. Then you value your place in Heaven very cheaply. ...You have always been kind to me, and I do not mean to be unkind to you. Affectionately, Your brother."

When Henry Clay died in June of 1852, Springfield stores closed, and after services in the Episcopal Church, a procession moved to the Hall of Representatives where, as the chief speaker, Lincoln reviewed Clay's life and suggested how on many occasions his moderation and wisdom had held the Union together when it seemed ready to break. He then quoted Clay on the slavery question: "There is a moral fitness in the idea of returning to Africa her children whose ancestors have been torn from her by the ruthless hand of fraud and violence. Transplanted in a foreign land, they will carry back to their native soil the rich fruits of religion, civilization, law and liberty."

With Clay, Lincoln hoped our government might become interested in purchasing the slaves from their masters, buying property and colonizing them in Africa. Later he was to learn how formidable a problem this might be, for over the south were 3,204,000 slaves valued on tax books at more than one and one-half billion dollars. Nevertheless, Lincoln considered slavery a moral evil which someday would be done away with in the United States.

In the last years of his law practice Abraham Lincoln rose higher and higher in the world of law and in the esteem of his fellow men. The wide variety of cases which he tried, the lawyers, the judges, ministers, and people with whom he was associated combined to make for him a most valuable period in the school of life. He learned as few men have in corresponding lengths of time, and added to his vast knowledge of human nature which was to stand him in hand in future years when he bore the responsibilities of a nation.

In all the ebb and flow of the life of a great lawyer he maintained his honesty, his integrity, and sense of fairness toward all men. "The framework of his mental and moral being was honesty," said Judge Davis, "and a wrong cause was poorly defended by him." Lincoln was "the fairest Lawyer I ever knew," declared Justice Sidney Breese of the Supreme Court. A reporter from the *Chicago Tribune* said, "Such has become the established integrity of Lincoln with us, that let a jury be empanelled from any part of our populous country, to try a case, and they will take his exposition of the law and the facts of a case without a scruple; for they know that as Lincoln has never misconstrued the law nor perverted the evidence, they can follow him and do no wrong. And when a man brings that kind of a reputation on the hustings his power with the people is almost omnipotent."[8]

He could not try a case with spirit or force unless he himself believed it was right. Once he brought suit for a client to collect an account. In the course of the trial Abe became suspicious of his client's honesty. Then the defendant introduced receipts in full, proving clearly that the entire account had been fully settled. Lincoln left the court room. When judgment was to be rendered, the judge sent for him, and he was found in the hotel washing his hands and refused to return. He told the messenger to say to the judge, "I can't come—my hands are dirty," and it became famous as "The Dirty Hands Case," and strengthened Lincoln's reputation for honesty.[9]

One of his would-be clients received the following advice: "I can win your case; I can get you $600. I can also make an honest family miserable. But I shall not take your case, and I shall not take your fee. One piece of advice I will give you gratis: Go home and think seriously whether you cannot make $600 in some honest way."

A few of his many cases have lived in the story of his life because they reveal phases of his character and the moral standards so tenaciously held throughout his life. Once when attending the trial of several women, indicted in Clinton County for having knocked in the head of a whiskey barrel and spilled the contents, Lincoln was asked to say a word in their defense. Although not employed in the case, he did speak against the evils of the liquor traffic, and insisted that the indictment should have read "The State versus Mr. Whiskey" instead of "The State against the Ladies."

In cases where Lincoln championed the cause of the needy, he expended his best efforts. On one occasion a poor crippled widow of a Revolutionary soldier came into the law office of Lincoln and Herndon; tearfully she told the senior partner how a pension agent named Wright had induced the government to grant her a pension of $400 but had charged her half the amount for his services. Her sincere protest over his exorbitant fee had availed her nothing and now she appealed to Lincoln for advice and aid.

The lawyer was thoroughly aroused as he listened. Then, when the sobbing old woman was gone, he went to the pension agent's office and requested the return of the money. When Wright refused, Lincoln reminded him that courts of justice existed to deal with such greedy rascals. Suit was brought to compel a refund.

The night before the trial, Lincoln carefully read the history of the Revolutionary War, and at the trial he had but one witness — the crippled little old widow. Through her tears to a crowded courthouse, she told what Wright had done. In that dramatic suspense of the moment Lincoln arose, peered straight into the eyes of the jury, and in a voice clear, distinct, and well modulated he reviewed the causes of the Revolution. Then straightening himself up and taking a few steps backward, he pictured eloquently and minutely the scene of patriots creeping with bleeding feet over the ice at Valley Forge.

As he reached the point in his speech where he narrated the hardened action of the defendant in fleecing the widow of her pension, "his eyes flashed, and throwing aside his handkerchief, which he held in his right hand. . .he shook his bony fingers at the pension agent with an effect that was indescribable and proceeded to 'skin' the rascal."

Then he recalled how the plaintiff's husband had kissed her and the baby and had departed for the war.

"Time rolls by; the heroes of 'seventy-six' have passed away and are encamped on the other shore. The soldier has gone to his rest; and now, crippled, blinded, and broken, his widow comes to you and to me, gentlemen of the jury, to right the wrongs. She was not always thus. She was once a beautiful woman. Her step was as elastic, her face as fair, and her voice as sweet as any that rang in the mountains of Virginia. But now she is poor and defenseless. Out here on the prairies of Illinois, many hundreds of miles away from the scenes of her childhood, she appeals to us who enjoy the privileges achieved for us by the patriots of the Revolution, for our sympathetic aid and manly protection."

Then, stretching out his long arms toward the jury, he concluded dramatically: "All I ask is, shall we befriend her?" The crowded courtroom sat gripped by a strange awe, half the jury was in tears, while the defendant sat "drawn up and writhing under the fire of Lincoln's invective." The jury returned the verdict for every dollar demanded, Lincoln became the widow's surety for court costs, paid her way home, and her hotel bill. When the judgment was paid he and Herndon remitted the proceeds to her, and made no charge for their services. [10]

Another example of services rendered by Lincoln without pay was his refusal to charge anything for saving the farm of a young woman, Rebecca Daimwood. She had inherited the farm from her uncle, Christopher Robinson. John Lane, who occupied the farm, was made administrator. For fifteen years Miss Daimwood made her home with the Lane family, then married a young farmer, William M. Dorman, and requested the farm be turned over to them. Whereupon Lane petitioned the court at Shawneetown for the sale of the property to satisfy his claim of more than a thousand dollars against the Robinson estate, which claim had been allowed him by the court some fifteen years earlier.

The young married couple resisted Lane's petition, but lost in the lower court. Their lawyer, Samuel D. Marshall, appealed the case to the Supreme Court and retained Lincoln to plead. Both sides were ably defended, but the Court, whose judge was none other than Justice James Shields, with whom Lincoln came near having a duel, sustained Lincoln's plea, reversed the decree of the trial court, and turned the farm over to the young couple. When asked the amount of his fee, Lincoln said his services were his wedding present to Rebecca and William. [11]

The case, *McCormick v. Manny* et al., afterwards called Lincoln's "Reaper Case," was most important because of its effect on Mr. Lincoln, and its historical implications.

Cyrus H. McCormick of Chicago sued John H. Manny and his associates of Rockford for $400,000 for alleged infringement of his patents in the manufacturing of their reaping machines. Other manufacturers, making machines similar to McCormick's, joined Manny in his defense against McCormick. Large sums of money were made available and leading attorneys employed on both sides. Edward M. Dickerson of New York, and Reverdy Johnson of Baltimore, represented McCormick, and George Harding of Philadelphia, and Edwin M. Stanton of Pittsburgh, for Manny.

Suit was brought in the U.S. District Court at Chicago, therefore the Manny group considered it wise to also employ an influential attorney who was conversant with Illinois laws and who stood well with Judge Drummond in whose court the case would be tried. Abraham Lincoln was chosen as the man best prepared to assist in the defense. It was arranged for him to be paid a substantial fee—supposedly $1000—and he was given a $500 cash retainer.

Lincoln prepared with great thoroughness in getting his brief ready to plead at this case. He not only studied the technical field of reaper mechanics and patent law, but he went to Rockford to study Manny's reaper and its intricate parts. However, it was finally arranged that the case should be heard in Cincinnati, instead of Chicago. Nevertheless, Lincoln went to Cincinnati with the fond hope of measuring swords with the famous lawyer, Reverdy Johnson of Baltimore. No such opportunity was given him, for when introduced to his fellow lawyers of the defense, he was not only given the cold treatment, but was treated very rudely by Edwin M. Stanton who looked down upon this strangely dressed country lawyer of the West. At the trial, the arguments were purposely limited to two on a side and Abe was not allowed to participate.

In spite of the affront Lincoln stayed in Cincinnati, and "sat as one entranced" or else walked back and forth in the rear of the court room as he heard and watched the talented Eastern lawyers deliver their carefully prepared briefs. It was a great experience for him. He was especially impressed with Stanton's masterly argument which closed and won the case. Yet neither Harding nor Stanton ever conferred with Lincoln, ever had him at their table, nor sat with him, nor asked him to their rooms, nor walked to and from the court with him. When the hearing was over Harding and Stanton left the city without saying good-bye to him. However Lincoln never remembered these men with bitterness and resentment, but with understanding and appreciation.[12]

After the trial Lincoln took a walk down to the river with a friend, and exclaimed with great fervor, "I am going home to study law." His companion expressed surprise at this and suggested that Lincoln was already at the head of the bar of Illinois. To which Abe replied: "Ah, yes, I do occupy a good position there, and I think that I can get along with the way things are done there now. But these college-trained men who have devoted their whole lives to study are coming West; don't you see? And they study their cases as we never do. They have got as far as Cincinnati now. They will soon be in Illinois. I am going home to study law! I am as good as any of them, and when they get to Illinois I will be ready for them!"[13]

From this time on his style and manner of speech and argument improved steadily.

On returning to Springfield, Lincoln received another check for $500 but returned it, saying that he had not earned it since he made no argument at the trial, and was entitled to no pay beyond the original retainer. Watson, who disbursed funds, again sent the check to Lincoln, insisting that, since he had prepared his argument and been present for the trial, he was as much entitled to the fee as if he had made the argument. Lincoln then accepted.

Lincoln's influence over a jury was shown in the case of Quinn "Peachy" Harrison who, in a fight at a country village, had fatally stabbed Greek Crafton. Both young men belonged to fine families, and the brother of one was married to the sister of the other. They had always been friends, but became involved in a hot political quarrel. In a moment of anger young Harrison stabbed Crafton with a knife causing his death three days later. Harrison's father was a rich man, and employed four lawyers, among them Lincoln, to defend his son. Prominent lawyers were employed to prosecute, and the case aroused great interest.

The trial was held in September 1859 in the Circuit Court of Sangamon County at Springfield. When the prosecution had finished its case against Harrison, it looked like wilful, premeditated murder. Yet when it came time for the defense, Lincoln led in a most effective manner. The dramatic crisis in the trial came when one of the main witnesses for the defense, the Reverend Peter Cartwright, the grandfather of the defendant, was called to the witness stand, and Lincoln questioned him. Cartwright had experienced a long and extremely useful life as an evangelist, a churchman, and "as a relentless fighter against wrong of every kind, and he was loved by the entire community."[14]

In most tender gentleness, Lincoln drew from him the story of his visit to the dying youth. In a deep solemn voice Cartwright told how he had held the defendant as a babe, laughing and crying on his knee. He told also of his visit to the dying Crafton, and how in almost the hour of death, the lad had said, "I am dying; I will soon part with all I love on earth and I want you to say to my slayer that I forgive him. I want to leave this earth with the forgiveness of all who have, in any way injured me."

With "moving power and pathos," Lincoln then made a graphic recital of the case, and pleaded with the jury to act in the magnanimous spirit of the deceased, and not to wrench from the dying man his last claim to Divine mercy, nor to burden with woe the last years of the venerable gray-haired minister. John M. Zane, a law student who was present, said of Lincoln's plea, "His listeners were moved to tears, as he described the repentant sinner on his deathbed, stretching out his hands with the hope of a farther shore, seeking to right his life with his salvation and imploring that he should have no part in bringing even his slayer to the scaffold." The jury acquitted Harrison.[15]

The most famous criminal case which Lincoln handled was his defense of William (Duff) Armstrong. Duff was the son of Jack Armstrong, Lincoln's old wrestling antagonist and friend of early New Salem days.

On Saturday night the 29th of August, 1857, about a half mile from a campmeeting in Mason County, a group of rough young men gathered around a wagon where whiskey was being sold. They drank, then quarreled and fought. James H. Norris and Duff Armstrong fought with and apparently beat up a drunken farmer by the name of James P. Metzker. The injured Metzker mounted his horse and rode off to his home, but supposedly fell from his mount twice. He died at his home three days later. Duff Armstrong and Norris were arrested and charged with his murder. Norris had already killed a man in Havana, Illinois, but had been acquitted. Now he was tried for Metzker's death, found guilty, and sentenced to the penitentiary for eight years.

Duff Armstrong, who was kept in prison, was to be tried later, and the attorneys secured a change of venue for his trial from Mason County to Beardstown in Cass County, where he was to be tried for murder the following May. The sorrow of the whole affair brought Jack Armstrong to his grave. Jack's last request to his wife, Hanna, was to sell everything and clear Duff.

Friends advised Hanna to get Lincoln's services, and she drove to Springfield to beg him to defend her son. Lincoln assured her that he could hardly believe Duff capable of the crime alleged against him, and that he would offer his services gratuitously to help in her deep affliction.

At the time of the trial, Lincoln was deeply engaged in both law and politics. His campaign for the senate against Stephen A. Douglas was just being launched, and at the time he was conducting proceedings in an outstanding divorce case. Yet, he dropped everything and hastened to Beardstown to defend the lad whose cradle he had rocked when a baby.

Lincoln assisted Judge Harriott in getting young men on the jury. They would understand the case better. The average age of the jurymen as finally picked was 23. During the trial Lincoln sat with his eyes fixed on the ceiling while the prosecution showed that Metzker had two wounds, one on the back of his head and the other over his right eye. Charles Allen, the prosecution's principal witness, swore that by the aid of a brightly shining moon, he had seen Norris strike Metzker in the back of the brain with a neckyoke of a wagon, and that he had seen Duff Armstrong hit Metzker with a slung-shot, then throw the slung-shot away. A slung-shot had been found nearby. The outlook for the defendant looked bleak.

When it came Lincoln's time to cross-examine Allen, he casually and with seeming unconcern asked as to the time of the attack, how far away Allen was standing, and how much light there was. The witness answered promptly that he was about 15 or 20 yards away from the combatants, that the hour was about eleven o'clock at night, and that he could see plainly for the moon was shining almost directly overhead at the time.

Thereupon Lincoln produced an *Almanac* for 1857, which showed that on the night of August 29, the moon had set and gone down out of sight at 11:57 P.M. Therefore at the precise hour of Armstrong's fight with Metzker, the moon was not in the position stated by Allen, but instead was low in the western sky—within an hour of setting. The jury broke into laughter. The *Almanac* was examined by Judge Harriott, by the attorneys for the prosecution and by the jury. Attorney Lincoln then pointed out to the jury that if this witness was so badly mistaken on so conspicuous a fact as the position of the moon, he might be in gross error on other relevant points.

William Watkins then took the witness stand and swore that the slung-shot belonged to him, that he had made it himself, but at the campmeeting the day before he had decided to throw it away, and had thrown it about where it had been found. The defense pointed out that Metzker had fallen from his horse once or twice on his way home, and struck his head on the ground. Dr. Charles E. Parker, a physician and surgeon, was then put on the stand, and by the aid of a skull, he showed the jury that such a fall and blow on the back of the head, or the stroke by Norris, might easily have caused the fracture near the right eye which helped to bring on Metzker's death. Several character witnesses testified to Duff Armstrong's good reputation. [16]

Lincoln concluded the trial, speaking for about an hour to the twelve jurymen who held Duff Armstrong's fate in their hands. He rose with grave impressiveness, took off his coat and vest and began to speak slowly, distinctly, sincerely as he reviewed the whole testimony, picking it to pieces, and concluded with a frank plea for sympathy. He told of his acquaintance with the Armstrongs; the accused, Duff Armstrong, he had held in his arms and rocked in the cradle "when Duff was a baby at Clary's Grove;" he told of the help and comfort given him by the parents, of "the pioneer hardships and struggles, of the recent death of the father, of the plight of the widow, and of the hopeless desolate life that would be hers if her son should be taken from her—the poverty, disgrace, and distress." Tears poured down Lincoln's face, and the jury was overcome and many of them wept with him in his desperate earnestness. Attorney Walker said, "I have never seen such Mastery exhibited of the feelings and emotions of men as on that occasion." [17]

The Court instructed the jury, and as they filed out of the

room, one of them heard Lincoln say, "Aunt Hanna, your boy will be cleared before sundown."

After one hour's deliberation the jury found Lincoln's client, Duff Armstrong, not guilty. Lincoln shook hands with Duff then led him to his mother and told him to care for and comfort her, "and try to make as good a man as your father has been."

The fees charged by Lincoln for his services were modest. His income from 1850 to 1860 averaged from two to three thousand dollars. In some cases, however, large monies were involved, and he accepted these fees accordingly.

In 1854 he was employed to represent the Illinois Central Railroad against McLean County. The State Constitution provided for uniform taxation of all property in proportion to its value, "and not otherwise." Only the Legislature could make exemptions in cases where persons or Corporations "were using or exercising franchises and privileges." The charter of the Illinois Central Railroad provided that the Company pay to the State, semiannually, five percent of its gross receipts, and be exempted from taxes for six years. Yet the officials of McLean County claimed that the exemption applied only to state taxes. They instituted court proceedings to force the railroad company to pay taxes on its property owned within that county in addition to the payment of five percent of its gross earnings which it paid to the state of Illinois by its charter terms. This would have endangered the financial stability of the railroad—probably causing inevitable bankruptcy; therefore they refused to pay the tax, and employed counsel to resist the suit.

Lincoln and his associate counsel argued the case in McLean County, and the case was decided against them. He appealed to the Supreme Court, and the case there was long and drawn out. In 1856 the case was reargued, and after Lincoln's final argument the court unanimously held that under the Constitution, the Legislature could make exceptions, and that the railroads charter provided an exception. Therefore the counties could not tax the Illinois Railroad. This saved the railroad hundreds of thousands of dollars, in that they would not have to pay county taxes for six years—until the financial crisis of the road had passed.

When Lincoln presented a bill of $2,000 at the Chicago office, an impertinent railway official there said, "Why, this is as much as a first class lawyer would have charged." Abe was angered by this contemptuous treatment. He obtained a signed statement from five leading lawyers to the effect that if he charged $5,000 it would be a reasonable fee for the services he had rendered. Thereupon Lincoln brought suit against the railway company for five thousand dollars. The company paid the fee, gave Lincoln a pass over their lines, and continued to use his services as attorney for their railroad.[18]

This generous fee was the largest Lincoln ever received, and was quite providential. Before too long he would be debating with Douglas, speechmaking as a candidate for the U.S. Senate and eventually running for the highest office in the land.

On his practice of law, Lincoln was frequently called on to prepare legal papers of various kinds. On one occasion he stood at the bedside of a dying woman to prepare her last will and testament. He had taken his friend Green with him as a witness. As she faced death, the dying woman expressed her confidence in God, and spoke of His faithfulness to her through life. Lincoln was deeply impressed and said, "Your faith in Christ is wise and strong. . . . You are to be congratulated on passing through life so usefully and into the life beyond so hopefully."

When the woman asked him to read a few verses out of the Bible, Lincoln quoted from memory the Twenty-Third Psalm. Then he quoted, "Let not your heart be troubled: Ye believe in God, believe also in me," and recited the words of "Rock of Ages." Later his friend Green said to him, "You have acted as a pastor as well as an attorney today." Lincoln replied, "God and eternity and heaven were very near me today."

CHAPTER VIII
The Giant Awakes

One evening after a very strenuous day in court, Abraham Lincoln and Ralph Emerson, a promising law student, went for a walk. Suddenly Emerson said, "Mr. Lincoln, I want to ask you a question. Is it possible for a man to practice law and always do by others as he would be done by?"

There was no answer. They walked for sometime in utter silence, then Lincoln heaved a sigh and began talking about something else. Later, in speaking of this, Emerson said, "I had my answer, and that walk turned the course of my life."

It was generally believed, not only by Emerson but by people at large, that Abraham Lincoln practiced the golden rule while he practiced law in Illinois for near twenty years. He liked the course of his life, and for the past five years had become more and more absorbed in his legal work, and less in politics.

Then, in the course of the years from 1850 to 1854, when the United States Congress and the whole nation was aroused over the slavery question, the Fugitive Slave Law, and what would be done concerning the further spread of slavery in the Western territories,

Senator Stephen A. Douglas became Chairman of the Committee on Territories. In an effort to gain for himself the goodwill of Southern members, he reactivated the question of what would be done with the territories of Kansas and Nebraska, from which slavery was excluded by the Missouri Compromise.

Being a remarkable man, a good orator, an accomplished parliamentarian, but morally willing to compromise, Douglas imposed himself on the Senate and effectively maneuvered through the Kansas-Nebraska Bill which empowered the people of Kansas at any time to vote whether they should be "slave" or "free." Thus the Missouri Compromise was virtually repealed, and slavery licensed to spread.

As the news spread across the nation, the majority of the people of the northern states were thoroughly aroused. In New England, 3,050 clergymen signed a widely publicized memorial to the U.S. Senate: "*In the name of Almighty God, and in His Presence,* we solemnly protest against the passage of the Kansas-Nebraska Bill." In Chicago 25 clergymen signed a similar protest, followed by 500 ministers in the Northwest. Douglas went forward with his iniquitous work, declaring that the ministers were striving to coerce Congress "In the name of Almighty God."

Nevertheless, immediately there followed a race to win Kansas for slavery or for freedom. Southerners came pouring into Kansas, and Northern settlers came in still larger numbers. When it became apparent that freedom was winning easily, the country began to suffer from stuffed ballot boxes, fights, bloodshed, and civil war between two classes of immigrants. The deep tragedy and shame of it all rapidly spread over the Nation.

Sensing the fact that he had helped set in motion forces which could well mean his ultimate undoing, Douglas hurried home to Illinois to explain his position. On the way, Douglas could see from his car window the burning of dummies bearing his name.

In Ohio a women's organization presented him with thirty pieces of silver and denounced him as "Judas." In Chicago, in front of North Market Hall where he was scheduled to speak, a crowd of 8,000 insulted him with questions, hisses, groans, boos, and catcalls. They howled and hooted him until finally, after two hours he looked at his watch, jammed his silk hat on his head, left the stand and went to Fremont House, followed by shouted insults.

News of the event was published throughout the United States. Many papers approved the outrage. The Democratic press denounced the disturbance. Douglas went to speak at other cities in the state. Everywhere he was received with indignity and insults. At some places there were burning effigies of himself hanging by the neck and the display of offensive mottoes and placards for the one who had broken a "sacred compact" and sacrificed freedom to gain the Presidency. However, Douglas spoke eloquently in city after city on the doctrine of "popular sovereignty," and gained back a measure of his former popularity.

On October 3, 1854, the State Fair opened at Springfield. For weeks it had been advertised that Douglas would speak on that day and it was rumored that Abraham Lincoln would answer him. Prize cattle, hogs, horses; exhibitions of corn and other farm products, along with housewifery skill; specimens of improved agricultural implements were features of the show. From all over Illinois political leaders came to the capital, and there was excitment over the prospect of hearing the "Little Giant," and possibly "Honest Abe."

In a grove near the city seats had been prepared for five thousand, but it rained and the meeting was moved to the Hall of the House of Representatives where Douglas spoke for three hours to a crowded house. The Keynote of his lecture was "popular sovereignty," and he drove home the simple question, "was not the real question whether the people should rule, whether the voters in a territory should control their own affairs." The people cheered, and when he closed it was announced that Lincoln would answer him the next day.

On the following afternoon the Hall of Representatives was again crowded, and with practically the same audience that had heard Douglas. Lincoln's friends expected him to do well in his reply, but his speech was to be a surprise even to those who knew him best. It was a hot, sultry afternoon and the air in the Hall was heavy when, at the appointed hour, the tall, thin lawyer somewhat awkwardly mounted the platform, and began haltingly, but soon his hesitation disappeared, and he rose with an earnest, profound, passionate eloquence which lasted for three hours. His hair was disordered, and as he proceeded, sweat poured down his face. Time and again the crowd burst into applause and when he closed the house rang with cheers. The next day the Springfield Journal said:

85

"Mr. Lincoln's speech was the profoundest, in our opinion, that he has made in his whole life. He felt upon his soul the truths burn which he uttered, and all present felt that he was true to his own soul. His feelings once or twice swelled within, and came near stifling utterance. He quivered with emotion. The whole house was as still as death as he pursued his masterly exhibition of the fraud and sophistry wrapped in Douglas' plan for 'popular sovereignty.' He attacked the Kansas-Nebraska bill with unusual warmth and energy; and all felt that a man of strength was its enemy, and that he intended to blast it if he could by strong and manly efforts. He was most successful, and the house approved the glorious triumph of truth by loud and continued huzzas."[1]

Senator Douglas was present, and the vigor, earnestness and truth of Lincoln's speech aroused the crowd to such enthusiasm that Douglas felt obliged to reply to him the next day. He achieved very little, for Lincoln had clearly emerged in public life, never again to return to obscurity.

In Peoria twelve days later, Douglas spoke and Lincoln replied to him in much the same three hour speech. This was preserved in its entirety, and came to be known as the "Peoria Speech." Excerpts show that in it he expressed the moral aspects of the subject as no one else had done.

I cannot but hate slavery. I hate it because of the monstrous injustice of slavery itself. I hate it because it deprives our republican example of its just influence in the world; enables the enemies of free institutions, with plausibility, to taunt us as hypocrites; causes the real friends of freedom to doubt our sincerity; and especially because it forces so many good men among ourselves into an open war with the very fundamental principles of civil liberty, criticizing the Declaration of Independence, and insisting that there is no right principle of action but self-interest. . . .Slavery is founded in the selfishness of man's nature — opposition to it is his love of justice. These principles are an eternal antagonism. Repeal the Missouri Compromise, repeal the Declaration of Independence, repeal all past history, you still cannot repeal human nature. It still will be in the abundance of man's heart that slavery extension is wrong, and out of the abundance of his heart his mouth will continue to speak. . . .

The doctrine of self-government is right — absolutely and eternally right — but it has no just application as here at-

86

tempted. Or perhaps I should rather say, that whether it has such application depends upon whether a negro is not or is a man. If he is not a man, in that case, he who is a man may, as a matter of self-government, do just what he pleases with him. But if the negro is a man, is it not to that extent a total destruction of self-government to say that he too shall not govern himself? When the white man governs himself, that is self-government; but when he governs himself and also governs another man, that is more than self-government — that is despotism. . . .I particularly object to the new position which the avowed principle of this Nebraska law gives to slavery in the body politic. I object to it because it assumes that there can be moral right in the enslaving of one man by another. I object to it as a dangerous dalliance for a free people — a sad evidence that, feeling prosperity, we forget right; that liberty, as a principle, we have ceased to revere. . . .Little by little, but steadily as man's march to the grave, we have been giving up the old for the new faith. Near eighty years ago we began by declaring that all men are created equal; but now, from that beginning, we have run down to the other declaration, that for some men to enslave others is a 'sacred right of self-government.' These principles cannot stand together. They are as opposite as God and Mammon. [2]

Douglas was so completely overwhelmed that he came to his opponent and said: "Lincoln, you understand this question of prohibiting slavery in the territories better than all the opposition in the Senate of the United States. I cannot make anything by debating it with you." And with this plea he begged Lincoln for a truce. Lincoln agreed, and both abandoned the field and returned to their work. Lincoln's speeches were widely reported alongside those of Douglas.

Forces were then in motion that shortly materialized in the organization of the Republican party. This new organization opposed the extension of slavery into the territories; stood for admitting Kansas as a free state; and for restoring the federal government to the principles of Washington and Jefferson. Its members were made up of groups from the Democratic Party, the Anti-slavery Whigs, the Abolitionists, the Free Soil, the Know Nothing Party, and others. For a time Lincoln avoided any possible connection with the new Republican party, but the logic of events, helped along by his active young partner, Herndon, finally brought him into membership.

The State Republican Convention met at Bloomington on May 29, 1856. Excitement over the turmoil in Kansas had grown to a frenzy, the newspapers were full of accounts of how, in the U.S. Senate, Congressman Brooks had attacked Senator Sumner and beaten him near to death for a speech against slavery. Paul Selby lay at home prostrated by a cowardly blow from a political opponent. The members were resolved to take radical action.

After the adoption of a platform, the appointment of delegates to the National Convention, and other necessary work was completed, there was a call for speeches. Various men were called to the platform and spoke without producing any marked effect; when suddenly the call was raised—"Lincoln"—"Lincoln"— "Give us Lincoln!" The crowd took it up and made the hall ring until a tall figure rose in the back of the audience and slowly strode down the aisle. As he turned to his audience there came an expression of intense emotion over his face—the emotion of a great soul moved by an unseen power. Even in stature he appeared greater. He seemed to realize it was a crisis—a parting of the ways in his political life. Beyond this, as he began to speak, he felt some strange "powerful amalgamating force" drawing together, for some great purpose, the discordent elements in that assembly. He was deeply moved with a profound sense of the importance of the hour, and the supporting strength of the One of whom Nancy Hanks Lincoln had taught him in childhood.

"He spoke slowly and haltingly at first, but gradually grew in force and intensity until his hearers arose from their chairs and with pale faces and quivering lips pressed unconsciously towards him. Starting from the back of the broad platform on which he stood, his hands on his hips, he slowly advanced towards the front, his eyes blazing, his face white with passion, his voice resonant with the force of his conviction. As he advanced he seemed to his audience fairly to grow, and when at the end of a period he stood at the front line of the stage, hands still on the hips, head back, raised on his tip toes, he seemed like a giant inspired. 'At that moment,' says Judge Scott, 'he was the handsomest man I ever saw.'"[3]

At the climax, he uttered these words, "We won't go out of the

Union and you SHAN'T." So powerful was the effect on his audience that men and women wept as they cheered, and "every one in that assemply came to feel as one man, to think as one man, and to purpose and resolve as one man." He had made every man of them pure Republican.[4]

At the Republican National Convention at Philadelphia June 17, 1856, Colonel John C. Fremont, famed explorer, was nominated for President. On the spur of the moment, Lincoln's name was put forward for Vice-Presidential candidate, and he received 110 votes on the first ballot. However, Judge William L. Dayton of New Jersey had organized forces of the eastern states back of him and was designated as Fremont's running mate. Lincoln presented contratulations to Dayton through a letter to his friend John Van Dyke, of New Jersey, saying: "When you meet Judge Dayton present my respects, and tell him I think him a better man than I for the position, and that I shall support both him and Colonel Fremont most cordially."[5]

In the spring of 1857, Lincoln's concern for slavery was deepened by the Dred Scott case in which the Supreme Court held that a negro could not sue in the United States courts and that neither Congress nor a territorial legislature could prohibit slavery in the territories. In effect, this meant that the "negro had no rights which the white man was bound to respect." The decision brought a violent uproar in the north. Douglas hurried to Illinois to calm his constituents. "What," he cried, "oppose the Supreme Court? Is it not sacred? To resist is anarchy."

Lincoln met him fairly on the issue in a speech at Springfield. "We believe as much as Judge Douglas (perhaps more) in obedience to and respect for the judicial department of government. . . . But we think the Dred Scott decision is erroneous. We know the court that made it has often overruled its own decision, and we shall do what we can to have it overrule this. We offer no resistance to it. . . ."[6]

In the early summer of 1858 Douglas was back in Illinois again. This time not merely to defend his policies, but as the Democratic candidate to plead for his reelection to the Senate. His task would not be easy, since the Democrats in the State and the Nation were widely divided over his sudden break with President Buchanan and his party.

The Republicans, jubilant over Democratic dissension, assembled in a state convention in the Hall of the House of Representatives at Springfield. They waved Lincoln banners, yelled for him, then unanimously nominated him as "the first and only choice of the Republicans of Illinois for the United States Senate." That same June evening, in his acceptance speech, Lincoln made his famous "House Divided Speech," which was to become the basis of his future political career. It began thus:

If we could first know where we are and whither we are tending, we could better judge what to do and how to do it. We are now far into the fifth year since a policy was initiated with the avowed object, and confident promise, of putting an end to slavery agitation. Under the operation of that policy, that agitation not only has not ceased, but has constantly augmented. In my opinion it will not cease until a crisis shall have been reached and passed. 'A House divided against itself cannot stand.' I believe this government cannot endure permanently half slave and half free. I do not expect the Union to be dissolved; I do not expect the house to fall, but I do expect that it will cease to be divided. It will become all one thing, or all the other. Either the opponents of slavery will arrest the future spread of it, and place it where the public mind shall rest in the belief that it is in the course of ultimate extinction; or its advocates will push it forward till it shall become alike lawful in the states, old as well as new, North as well as South. [7]

Lincoln's nomination and his speech brought Douglas and Lincoln face to face as opposing candidates. Each respected the strength and ability of the other. Douglas who was then in Washington, told a group of Republicans, "You have nominated a very able and a very honest man." To John W. Forney he said: "I shall have my hands full. Lincoln is the strong man of his party, the best stump speaker in the west."

Senator Douglas, accompanied by his beautiful and accomplished wife, started west in June. Sixty miles out of Chicago, a special Illinois Central train with a brass band, flags and pennants met the Douglas party and escorted them to Chicago. As he stepped out on the Lake Street balcony of the Tremont House that night, fiery rockets lit the street, and the statesman began an hour and a half speech. Lincoln was in the crowd of thousands that swarmed the street, and heard Douglas refer to him as "a kind, amiable, and intelligent gentleman, a good citizen and an honorable opponent." He also heard him say: "Mr. Lincoln advocates boldly and clearly a war of sections, a war of the North against South, of the free States against the slave States — a war of extermination — to be continued relentlessly until the one or the other shall be subdued, and all the States shall either become free or become slave."[8]

The next night Lincoln spoke to a large crowd from the same Tremont House balcony. He adroitly denied the charge as it had been stated, and carefully explained the importance of settling the "mighty issue" of slavery — "whether or not Judge Douglas or myself shall ever be heard of after this night."

From Chicago the Lincoln-Douglas senatorial campaign moved down-state. In city after city they spoke to crowds numbering into the many thousands — speaking from the same platform, but at different times. Lincoln's strategy was to stay on Douglas's trail and answer him to audiences in the same places.

> "The well-tailored Senator traveled in a gaudily bannered private railroad car, accompanied by his attractive wife and busy secretarial staff. The lone Lincoln, with his wife Mary at home with the boys, followed closely behind in another car. He wore a weather-beaten 'stove-pipe' hat and dusty coat and carried a carpet bag and cane made from the wood of Henry Clay's house. Hitched to Douglas's train was a flat car on which was mounted a brass cannon. As the Senator's car approached a town, the cannon would be fired to inform the townspeople that the 'Little Giant' was coming. 'Wherever the Little Giant happened to be,' came one report, 'Abe is sure to turn up and be a thorn in his side.'"[9]

With Lincoln the "profound central truth" of the day was "slavery is wrong and ought to be dealt with as wrong." When, therefore, it was clear that Douglas did not mean to meet the issue squarely, Lincoln resolved to force him into open forum, and challenged him to a series of joint debates where they would speak face to face from the same platform on the same occasions. Their respective managers felt well of the matter, yet Douglas was reluctant. To the State Democratic leaders he said:

> Gentlemen, you do not know Mr. Lincoln. I have known him long and well, and I know that I shall have anything but an easy task. I assure you that I would rather meet any other man in the country, in this joint debate, than Abraham Lincoln.

But Douglas was not a man to shirk a fight, whatever the odds.

On July 29, 1858, Lincoln and Douglas met at a certain point on the road between Monticello and Belmont, Illinois and talked the matter over. That night the final arrangements for the debates were closed at the Belmont home of Mr. F. E. Bryant where Senator and Mrs. Douglas were spending the night at the home of their friends.[10]

According to the schedule they were to meet once in each Congressional district except those of Chicago and Springfield, where both had already spoken. The time and places designated were:

Ottawa, La Salle County	August	21, 1858
Freeport, Stephenson County	August	27, 1858
Jonesboro, Union County	September	15, 1858
Charleston, Coles County	September	18, 1858
Galesburg, Knox County	October	7, 1858
Quincy, Adams County	October	13, 1858
Alton, Madison County	October	15, 1858

The arrangement was that they should alternately open and close the discussion. Douglas was to speak at Ottawa one hour, Lincoln was to occupy an hour and a half in his reply, then Douglas would follow for half an hour. At Freeport Lincoln was to open the discussion and speak one hour. Douglas was to follow for an hour and a half, then Lincoln use one half an hour for his reply. They were to alternate in that manner in each successive place. The terms gave Douglas four openings and closes to Lincoln's three. Yet Lincoln agreed. The debates took place exactly as scheduled.[11]

Never before nor since has there ever been anything like these debates in American history—two intellectual giants, proceeding from city to city discussing in public forum the vital, burning issues of the day. The people sensed the greatness of the occasions, and came by special trains, in wagons, hayracks, buggies, oxcarts, on horseback, or afoot until hotels, rooming houses, and private homes were crowded. In some places tent encampments were set up outside the cities. Ten thousand people heard the first debate at Ottawa, fifteen thousand at Freeport, twelve thousand at Charleston, and twenty thousand at Galesburg. At Jonesboro the crowd was small—only about 1,400.

Bands, military companies, and cavalcades of horsemen headed long processions escorting the speakers from the railway stations to the platforms where they were to speak. The Douglas promoters usually put on the greater show. Yet at one place Lincoln rode in a Conestoga wagon drawn by six white horses.

There were no loud speaking systems in those days, yet Douglas had a splendid voice, and Lincoln spoke in clear trumpet tones that could be heard at an "immense distance."

For the most part each speaker respected the other, and observed the usual amenities, but "once or twice Douglas lost his temper and used such words as 'slanderer,' 'wretch,' 'sneak,' while Lincoln holding his anger in check, applied 'fraud,' 'forgery,' 'perversion,' 'falsehood' to some of Douglas' arguments." 12

But there was a marked difference in the manner of the two men. Douglas was speaking directly to his audiences. Lincoln was speaking not only to the people before him, but also over and beyond them to the people of America.

In the opening speech, Douglas paid tribute to Lincoln as "one of those peculiar men who perform with admirable skill everything they undertake." Yet, he was unfair to him in that he represented him as a former groceryman who not only sold liquor, but "could ruin more liquor than all the boys of the town." On another occasion, so the tradition persists, in the opening of one of his first speeches Douglas tried to be somewhat humorous at Abe's expense: "When I behold my honorable opponent, I am reminded of the Holy Writ where it says, 'How long, O Lord, how long.'" The people laughed rather heartily. When Douglas had finished his speech and Lincoln took the platform he said, "When I behold my honorable opponent, I, too, am reminded of the Scripture where it says, 'The wicked shall be cut short in his day.'" The retort was so apt that the people gasped rather than laugh.

However, for the most part the debates kept a desperately serious vein. So much was at stake. The speakers met each other blow for blow. Douglas hammered incessantly in his subject of "Popular Sovereignty"—that the people in each state had the right to vote slavery up or vote it down. He didn't care, he said, just so the people had their way. On the other hand, he attacked Lincoln's "House Divided Speech" and then went on to charge him with advocating "equality of the races."

In answering Douglas attack on his "House Divided Speech," Lincoln said:

> He has read from my speech in Springfield, in which I say that "a house divided against itself cannot stand." Does the

93

judge say it can stand? I don't know whether he does or not.
The judge does not seem to be attending to me just now, but
I would like to know if it is his opinion that a house divided
against itself can stand. If he does, then there is a question of
veracity, not between him and me, but between the judge and
an authority of a somewhat higher character.

Now, my friends, . . . I leave it to you to say whether in the
history of our government this institution of slavery has not
always failed to be a bond of union, and on the contrary has
been an apple of discord and an element of division in the
house. I ask you to consider whether, so long as the moral
constitution of men's minds shall continue to be the same
after this generation and assemblage shall sink into the grave,
and another race shall arise with the same moral and intellec-
tual development we have,—whether, if that institution is
standing in the same irritating position in which it now is, it
will not continue an element of division?

If so, then I have a right to say that in regard to this ques-
tion the Union is a house divided against itself. . . .

Now I believe if we could arrest the spread of slavery, and
place it where Washington and Jefferson and Madison placed
it, it would be in the course of ultimate extinction, and the
public mind would as for eighty years past believe that it was
in the course of ultimate extinction. The crisis would be past,
and the institution might be let alone for a hundred years —
if it should live so long — in the states where it exists, yet it
would be going out of existence in the way best for both the
black and the white races. [13]

In answering Douglas's accusation that he believed in social
equality, Lincoln read from one of his speeches which Douglas had
misquoted, then said:

Now, gentlemen, I don't want to read at any great length;
but this is the true complexion of all I have ever said in regard
to the institution of slavery and the black race. This is the
whole of it; and anything that argues me into his idea of per-
fect social and political equality with the negro is but a spec-
ious and fantastic arrangement of words, by which a man can
prove a horse-chestnut to be a chestnut horse. I will say here
while upon this subject that I have no purpose, either directly
or indirectly, to interfere with the institution of slavery in the

states where it exists. I believe I have no lawful right to do so, and I have no inclination to do so. I have no purpose to introduce political and social equality between the white and black races. There is a physical difference between the two, which in my judgment will probably forever forbid their living together upon the footing of perfect equality; and, inasmuch as it becomes a necessity that there must be a difference, I as well as Judge Douglas am in favor of the race to which I belong having the superior position.

I have never said anything to the contrary, but I hold that notwithstanding all, there is no reason in the world why the negro is not entitled to all the natural rights enumerated in the Declaration of Independence, — the right to life, liberty, and the pursuit of happiness. I hold that he is as much entitled to these as the white man. I agree with Judge Douglas he is not my equal in many respects — certainly not in color, perhaps not in moral or intellectual endowment. But in the right to eat the bread without the leave of anybody else, which his own hand earns, he is my equal and the equal of Judge Douglas, and the equal of every living man. [14]

Douglas tried cleverly to avoid discussing the right and wrong of slavery — said he didn't care "whether slavery is voted down or voted up." Yet, he defended the Dred Scott Decision which, in effect, said that the negro was "only property" and had no rights. But Abe "drove him mercilessly to the wall" on the moral issue when he said:

Judge Douglas is going back to the era of our Revolution and to the extent of his ability muzzling the cannon which thunders its annual joyous return. When he invites any people, willing to have slavery, to establish it, he is blowing out the moral lights around us. When he says he "cares not whether slavery is voted down or voted up," — that it is a sacred right of self-government, — he is, in my judgment, penetrating the human soul and eradicating the light of reason and the love of liberty in this American people . . . the slavery controversy is simply a phase of that eternal world-wide struggle between right and wrong that runs through all human history.

At Freeport Lincoln made one of his greatest political strokes when he put a series of questions to Douglas, the most important of which was:

Can the people of a United States territory, in any lawful way, against the wish of any citizen of the United States, exclude slavery from its limits prior to the formation of a state constitution?

In company with a number of political friends Lincoln had suggested that he intended putting this most important question to Douglas. They advised that he should not put it, for Douglas would answer "yes" in such a way as to win the senatorship. Lincoln knew that the people of the South agreed with the decision of the Supreme Court in the Dred Scott case that slaves, being property, could *not* under the Constitution be excluded from a territory. Thus, if Douglas said *yes,* the people of the South would never vote for him for President of the United States. This led Lincoln to say, "I am after larger game; the battle of 1860 is worth a hundred of this."

As expected Douglas answered unqualifiedly, "Yes." Then went on to explain at length how "the people have the lawful means to introduce it or exclude it as they please, for the reason that slavery cannot exist a day or an hour anywhere unless it is supported by local police regulations. Those police regulations can only be established by the local legislature; and if the people are opposed to slavery, they will elect representatives to that body who will by unfriendly legislation effectually prevent the introduction of it into their midst. If, on the contrary, they are for it, their legislature will favor its extension. Hence, no matter what the decision of the Supreme Court may be on that abstract question, still the right of the people to make a slave territory or a free territory is perfect and complete under the Nebraska bill."

The answer won Douglas considerable favor throughout Illinois, for it sounded good as a temporary measure. But it raised such a storm of opposition to him in the South that the dye was cast — he could never be elected President.

Thus the "battle of the giants" raged throughout Illinois. The papers printed their speeches, and the whole nation watched with the deepest of interest. Letters came from afar. One came from a prominent Eastern statesman, saying: "Who is this man that is replying to Douglas in your State? Do you realize that no greater speeches have been made on public questions in the history of our country; that his knowledge of the subject is profound, his logic unanswerable, his style inimitable?" "No man of this generation," said the *Evening Post,* "has grown more rapidly before the country than Lincoln in this canvass."[15]

Lincoln's great strength and temperate habits "showed to advantage over the fast-living Douglas. Abe made the rounds on common trains, sometimes driving across country, but always living simply; while Douglas traveled on a special train with his beautiful young bride, indulging in much merry-making and feasting." In the last debate at Alton, Douglas was worn and worried; and although he fought gamely to the last, his voice had lost the famous Douglas "bark". In his last speech he endeavored to attack Lincoln's poor showing in Congress, but he finished almost in a whisper. Abe, "as fresh and cool as ever" handed his old linen duster to a bystander and with his quaint good humor said, "Hold this while I stone Stephen."[16]

On election day, November 2, Lincoln had a majority of 4,085 votes over Douglas, yet under the apportionment law then in effect in Illinois, Douglas received fifty-four electoral votes and Lincoln forty-one. Douglas was elected and Abe was deeply disappointed. He said he felt like the boy who stubbed his toe and said that "it hurt too bad to laugh, and he was too big to cry."[17]

But he did not feel that all was lost. "I am glad I made the late race," he wrote Dr. A. G. Henry. "It gave me a hearing on the great and durable question of the age which I would have had in no other way; *and though I now sink out of view and shall be forgotten, I believe I have made some marks which shall tell for the cause of civil liberty long after I am gone.*"

However, Lincoln was far from "sinking out of view and being forgotten." Scarcely had the outcome of the campaign become known when letters of congratulation and encouragement came pouring in from all parts of the Union. He was besieged with invitations for lectures, and a number of Republican journals suggested him as the next President of the United States.

The greater number of the speaking invitations he declined, seeing he felt it necessary to take care of the many legal cases which awaited his attention. But certain calls to speak could not be declined. Douglas had been speaking for the Democrats in the governor's race in Ohio in 1859, and Lincoln was asked to reply. He spoke to two great audiences, one at Columbus on September 16, and the other at Cincinnati on September 17. At Columbus he answered Douglas' speech which had been printed in the September number of *Harper's Magazine*, and which began by asserting that—"Under our complex system of government it is the first duty of American statesmen to mark distinctly the dividing-line between Federal and Local authority." It was Douglas's best argument for "popular sovereignty" and at the time was attracting national attention. In attacking the speech, Lincoln used these and other words:

"What is Judge Douglas' popular sovereignty? It is, as a principle, no other than that if one man chooses to make a slave of another man, neither that other man nor anybody else has a right to object. Applied in government, as he seeks to apply it, it is this: If, in a new territory into which a few people are beginning to enter for the purpose of making their homes, they choose to either exclude slavery from their limits or to establish it there, however one or the other may affect the persons to be enslaved, or the infinitely greater number of persons who are afterward to inhabit that Territory, or the other members of the familes of communities, of which they are but an incipient member, or the general head of the family of States as parent of all—however their action may affect one or the other of these, there is no power or right to interfere. That is Douglas's popular sovereignty applied."

It was in this address that Lincoln uttered the oft-quoted paragraphs:

"I suppose the institution of slavery really looks small to him. He is so put up by nature that a lash upon his back would hurt him, but a lash upon anybody else's back does not hurt him. That is the build of the man, and consequently he looks upon the matter of slavery in this unimportant light.

"Judge Douglas ought to remember, when he is endeavoring to force this policy upon the American people, that while he is put up in that way, a good many are not. He ought to remember that there was once in this country a man by the name of Thomas Jefferson, supposed to be a Democrat—a man whose principles and policy are not very prevalent amongst Democrats to-day, it is true; but that man did not take exactly this view of the insignificance of the element of slavery which our friend Judge Douglas does. In contemplation of this thing, we all know he was led to exclaim, 'I trem-

ble for my country when I remember that God is just!' We know how he looked upon it when he thus expressed himself. There was danger to this country, danger of the avenging justice of God, in that little unimportant popular-sovereignty question of Judge Douglas. He supposed there was a question of God's eternal justice wrapped up in the enslaving of any race of men, or any man, and that those who did so braved the arm of Jehovah—that when a nation thus dared the Almighty, every friend of that nation had caused to dread his wrath. Choose ye between Jefferson and Douglas as to what is the true view of this element among us.'' [18]

Southern Senate leaders deposed Douglas from the chairmanship of the Committee on Territories, which he had held for eleven years. Senator Benjamin of Louisiana denounced him in the Senate for his treason to the South, and predicted Lincoln's ultimate success.

CHAPTER IX

Lincoln Nominated and Elected President

Step by step Lincoln became an acknowledged leader of the Republican party throughout the nation. He wrote to his political allies, and made numerous public appearances in Illinois, Indiana, Iowa, Ohio, Wisconsin, and Kansas. His prospects continued to brighten. On February 16, 1860, the *Chicago Press and Tribune* joined smaller newspapers with a direct endorsement of Abraham Lincoln for President.

In the fall of 1859, Lincoln received an invitation to lecture on a lyceum program at the Plymouth Church in Brooklyn, where Henry Ward Beecher was the pastor. The lecture was scheduled for Feb. 27, 1860. He accepted providing they would take a political speech if he could not find time to develop another.

On arriving in New York he learned that the Young Men's Republican Union had assumed control of his coming; arrangements had been made for him to speak at the Cooper Union Institute in New York. At the Astor House he met with visitors, worked on his speech, and noticed the wide publicity given him in the papers.

The *Tribune* called him "a man of the people, a champion of free labor."

A snowstorm came up that afternoon, interfering with traffic, yet about 1,500 people came, most of them paying 25 cents admission. The *Tribune* said that "since the days of Clay and Webster there hadn't been a larger assemblage of the intellect and moral culture" of the city of New York. Many distinguished guests were in the audience, including Horace Greeley, and Henry Ward Beecher. David Dudley Field escorted the speaker to the platform. William Cullen Bryant, editor of the *Evening Post,* and author of "Thanatopsis," presided. He told the audience of a few of the speaker's accomplishments, especially of Lincoln's majority vote over Douglas for the Senate-seat in Illinois, then closed with these words: "I have only, my friends, to pronounce the name of Abraham Lincoln of Illinois to secure your profoundest attention."

The tall Illinois lawyer arose and came forward, holding his manuscript in trembling hands. The audience cheered. After courteously addressing the chair, Mr. Lincoln began to read. As he turned the pages of his paper, a sheet dropped unseen to the floor. A few moments later he reached that point in his reading and saw something was missing. For a moment he stood there embarrassed. Then, he cast the manuscript aside, threw out a long arm, looked full into the face of his audience, and suddenly he seemed a transformed man. "His eyes kindled, his voice rang, his face shone and seemed to light up the whole assembly."

It was as if some unseen influence was making itself felt as he played at will upon his audience for an hour and a half. His style of speech and manner of delivery were severely simple — "the grand simplicities of the Bible, with which he was so familiar." He showed a profoundness of thought, a mastery of logic, and a power of lucid statement not possessed by any of his rivals. His audience came to love and trust him as he spoke conciliatory words of the South; cleared the Republican party of insurrection tendencies such as that at Harper's Ferry by John Brown; yet declared slavery to be wrong, and that it was idle to seek for common ground with men who say it is right. He ended his address on the noble note; "Let us have faith that right makes might, and in that faith, let us, to the end, dare to do our duty as we understand it." [1]

The audience was soon on its feet in wild applause. There were cheers, outcries; hats went into the air and handerchiefs waved.

They crowded to shake the speaker's hand, and to inquire how he had come by such powers of speech. A reporter said, "He's the greatest man since St. Paul," and hurried away to write: "No man ever before made such an impression on his first appeal to a New York audience." [2] Four New York papers printed the speech in full. Editors were lavish with praise. The *Chicago Tribune* brought out the speech in pamphlet form.

Early next morning Mr. Erastus Corning, President of the New York Central Railroad, visited Mr. Lincoln at the Astor House. "Mr. Lincoln," he said, "I understand that in Illinois you win all your law suits." Laughingly Lincoln answered, "Oh, no, Mr. Corning, that is not true; but I do make it a rule to refuse cases unless I am convinced the litigant's cause is just." Then came the inquiry, "Mr. Lincoln, will you entertain an offer from the New York Central Railroad to become its general counsel at $10,000 a year?" The generous offer was courteously declined, and when renewed in writing after Lincoln had returned home, was again finally refused.

Lincoln visited his son, Robert, in school at Exeter, New Hampshire, and spoke for his party in Providence, Hartford, Concord, Manchester, Dover, New Haven, Meridian, Norwich, and Bridgeport. Being "worn down," he turned down invitations to speak in Philadelphia, Reading and Pittsburgh.

At Manchester Lincoln was introduced as the next President. At Hartford, where the shoemakers were on strike, he declared:

"I am glad to see that a system of labor prevails in New England under which laborers can strike when they want to, where they are not obliged to work under all circumstances, and are not tied down and obliged to labor whether you pay them or not! I like the system which lets a man quit when he wants to, and wish it might prevail everywhere. . . . I don't believe in a law to prevent a man from getting rich; it would do more harm than good. So while we do not propose any war upon capital, we do wish to allow the humblest man an equal chance to get rich with everybody else. When one starts poor, as most do in the race of life, free society is such that he knows he can better his condition; he knows that there is no fixed condition of labor, for his whole life."[3]

On March 11, he went with James A. Briggs to hear Henry Ward Beecher preach in Brooklyn, to attend a prayer meeting, and then a service at the Universalist Church of Edwin H. Chapin in New York. The next day he took the train for Chicago, and two days later was home in Springfield, arriving "in excellent health and in his usual spirits."

Soon after Lincoln's dazzling Eastern trip, a Republican meeting was called in Springfield, and Milton Hay addressing him on behalf of the local club said:

> "No inconsiderable portion of your fellow citizens in various portions of the county have expressed their preference for you as the candidate of the Republican party for the next Presidency. . . .There are those around you, sir, who have watched with manly interest and pride your upward march from obscurity to distinction. There are those here who know something of the obstacles which have lain in your pathway. Our history is prolific in examples of what may be achieved by ability, perseverance and integrity . . . but in the long list of those who have thus from humblest beginnings won their way worthily to proud distinction there is not one can take precedence to the name of Abraham Lincoln. . ."4

The Illinois Republican convention met at Decatur on May 9, 1860, in preparation for the general Republican Convention which was to meet in Chicago. Lincoln came in late and received a tumultuous ovation as he was invited to a seat on the platform. Soon the chairman announced that an old Macon County Democrat wished to offer a contribution. "Receive it," roared the delegates. Then, amid cheers, in marched Lincoln's country cousin, old John Hanks, and another pioneer bearing on their shoulders two long fence rails labelled: *"Two rails from a lot of 3,000 made by Abraham Lincoln and John Hanks in the Sangamon Bottom in the year 1830."* The crowd broke loose in a pandamonium of cheers and calls.

"Gentlemen," said Lincoln, in response to the loud calls, "I suppose you want to know something about those things. Well, the truth is, John Hanks and I did make rails in the Sangamon Bottom. I don't know whether we made those rails or not; fact is, I don't think they are a credit to the makers. But I do know this; I made rails then, and I think I could make better ones than these now." Lincoln sat down and the cheering broke out afresh. Thus Lincoln gained the nickname of the "Rail-splitter" candidate; it symbolized his humble origin and kinship with the workingman.5

The Republican National Convention met in Chicago in the "Wigwam" — a lumber structure seating 10,000 people — on

Wednesday, May 16, 1860, and adopted its platform the next day. Overshadowing all else was the nomination of a candidate for President. Behind the scenes skilled emissaries worked tirelessly. Judge David Davis, of the Eighth Judicial Circuit, and State Chairman Norman Judd led the Lincoln forces. Lincoln waited in down-state Springfield for word about his candidacy.

On the *first* ballot William H. Seward had 173½ votes, Abraham Lincoln 102, Cameron 50½, Chase 49, Bates 48, and favorite sons and others the remaining votes. On the *second* ballot Seward had 184½ and Lincoln 181. Pennsylvania had switched to Lincoln and other delegates had joined the bandwagon.

On the *third* ballot Lincoln had risen to 231½ while Seward had dropped to 180. When the third ballot showed Lincoln so close to the nomination, Mr. Carter, of Ohio, arose and announced that Ohio had four more votes for Lincoln. Other changes followed until the *fourth* ballot, as officially announced, gave Lincoln 354 votes. On motion of Mr. Evarts, of New York, the nomination was made unanimous amid intense excitement. The chairman announced: "Abraham Lincoln, of Illinois is selected as your candidate for President of the United States."

"Strong men hugged each other, wept, laughed and shrieked in each other's faces through tears," says Sandburg. "Judge Logan stood on a table, brandished his arms and yelled, swung wild his new silk hat and on somebody's head smashed it flat. Inside and outside the Wigwam there was wild applause. Hats, handkerchiefs, and umbrellas were thrown in the air; brass bands blared, cannons exploded, bells rang and railroad and river boats whistled."[6]

Delegate Nathan Knapp wired Lincoln: "We did it. Glory to God." Jesse Fell wired: "City wild with excitement. From my inner heart I congratulate you." Chairman Judd wired advising the exact votes cast, and that the nomination had been made unanimous, then added, "Do not come to Chicago." Lincoln knew that "a great moment had come to him." He read many telegrams, shook hands with wellwishers, and went home to tell Mary. That Friday night was a time of rejoicing in Springfield. Bonfires were lit, bands played, and a cheering crowd came to the Lincoln home to congratulate him.

The Republican National Convention of Chicago appointed a committee to journey to Springfield to notify Mr. Lincoln, in person, of his nomination. While they were in route, a number of citizens of Springfield, knowing Lincoln's habit to total abstinence, and believing, in all probability, that he would have no liquor in his house, called upon him, and suggested that perhaps some members of the committee would be in need of some refreshment — wine, or other liquors.

"I haven't any in the house," said Mr. Lincoln.

"We will furnish them," said the visitors.

"Gentlemen," replied Lincoln, "I cannot allow you to do that which I will not do myself."

Some Democratic citizens, however, who felt that Springfield had been honored by the nomination, sent several baskets of wine to Lincoln's home; but he returned them, thanking them for their intended kindness.

After the formal ceremonies connected with the business of the committee of notification had passed, Lincoln remarked that, as an appropriate conclusion to an interview so important and interesting, he supposed good manners would require that he furnish the committee something to drink; and, opening a door, he called the name of the house maid.

The girl responded to the call. Lincoln spoke to her in an undertone.

In a few minutes the maid re-entered, bringing a large tray containing several glass tumblers and a large pitcher, and placed it upon the center table. Lincoln arose and gravely addressing the distinguished gentlemen, said:

"Gentlemen, we must pledge our mutual healths in the most healthful beverage I have ever used, or allowed in my family. I cannot conscientiously depart from it on the present occasion; it is pure Adam's ale, fresh from the spring."

Taking a tumbler, he touched it to his lips and pledged them his highest respects in a cup of cold water.

Congratulations and promises of support came from eminent men and women of the nation. The people were thrilled with the bright prospects of a soon-coming day when a man of such honesty, integrity, and eloquence would head the government of the United States. Joshua Giddings wrote saying:

> Dear Lincoln: You are nominated. You will be elected. After your election, thousands will crowd around you, claiming rewards for services rendered. I, too, have my claims upon you. I have not worked for your nomination, nor for that of any other man. I have labored

105

for the establishment of principles; and when men came to me asking my opinion of you, I only told them, 'Lincoln is an honest man.' All I ask of you in return for my services is, *make my statement good* through your administration.

Yours, Giddings.

The nominee for President was heralded far and wide as "Honest Old Abe," "the Rail-splitter." His Republican rivals—Seward, Chase, and others—swung in line and campaigned for him. The poets—Bryant, Whittier, Stedman, etc.—represented him as "A Real Representative man," and wrote poems in his honor. Books telling the people of his life were written and distributed by the millions. His mail grew so heavy that he employed John G. Nicolay as his secretary. Representative men from over the nation came to visit him, but he did not travel, nor did he lecture, nor even write on the issues of the day. His confidential letter to William S. Speer, of Tennessee, explained his views:

"Yours of the 13th was duly received. I appreciate your motive when you suggest the propriety of my writing for the public something disclaiming all intention to interfere with slaves or slavery in the States; but in my judgment, it would do no good. I have already done this many—many times; and it is in print, and open to all who will read. Those who will not read, or heed, what I have already publicly said, would not read, or heed, a repetition of it.

"If they hear not Moses and the prophets, neither will they be persuaded though one rose from the dead."[7]

The presidential contest on November 6 was a national election like no other in American history. There were four candidates for President in the final race: Lincoln, Douglas, Breckenridge, and Bell. Lincoln's three rivals represented three different parties— splits in national thought—thus they were hopelessly divided.

On election day, Lincoln went to his temporary offices—those of the Governor which had been placed at his disposal—in the State Capitol. Crowds gathered and some one suggested that he close the door. He said he had never closed his door on anyone and didn't intend to start doing it now.

By midnight, returns of telegrams indicated a victory. The popular New York vote in his favor decided the issue. The final tally, in electoral votes, stood as follows: Lincoln 180, Breckenridge 72, Bell 39, and Douglas 12.

106

Mr. Lincoln shook hands around with the people, then walked home, entered his bedroom, found Mrs. Lincoln fast asleep. Gently he touched her on the shoulder and whispered, "Mary, Mary, we are elected."

The rejoicing of the people knew no bounds. They threw up their hats, hurrahed, cheered for Lincoln, and shouted themselves hoarse as they surged around the Statehouse. Bonfires were lighted, whistles blew, bells rang, and crowds marched the streets shouting and singing "Ain't I glad I joined the Republicans" until near the morning hour. Much of the same spirit of rejoicing went on in other cities where there was gladness that "Honest Abe, the man of the common people" had been elected to the Presidency of our country.

In the South, however, Lincoln's election was the occasion for terrible threats, the direst prophecies, and in some quarters the nation's dirtiest propaganda. Lincoln had always taken a stand against slavery as a *moral evil* but had held the opinion that property in slaves was entitled to protection under the Constitution, but he had never formulated a political program that comprehended more than the prevention of slavery's extension. Certain newspapers had misquoted and misrepresented him. Many misguided leaders in the South vowed that they would not submit to "such humiliation and degradation as the inauguration of Abraham Lincoln."[8]

In a letter to Senator Zachariah Chandler of Michigan, Lincoln expressed his satisfaction with the results at the polls: *"I am very glad the elections this autumn have gone favorably, and that I have not, by native depravity, or under evil influence, done anything bad enough to prevent the good results.*

"I hope to 'stand firm' enough not to go backward, and yet not go forward fast enough to wreck the country's cause."[9]

Abraham Lincoln as he opened the fourth debate with Stephen A. Douglas.

Abraham Lincoln in the summer of 1860, in Springfield Ill. Photographer unknown.

Abraham Lincoln and his family.

The tomb of Nancy Hanks Lincoln, the mother of President Lincoln.

This tomb of Abraham Lincoln at Springfield is the finest and most meaningful ever erected on the American continent. In it are the remains of Abraham Lincoln, Mrs. Lincoln and three of their four sons, Edward, William, and "Tad." On three bronze tablets inside the tomb are the immortal words of his Gettysburg and Second Inaugral addresses, and of his farewell address to Springfield. More than a hundred thousand people visit the tomb annually.

Lincoln's home at 8th and Jackson St. It is open from 9 to 5 daily and many thousands visit it each year, and view many of its original furnishings.

CHAPTER X
From Springfield To Washington

Abraham Lincoln had been elected President of the United States on November 6, 1860, yet he could exercise no direct influence on the affairs of the country until his inauguration on March 4, 1861. All this time he spent in Springfield, with the exception of a trip to Chicago for a brief conference with Vice President-elect Hannibal Hamlin, and a visit which he made to his stepmother and to his father's grave in Cole's County. These were the busiest, and in many respects the most trying times of his life up to then.

Almost every day the trains into Springfield unloaded hundreds of people who came to see the President-elect. The majority were well-wishers who just wanted to "look at him and tell him they hoped to God he'd live and have good luck;" many groups merely shook hands with him, then went away singing "Ain't we glad we joined the Republicans;" but the ones who wore him most and tried his patience were the long lines of seekers who said they helped nominate and elect him President, and inquired what he could do about appointing them or their friends to post offices, revenue collectorships, clerkships, secretaryships, and other such positions.[1]

In Washington, certain leaders were working to bring about a compromise on the slavery issue with the slave states. But the penetrating foresight of the President-elect caused him to write privately to Senators and Congressmen, saying: "Entertain no propposition for a compromise in regard to the *extension* of slavery. The instant you do . . . all our labor is lost, and sooner, or later must be done over."[2]

The important duty of choosing his official Cabinet weighed heavily upon Mr. Lincoln, and many of the most important leaders of the nation were summoned to Springfield to confer with him. Judges, consuls, generals, and other like officials had to be considered for appointment. Final action would, of course, await his being President.

The writing of his inaugural address required such precision of thought, meditation, and divine aid that he locked himself up in an upper room across from the State House, during the hours of a number of afternoons, and there, with a copy of the Constitution, Henry Clay's Speech on the Compromise of 1850, Andrew Jackson's "proclamation of 1832 against Nullification," and Webster's "Reply to Hayne," he prepared the draft of his first inaugural address. Twenty copies were printed in strict secrecy in order that no one should know its contents until given.

The weightiest burden which bore on Lincoln's mind was the fact that secession was already in process in the southern states. South Carolina had passed an ordinance of secession on December 20; Mississippi, January 9; Florida, January 10; Alabama, January 11; Georgia, January 19; Louisiana, January 26; and Texas, February 1.[3]

To add to the general consternation, there were reliable reports that quantities of arms and ammunitions were being shipped from United States Arsenals to the secessionists in the South. Then, there were numerous threats that the President-elect would never live to take the oath of office.

Judge Gillespie, a long-time friend, spent the night at Mr. Lincoln's home. While discussing the difficult situation of the country, Lincoln suddenly roused himself.

"Gillespie," he said, "I would willingly take out of my life a period of years equal to the two months which intervene between now and my inauguration to take the oath of office."

"Why?" asked Gillespie.

"Because every hour adds to the difficulties I am called upon to meet, and the present administration does nothing to check the tendency toward dissolution. I, who have been called to meet this awful responsibility, am compelled to remain here, doing nothing to avert it or lessen its force when it comes to me . . .Every day adds to the difficulty of the situation, and makes the outlook more gloomy. . . .I have read, upon my knees, the story of Gethsemane, where the Son of God prayed in vain that the cup of bitterness might pass from him. I am in the garden of Gethsemane now, and my cup of bitterness is full and overflowing."

Judge Gillespie said when he retired, it was the master of the house and chosen ruler of the country who saw him to his room.

"Joe," he said, as he was about to leave me, "I suppose you will never forget that trial down in Montgomery County, where the lawyer associated with you gave away the whole case in his opening speech. I saw you signaling to him, but you could't stop him. Now, that's just the way with me and President Buchanan. He is giving away the case, and I have nothing to say, and can't stop him. Good night."

On the night of February 6, between seven and twelve o'clock, seven hundred people attended a public reception at the Lincoln home. The President-elect greeted guests at the door. Mrs. Lincoln, as "a lady of fine figure and accomplished address," met well-wishers in the parlor. It was the Lincoln's good-by house party. The next day they took rooms in the Chenery House. Their house was already leased, and they sold most of the furniture at private sale. Lincoln cleaned out files, threw away odds and ends, and packed personal belongings in trunks and boxes, roped them with his own hands, and addressed them. "A. Lincoln, White House, Washington, D.C."

Among the many who came to bid him farewell was an old farmer, in butternut jeans, who had ridden horseback many miles since daybreak. The old gentleman was bent and worn with age, and nearly blind. He had been a close friend of the Armstrongs, and knew what Lincoln did for Duff Armstrong. He came and put his old eyes close to Lincoln's face, and after studying the lines of the face, burst into tears, and murmured, "It *is* him-it's

116

the same." And after mentioning the Duff Armstrong case, shook the hand of the President-elect and said solemnly two or three times, "God preserve you, Mr. Lincoln."[4]

Hanna Armstrong, who had mended Lincoln's trousers and cooked meals for him in Old New Salem days and whose boy Lincoln had saved from a murder charge, came laying her hands in Lincoln's while she wept and doubted if she would ever see him again. Lincoln said: "Hanna, if they do kill me I shall never die again."

His last act in Springfield was to call on Herndon in the offices they had so long shared. After visiting for a time, Lincoln said, "Billy, how long have we been together?" "Over sixteen years," answered Herndon. "And we have never had a cross word during all that time, have we?" He then gathered up an armful of books, and the two men walked slowly down the stairs. Outside the street door they stopped and Lincoln looked wistfully at the "Lincoln and Herndon" sign. "Let it hang there undisturbed," he said. "Give our clients to understand that the election of a President makes no change in the firm of Lincoln and Herndon. If I live I'm coming back some time and then we'll go right on practicing law as if nothing had ever happened."[5]

Precisely five minutes before eight o'clock on Monday morning, February 11, 1861, President-elect Lincoln left the waiting-room of the Great Western railway station at Springfield, and slowly worked his way through the crowd of friends and townspeople who had gathered to bid him good-by. Mounting the rear platform of his special train, and looking down into the faces of more than a thousand of his fellow citizens which had closed about him, he drew himself up to his full height, removed his hat, and stood for several seconds in profound silence. Then there came an unusual quiver on his lips, and tears in his eyes, as with strong emotion he solemnly said:

> *My Friends: No one, not in my situation, can appreciate my feeling of sadness at this parting. To this place and the kindness of these people, I owe everything. Here I have lived a quarter of a century, and have passed from a young to an old man. Here my children have been born, and one is buried. I now leave, not knowing when or whether ever I may return, with a task before me greater than that which rested upon Washington. Without the assistance of that Divine Being who*

117

ever attended him, I can not succeed. With that assistance, I can not fail. Trusting in Him who can go with me, and remain with you, and be everywhere for good, let us confidently hope that all will yet be well. To His care commending you, as I hope in your prayers you will commend me, I bid you an affectionate farewell.[6]

An uncontrollable burst of applause greeted Mr. Lincoln when he said that *with God's help he would not fail,* and a sob of response "We will do it! We will do it!" went through the listening crowd when with a broken voice he climaxed by requesting their prayers.

When the speech was telegraphed over the country, the skeptics sneered, but the people were touched. They felt that he had appealed to one of their deepest convictions — the belief in a Providence whose help was given to those who sought it in prayer.

"The new President," they said one to another, "was not only a man who had struggled with life like common people, but he was a man who believed, as they did, in God, and was not ashamed to ask the prayers of good men."[7]

On leaving Springfield, Lincoln was further strengthened and encouraged by a flag given him by an admirer. On its silken folds was embroidered an inscription from the first chapter of Joshua.

"Be strong and of a good courage; be not afraid, neither be thou dismayed: for the Lord thy God is with thee whithersoever thou goest. There shall not any man be able to stand before thee all the days of thy life. As I was with Moses, so shall I be with thee."

In recognizing this gift he told the people that he felt that he did have a mission from God to fulfill, and again requested their prayers in his behalf.[8]

The trip to Washington was a triumphant, and in many respects a pleasant twelve days journey. Instead of traveling directly to Washington, Lincoln had agreed to make numerous stops, and to deliver short speeches in route through Indiana, Ohio, Pennsylvania, New York, and New Jersey.

The beginning of the journey — eastward through Illinois — was graphically described by Thomas Ross, a brakeman on the Presidential train.

"The enthusiasm all along the line was intense," he said. "As we whirled through the country villages, we caught a cheer from the people and a glimpse of waving handkerchiefs and of hats tossed high in the air. Wherever we stopped there was a great rush to shake hands with Mr. Lincoln, though of course only a few could reach him. The crowds looked as if they included the whole population. There were women and children, there were young men, and there were old men with gray beards. It was soul-stirring to see those white-whiskered old fellows, many of whom had known Lincoln in his humbler days, join in the cheering, and hear them shout after him, 'Good-by, Abe. Stick to the Constitution, and we will stick to you. . . .' I never knew where all the people came from. They were not only in the towns and villages, but many were along the track in the country, just to get a glimpse of the President's train. . . .The people everywhere were wild. . . .At the State line, I left the train, and returned to Springfield, having passed the biggest day in my whole life."9

At five o'clock in the afternoon the Presidential party reached Indianapolis, where it was received by Governor Morton, and in a brief speech Lincoln spoke of himself as "a mere instrument . . . of a great cause."

On his 52nd brithday, the President-elect arrived in Cincinnati, Ohio. He entered a carriage drawn by six white horses, and rode in a procession in his honor. Bands played, military units marched, and the people followed on horseback, in carriages, and afoot. The Mayor introduced Lincoln and in his speech he said, "To the Kentuckians just across the river, we will say that we mean to treat you, as near as we possibly can, as Washington, Jefferson, and Madison treated you, that under the Providence of God, who has never deserted us . . . we shall again be brethren, forgetting all parties — ignoring all parties." Speaking further, he said, "It is not my nature, when I see a people borne down by the weight of their shackles — the oppression of tyranny — to make their life more bitter by heaping upon them greater burdens; but rather would I do all in my power to raise the yoke, than to add anything that would tend to crush them." 10

At Pittsburgh, on February 14, he thanked Mayor Wilson and the citizens for a "flattering reception," and said he would speak on the country's "present distracted condition" when the time arrived.

When the Presidential train stopped at the small mining town of Freedom, a coal miner called from the crowd, "Abe, they say

119

you are the tallest man in the United States, but I don't believe you're any taller than I am." Lincoln replied, "Come up here and let's measure." The dusty miner in work clothes pushed through the crowd, stood back to back with the President-elect and they were exactly the same height. The crowd cheered, but some reporters thought it unbecoming.

When the train stopped at Westfield, New York, and the crowd gathered around, Lincoln said, "I have a correspondent in this place, and if she is present I would like to see her." "Who is it? Give us her name," came from the crowd. "Her name is Grace Bedell." Eleven year old Grace was led and carried to the platform, when Lincoln said, "She wrote me that she thought I would be better looking if I wore whiskers." Then looking down at the little girl, "You see, I let these whiskers grow for you, Grace." Then he kissed her, and the people cheered.

On February 18, they arrived at New York City, and Lincoln rode in a procession of thirty carriages led by a platoon of mounted police. At the Astor House 500 policemen held a curious crowd in check. That evening he heard the grim news that the Congress of seceding states had met at Montgomery, Alabama, and adopted a provisional Constitution modeled largely upon that of the United States; that the West Point-educated Jefferson Davis, who had retired to his farm, had been sent for to become President; and that Alexander H. Stephens was made Vice-President of the Confederate States of America.

In the City Hall next morning, surrounded by the Mayor, Aldermen and representatives of the press, Lincoln said:

> . . . *If we have patience, if we restrain ourselves, if we allow ourselves not to run off in a passion, we still have confidence that the Almighty, the Maker of the universe, will, through the instrumentality of this great and intelligent people, bring us through this as He has other difficulties of our country. Relying on this, I again thank you for this generous reception.* [11]

Lincoln's arrival in Philadelphia was on February 21—the day before George Washington's birthday. Through the dark, cold streets he was obliged to ride in state to the Continental Hotel, where hundreds of visitors were waiting to shake his hand. Soon after being settled in his room, he was summoned to the room of Mr. Norman Judd, one of his party. There he was introduced to

Mr. Allen Pinkerton, former deputy sheriff of Chicago, and now Chief of a private detective agency, who said: "We have come to know, Mr. Lincoln, and beyond the shadow of a doubt, that there exists a plot to assassinate you. The attempt will be made on your way through Baltimore, day after tomorrow. I am here to help in outwitting the assassins."

Mr. Lincoln listened while Pinkerton told of being employed by the Philadelphia, Wilmington and Baltimore Railroad to ferret out the facts about rumors that by fires and explosions secessionists were expecting to destroy their bridges and wreck their trains. He had adopted a Southern accent, posed as one John H. Hutchinson, and opened a brokerage office as cover. Then he had established himself as a nightly figure at the bar of Barnum's Hotel, the favorite haunt of the secessionists. He soon learned that far more was at stake than burning bridges and wrecking railway cars — in fact nothing less than the life of the President-elect. Tongues had been loosed by drink, and they had stated definitely that Lincoln would be assassinated as he passed through Baltimore on Saturday, February 23. Lots had already been drawn to decide who was to do the actual killings.

They had alternate plans but their master plan was that on the coming Saturday, when Lincoln arrived in Baltimore on the 12:30 p.m. train from Harrisburg, crowds were sure to gather in the narrow vestibule. Lincoln would walk through to the receiving point at the waiting room. The conspirators were to mingle with the crowd. Just before Lincoln entered the vestibule, other secessionists would create a disturbance on the street outside the passageway, thus drawing away the station police. At that moment, the assassin was to step close to the President-elect and either stab or shoot him to death.

Twenty men were involved. Their chief leader was Cypriano Fernandina, the Barnum Hotel's head barber and an Italian immigrant with anarchistic sentiments. He had two assistants; one boasted that his group would make certain that Lincoln left Baltimore in a coffin.

When Pinkerton had finished outlining the Baltimore plot, Judd and Lincoln asked what he thought should be done. Pinkerton glanced at his watch, and seeing it was a few minutes after 9 p.m., replied, "There is a Washington car on the last train out of here for Baltimore at 10:50 tonight, and I think Mr. Lincoln should be on it."

"So do I," said Judd.

Lincoln sat in a studied mood. "No," he said at last, "I cannot consent. Tomorrow, Washington's Birthday, I must be at a flag-raising ceremony at Independence Hall and then go on to Harrisburg." Then turning to Judd, he said, "If you both think there is real danger in my going through Baltimore openly, I shall try to get away quitely from the people at Harrisburg tomorrow evening. *Then* I'll place myself in your hands."

On leaving Mr. Pinkerton and starting for his room, Mr. Lincoln met Ward Lamon, also a member of his party. Lamon introduced Frederick Seward, son of Senator Seward and handed a letter to Lincoln from his father. Mr. Lincoln slowly read it through twice. The letter informed Mr. Lincoln that General Scott and Colonel Stone, who commanded the District of Columbia militia, had just received information that a plot existed in Baltimore to murder him on his way through the city. "All risk might be easily avoided by a change in traveling arrangements," the letter said.

After discussing the subject briefly, Lincoln advised Seward of the detectives report. "Surely, Mr. Lincoln," said Mr. Seward, "that is a strong corraboration of the news I bring you." Lincoln replied, "I shall think it over carefully, and try to decide it right; and I will let you know in the morning."

At seven o'clock the next morning, on Washington's Birthday, Mr. Lincoln made a brief speech in front of Independence Hall, where he raised the new flag with its thirty-four stars—the thirty-fourth representing the free State of Kansas. He said:

> *I am filled with deep emotion at finding myself standing in this place, where were collected together the wisdom, the patriotism, the devotion to principle from which spring the institutions under which we live.*
>
> *You have kindly suggested to me that in my hands is the task of restoring peace to our distracted country. I can say in return, sir, that all the political sentiments I entertain have been drawn, so far as I have been able to draw them, from the sentiments which originated in and were given to the world from this hall. I have never had a feeling, politically, that did not spring from the sentiments embodied in the Declaration*

of Independence. I have often pondered over the dangers which were incurred by the men who assembled here and framed and adopted that Declaration. I have pondered over the toils that were endured by the officers and soldiers of the army who achieved that independence. I have often inquired of myself what great principle or idea it was that kept this Confederacy so long together. It was not the mere matter of separation in the Declaration of Independence which gave liberty not alone to the people of this country, but hope to all the world, for all future time. It was that which gave promise that in due time the weights would be lifted from the shoulders of all men, and that all should have an equal chance. This is the sentiment embodied in the Declaration of Independence.

Now, my friends, can this country be saved on that basis? If it can, I will consider myself one of the happiest men in the world if I can help to save it. If it cannot be saved upon that principle, it will be truly awful. But if this country cannot be saved without giving up that principle, I was about to say I would rather be assassinated on this spot than surrender it. Now, in my view of the present aspect of affairs, there is no need of bloodshed and war. There is no necessity for it. I am not in favor of such a course, and I may say in advance that there will be no bloodshed unless it is forced upon the government. The government will not use force, unless force is used against it.

My friends, this is wholly an unprepared speech. I did not expect to be called on to say a word when I came here. I supposed I was merely to do something toward raising a flag. I may, therefore, have said something indiscreet. (Cries of "no, no.") But I have said nothing but what I am willing to live by, and, if it be the pleasure of Almighty God, to die by. With these few remarks, I proceed to the duty assigned me.[12]

After the flag-raising, Lincoln told his friends in privacy that he had decided to go on to Washington at whatever time they thought best after he met and addressed the Pennsylvania Legislature at Harrisburg that afternoon.

At six o'clock that evening Lincoln was called from the dinner table on pretext of official business. In his room he changed his dinner dress for a traveling suit, put on an overcoat, and slipped out at the back door with a soft felt hat in his pocket and a folded shawl on his arm. He and Mr. Lamon entered a carriage and drove away in the darkness to a special car and engine train waiting for them on a siding about two miles outside Harrisburg. The "special train," provided for them by the president of the railway company, pulled away unlighted save for a dim headlight, and made the 100 mile trip to Philadelphia by eleven o'clock where the night train for Washington was being held by order of the Superintendent of the road for an "important package."

Superintendent Kenny and Detective Pinkerton met the special at the Pennsylvania Railway Station, and took Lincoln and Lamon across the city to the P.W. & B. railway station where they were directed to special reserved berths on the last sleeping car on the New York-Washington train. The berths had been booked by one of Pinkerton's agents for her "invalid brother" who would be accompanied by another brother. After an undisturbed night's rest, Lincoln reached Washington at six o'clock the next morning. He was met by Mr. Seward and Mr. Washburne, and taken to his special suite in the Willard Hotel, where he remained until after the inauguration.

Lincoln breakfasted at Willard's with Seward, and at eleven the two men called at the White House, chatted with President Buchanan, and shook hands with the Cabinet. In the afternoon he met the Illinois Congressmen and Senators, headed by Stephen A. Douglas. Later, in the Parlor at Willard's, he received the delegates from twenty-one states who had gathered at a "Peace Conference" at the Hotel. During the brief interview one Southern delegate suggested to Lincoln: "Everything now depends upon you." He replied: *"I cannot agree to that. My course is as plain as a turnpike road. It is marked out by the Constitution. I am in no doubt which way to go. Suppose now we all stop discussing and try the experiment of obedience to the Constitution and the laws. Don't you think it would work?"*

During Lincoln's first evening in Washington he received calls from the Buchanan Cabinet members, and held interviews with General Scott and others "who were intent on obtaining an opportunity to say a few words to him *privately*." [13]

That Saturday night the train bearing the Lincoln family arrived, and Mrs. Lincoln and the three boys took their first Washington breakfast with husband and father. The President-elect went with Seward to St. John's Church near the White House that Sunday morning.

The week before inauguration was filled with the many duties and responsibilities incident to the beginning of a four year term of guiding the destinies of a divided nation. Engagements connected with getting acquainted, the appointment of people to fill certain strategic positions, and just being nice to the many callers with their many requests constituted an enormous drain on the physical, mental, and emotional energies of even a strong man like Lincoln. But that which took the most out of him was the many conflicts which arose over who should constitute his future Cabinet. During this week he sought counsel on his proposed appointments from many of the leading men of the country—especially the representative men of the Republican party. If they did not come to him, he went to them. Many were pleased to let him choose, others hotly contested certain appointments, and the struggle over one or two proposed members culminated in prolonged encounters.

Mr. Lincoln listened "candidly and patiently" to all the arguments from earnest men; then found himself on the eve of his inauguration with much the same selections he had made before leaving Springfield. The final cabinet which he sent to the Senate for confirmation was made up of:

William H. Seward, of New York, for Secretary of State.
Salmon P. Chase, of Ohio, for Secretary of the Treasury.
Simon Cameron, of Pennsylvania, for Secretary of War.
Gideon Welles, of Connecticut, for Secretary of the Navy.
Edward Bates, of Missouri, for Attorney General.
Caleb B. Smith, of Indiana, for Secretary of the Interior.
Montgomery Blair, of Maryland, for Postmaster-General. [14]

CHAPTER XI

The Inauguration of
Mr. Lincoln

At high noon, March 4, 1861, President Buchanan called on Mr. Lincoln at Willard's hotel. Soon the two returned arm in arm and passed through a path packed on either side with people, and entered an open carriage. The venerable form, pallid face, and perfectly white hair of Mr. Buchanan contrasted strikingly with the tall figure, coal-black hair, and rugged features of Mr. Lincoln. The procession which moved along Pennsylvania Avenue was led by Chief Marshal Major French "with aids in blue scarfs and white rosettes, carrying blue batons with gilt ends, their saddle cloths blue and white."

In the presidential carriage Buchanan and Lincoln sat side by side facing forward and Senators Baker and Pearce seated opposite. A company of West Point soldiers marched in front of the carriage, a squadron of cavalry rode alongside, and infantry and riflemen of the District of Columbia followed. Behind these came representatives from the judiciary; the clergy; foreign Ministers, the diplomatic corps; members of Congress; the Peace Convention delegates; heads of bureaus; governors of States; the army, navy, marine corps, militia; veterans of the Revolutionary War and the War of 1812 in carriages, followed by a variety of organizations and citizens afoot."[1] Bringing up the rear of the procession was the float representing the Republican Association drawn by four milk-white horses. On the float were thirty-four pretty girls in white frocks — one beautiful girl for each of the States in the Union.

Everywhere, that day, there were police, armed soldiers, and riflemen — even on the housetops. General Scott was determined that the inauguration should go off peaceably. And it did.

At the end of the way, President Buchanan and Mr. Lincoln, arm in arm, passed through the long tunnel erected for his protection, entered the Capitol, and walked into the Senate Chamber filled to overflowing with Senators, members of the Diplomatic Corps, and distinguished visitors. From here the justices of the Supreme Court, in cap and gown, led the way as the large company of the nation's greatest men moved to the East Portico of the Capitol, and took seats on the platform especially erected for the occasion.

Lincoln in a new black suit of clothes, black boots, and a new high silk hat, paused before taking a seat, and helplessly looked for a spot where he might place his hat. Quickly Stephen A. Douglas, stepped forward, took the hat from Lincoln's hands, and graciously held it for the duration of the ceremony. "If I can't be President," he said in an undertone, "I at least can hold his hat." Thus in such simple form came the dramatic climax to their last, long race.

At the proper moment Lincoln arose and advanced to the front, whereupon his friend Senator Baker, of Oregon, stepped to his side, and in tones clear as a silver-bell, said: "Fellow-citizens, I introduce to you Abraham Lincoln, the President-elect of the United States." The crowd of more than 10,000 gave moderate applause as they intently watched the great and kindly man draw his inaugural address from his inside coat pocket and, addressing them as "Fellow Citizens of the United States," talked to them in a heart-to-heart fashion for thirty minutes.

He told them that there had never been any real cause for the apprehension which seemed to exist among the Southern States regarding the accession of the Republican Administration; that neither he, nor those who elected him, had any thought of interfering with their affairs only as the Constitution directed, and that it states "the citizens of each State shall be entitled to all priviliges and immunities of the citizens in the several states." He spoke calmly, yet firmly of the perpetuity of the Union, and against any legal right of a minority secession. He said it was the majority who should rule, and therefore there should be no hurry or "hot haste," but "a patient confidence in the ultimate justice of the people." *"Intelligence, patriotism, Christianity, and a firm reliance on Him, who has never yet forsaken this favored land are still competent to adjust in the best way, all our present difficulties."* In the meantime, however, he said, he deemed it only his "simple duty" to use the power confided to him "to hold, occupy, and possess the property and places belonging to the government."

"In your hands, my dissatisfied fellow countrymen, and not in mine, is the momentous issue of civil war. The government will not assail you. You can have no conflict, without being yourselves the aggressors. You have no oath registered in Heaven to destroy the government, while I shall have the most solemn one to 'preserve, protect and defend' it."

He then concluded with that magnificant concilatory paragraph so rich in "prose of Biblical beauty:"

"I am loath to close. We are not enemies, but friends. We must not be enemies. Though passion may have strained, it must not break our bonds of affection. The mystic chords of memory stretching from every battle-field, and patriot grave, to every living heart and hearthstone, all over this broad land, will yet swell the chorus of the Union, when again touched, as surely they will be, by the better angels of our nature." [2]

Then turning about, he said, "I am now ready to take the oath." Chief Justice Taney, old, worn, and shrunken, stepped forward with trembling hands as he held an open Bible toward the ninth President to be sworn in. Mr. Lincoln laid his left hand on the Bible, raised his right hand, and after the Chief Justice repeated the words of the oath:

I do solemnly swear that I will faithfully execute the office of President of the United States, and will, to the best of my ability, preserve, protect, and defend the Constitution of the United States. So help me God!

A burst of applause arose from the people, and the artillery over on the slope boomed with its guns a salute to the sixteenth President of the United States. The inaugural ceremony was over.

Those upon the broad platform rose and remained standing as the President and his party passed back into the Senate Chamber The procession reformed in the same order as before, then went to the carriages, and returned, by the way of Pennsylvania Avenue, leaving at the White House Abraham Lincoln, the son of Thomas and Nancy Hanks Lincoln. There he was rejoined by his family.

Late that night, after the days exhausting activities, Abe lay quiet on his bed and retraced, in memory, the long road from the loft in the log cabin to the comfortable canopied bed in the White House.

CHAPTER XII
President of the United States

Never did an incoming President of the United States face so many seemingly insurmountable problems—human crisis, uncertainty, a divided world. Yet, during the first few days in office self-seeking men demanded much of his priceless time and energy.

Office seekers and their sponsoring senators, representatives, and governors, "lay in wait for him in every nook and cranny inside and outside the White House, all endeavoring to obtain a secret interview." All but innumerable were the notes he was obliged to write, such as to Attorney General Bates: "Please let Senator Wade name the men to be District Attorney for the Northern District of Ohio." Or, to Secretary of State Seward, about a Mr. Carl Schurz: "I wish you would give Mr. Schurz a full interview." Or, to Postmaster-General Blair about Postmaster appointments.[1]

There were many, many other problems, such as the proper channeling of the unbounded energies of his Cabinet officers, and the crying demands for solving domestic problems. But the fact of a divided nation demanded immediate and constant attention.

On the very day following the inaugural, there came a letter from Major Robert Anderson, officer in command of Fort Sumter in Charleston Harbor, saying that he had food supplies for only about four weeks longer. On January 9, the Confederates in Charleston had fired on the *Star of the West,* and driven it back as it was attempting to supply the fort. Now they were demanding that the fort be evacuated.

President Lincoln consulted with the War Department, the Senate, and his cabinet about sending food, but no military supplies, to Fort Sumter. The advice he received was mixed. Some said yes; most advised no. All agreed that a gun fired at Fort Sumter made war inevitable.

The President continued to confer with the Senate, with General Scott, and others. Then on April 6, he notified Governor Pickens, by letter at Charleston, that an attempt would be made to supply Fort Sumter "with provisions only." General Beauregard, Confederate Commander at Fort Sumter, telegraphed the Confederate Secretary of War that he had been notifed that the supplies would be sent, either peaceably or by force.

Jefferson Davis called his advisers into session at Montgomery to consider Lincoln's message to Governor Pickens, and said, "The firing on the fort will inaugurate a civil war greater than any the world has yet seen; and I do not feel competent to advise you. . . . You will want—only to strike a hornet's nest which extends from mountains to ocean; legions, now quiet, will swarm out and sting us to death. . . ." Yet President Davis and his advisers instructed Beauregard to demand the surrender of the fort. Thus they decided in favor of attacking the fort, leaving it to General Beauregard the time and method of attack.

On April 11, Beauregard sent two messengers in a boat with a note to Major Anderson—his former teacher in artillery at West Point—demanding that he evacuate the Fort. Major Anderson wrote in answer, ". . .It is a demand with which I regret that my sense of honor, and my obligations to my Government, prevent my compliance. . . ." As Major Anderson handed his note to Beauregard's aides, he remarked, "Gentlemen, if you do not batter us to pieces, we shall be starved out in a few days." [2]

That night, beyond the mid-night hour, four aids from Beauregard, went in a boat to the Fort with a note saying there would

131

be no "useless effusion of blood" if he would fix a stated time for his surrender. Anderson consulted with his fellow officers, and at 3:15 that morning gave his answer: "Cordially uniting with you in the desire to avoid the useless effusion of blood, I will, if provided with the proper and necessary means of transportation, evacuate Fort Sumter by noon on the 15th instant, and I will not in the meantime open my fire on your forces unless compelled to do so by some hostile act against this fort or the flag of my country. . .should I not receive prior to that time controlling instructions from my Government or additional supplies."

Within five minutes they gave Anderson a written answer, notifying him that "By authority of Brigadier-General, commanding the Provisional Forces of the Confederate States, we have the honor to notify you that he will open the fire of his batteries on Fort Sumter in one hour from this time." To the four men who got in their boat, Major Anderson's parting words were: "If we do not meet again on earth, I hope we may meet in Heaven."[3]

At 4:30, on that same morning of April 12, 1861, General Beauregard ordered the attack, and there came a flash of light and the booming of a cannon across at Charleston Harbor. Encircling batteries let loose their mortars and howitzers, and the Confederate guns pounded Fort Sumter for thirty-four hours. When finally the Stars and Stripes had been shot down, no provisions but pork remained, the gates destroyed, the bastion walls seriously injured, and the magazines surrounded by flames, Major Anderson hoisted the white flag, accepted terms of evacuation, and marched out of the fort. On Sunday afternoon, the 14th, with his men he sailed for New York.

"They had lost one man, killed in the accidental explosion of one of their own cannons. In their last glimpse of Fort Sumter they saw the new Confederate flag, Stars and Bars, flying. In his trunk Major Anderson had the flag he had defended; he wished to keep this burnt and shot flag and have it wrapped round him when laid in the grave."[4]

Telegrams were sent, and bulletins were posted of the firing on Fort Sumter. Over the northern states the cry went up "Avenge the Insult!" and "Vindicate the nation's honor!" That Sunday was a crucial day, for no one talked of anything but Fort Sumter and the war that was probably coming.

The President had many visitors. Senators and Congressmen

came to say their people would stand by the government and the President. The Cabinet met, and a proclamation was framed whereby the seceding states were proclaimed as "too powerful to be suppressed" by ordinary procedure of government. The President issued a proclamation calling forth "the militia of the several States of the Union, to the aggregate number of seventy-five thousand, in order to suppress said combinations, and to cause the laws to be duly executed."

That Sunday evening, Stephen A. Douglas, the acknowledged leader of the Democrats of the northern States, called on the ᴰresident. After a cordial visit, in which the crisis was discussed, Lincoln read to Douglas the proclamation he intended sending out the next day calling for 75,000 volunteers to serve the nation for the next three months.

As soon as the reading was ended, Mr. Douglas rose from the chair and said: "Mr. President, I cordially concur in every word of that document, except that instead of a call for seventy-five thousand men I would make it two hundred thousand. You do not know the dishonest purposes of those men (the Rebels) as well as I do —" He then asked the President to look with him at a map which hung on the wall, where in considerable detail he pointed out the principal strategic places which should be strengthened at once for the coming contest — Fort Monroe in Virginia, Harper's Ferry on the Potomac, Cairo on the Mississippi, and Washington. The two men discussed at length the manner by which the nation should be placed on a firm warlike footing, and parted that night with a more cordial and united purpose than ever before in their lives.

The President's call for seventy-five thousand militia went out the next day, and with it an order for the person's disturbing the public peace "to disperse and retire peacefully to their respective abodes within twenty days from date." The quota for which he called was immediately over-subscribed. The enthusiasm to enlist was so great that Horace Greely believed that 500,000 men would have responded, had they been called. Banks, corporations, and individuals offered money, supplies and credit. The sad fact, however, was that the South endeavored to shift the blame for firing on Fort Sumter and the war in general on Lincoln; his call for troops only moved them to deeper anger and to unified action.

The Virginia state convention passed an ordinance of secession, and the Virginia militia marched on Harper's Ferry, where the small Union garrison put to the torch several million dollars worth of arms and ammunition as they marched out. Likewise the Union Navy Yard at Norfolk was abandoned, and some thirty million dollars worth of Federal property destroyed when they considered the place under attack.

Mr. Douglas, who had warned the President against such maneuvers, went on a lecture tour through Western Virginia, Ohio and Illinois rallying support for the Union. In Chicago, Douglas spoke to a large crowd, saying: "Before God it is the duty of every American citizen to rally around the flag of his country." This was his last speech. Worn and exhausted he fell ill with fever and retired to his Oakenwald estate, overlooking Lake Michigan. He died on the third of June. His last words were for his sons, "Tell them to obey the laws and support the Constitution of the United States." Lincoln hung crepe in the White House, and his passing was mourned throughout the Union.

Within a short time Arkansas, North Carolina and Tennessee joined the states that had already seceded. To facilitate action the Confederates moved their capitol from Montgomery to Richmond, Virginia — only 109 miles south of Washington.

President Lincoln was not by nature a man of war, and had hoped that difficulties might be settled without further shedding of blood, but rebel intentions were now too plain to be misread. He, therefore, acted boldly and energetically in setting in motion every possible force and agency to save the Union. To the members of his Cabinet he said: "It will require the utmost skill, influence, and sagacity for all of us to save the Republic. If we succeed, there will be glory enough for us all."

In a brief time he expanded the regular army; raised a volunteer army of over 300,000; imposed a blockade on Southern ports; built up a Navy of Warships, merchant vessels, gunboats and men sufficient to guard the coastline for 3,550 miles; closed the Post Office to "treasonable correspondence"; suspended the writ of habeas corpus in areas where Southern sympathizers were active, and ordered the spending of unappropriated funds for the prosecution of the war. The South had made the fatal mistake of forcing war upon the Nation. They had generals and soldiers, but no leader to match the moral strength of Abraham Lincoln with his masterly ability in statecraft.

At the beginning, however, military affairs for the Union moved painfully slow. Yet Southern papers had been calling for the capture of Washington. Jefferson Davis had been rumored as the possible leader, and some 15,000 Confederate troops were already reported near Alexandria. The flicker of campfires of their Army on Arlington Heights across the Potomac could already be seen from Washington. Who knew what could or would happen any day here or elsewhere? Problems piled high for the new President.

The first Union regiment to start for Washington was the Sixth Massachusetts. As they were changing trains in Baltimore on April 19, they were attacked by a mob of secession sympathizers. Four enlisted men were killed and seventeen wounded. Twelve civilians were killed. Dusty and dispirited they reached Washington at five o'clock and marched to the capitol through a great crowd of silent people.

Early the next day a delegation from Baltimore called on Mr. Lincoln requesting that no more troops should be sent through Baltimore. Lincoln's reply was "If I grant you this concession that no troops shall pass through the city, you will be back here tomorrow, demanding that none shall be marched around it."

The President was right, for again on Sunday and Monday committees sought him, protesting that Maryland soil should not be "polluted" by the feet of soldiers marching against the South. Lincoln's reply was, "We must have troops; and as they can neither crawl under Maryland nor fly over it, they must come across it." They responded by destroying certain bridges on the railroads running from Baltimore to Harrisburg and Philadelphia. To make matters worse, they cut the telegraph lines connecting Washington with the north.

The Seventh Regiment from New York was due to arrive in Washington, but day by day it did not come, nor was there news of its whereabouts. Time dragged on, and when more than a week had passed, with no news, tensions mounted, yet Lincoln remained "calm and collected." Then one day, Mr. Hay, his secretary, heard him exclaim in an anguished tone, "Why don't they come? Why don't they come?"

Then on Thursday, the 25th, the whole city was made glad by the shrill whistle of a locomotive. A great crowd gathered at the station and cheered while the troops of the Seventh New York Regiment left the train and marched up Pennsylvania Avenue to the White House. Bridge building and the laying of tracks had caused the delay. Washington now had seventeen thousand troops, and more were coming. The capitol would be defended, and the President could give attention to the prosecution of the war.

Some of Lincoln's most trying problems were within his own Cabinet family. Those had been chosen largely from among the President's political rivals, and although they were able men, they were all ambitious. Some, like Joseph's brethren, were envious of the President. They were rather certain that their training and experience were superior to his. And, when he consulted freely with the entire Cabinet, and with others who were well-qualified in their respective fields, there were those who gained the false impression that he just did not know.

Secretary of State Seward, "felt certain that the responsibilities of conducting the government in the great crisis that confronted the administration devolved upon him. And he took little pains to conceal his views." Lincoln's kind patience, coupled with firmness, soon convinced Seward that Lincoln was President and would have the advice of all the Cabinet, and in the end would follow the course which seemed best to him. In the final days it was Seward who said, "Lincoln was the best man I ever knew."

Salmon P. Chase, Secretary of the Treasury, however, always held the opinion that he should have been President instead of Lincoln, and he continued to aspire to that position, and at times to indulge in political intrigue. Yet he was a good secretary who knew how to raise money. Lincoln "controlled" him until near the end of the war, and then appointed him Chief Justice of the Supreme Court.

Simon Cameron, Secretary of War, became involved in scandals over cheap merchandise delivered in war contracts, and after only seven months in office, he was appointed minister to Russia. In his place Lincoln chose Edwin M. Stanton, former Attorney General in Buchanan's Cabinet, and at the time legal adviser to Cameron. People wondered at this appointment, for he was an unswerving Democrat, and it was Stanton who had snubbed Lincoln at Cincinnati in the McCormick reaper case. During the early months of his presidency, Lincoln had no critic more bitter than Edwin M. Stanton. He had looked upon Lincoln's rise to the

Presidency as a national disaster. He deplored what he called his "painful imbecility" and habitually referred to the President as "the original gorilla." After the battle of Bull Run, Stanton charged the "catastrophe" to the "imbecility of the Administration," and suggested that "Jeff Davis" might soon "turn out the whole concern."

Yet in January, 1862, nine months after Lincoln's inauguration, Stanton was invited to become Secretary of War. A strong man was needed, and Lincoln, seeking only ability and willing to overlook personal thrusts, saw in Stanton the qualities required for the War Department's enormous responsibilities.

Stanton accepted "with supreme confidence in himself" and only small lessening of his contempt for Lincoln. He looked upon the call to duty "solely as a personal obligation to save the country." Upon the task before him he centered all his great talents and energies.[5]

When Lincoln's friends warned him that Stanton would give him constant trouble, and would run away with the whole War Department, Lincoln showed no signs of alarm, but said, *"We may have to treat him as they are sometimes obliged to treat a Methodist minister I know of out West. He gets wrought up to so high a pitch of excitement in his prayers and exhortations that they are obliged to put bricks in his pockets to keep him down. We may have to serve Stanton the same way, but I guess we'll let him jump awhile first."*

The war took on a different tempo under Stanton — as indicated by the following incident which took place soon after he took over: Stanton discovered that an order for heavy guns had been neglected. With his own hands he helped drag heavy guns from the Washington arsenal and put them on cars for Harper's Ferry. The next day the commander of the arsenal reported that he had not found it convenient to forward the guns on the preceding day, but would get them off immediately. Stanton stared at him scornfully. "The guns are now at Harper's Ferry," he roared, "and you, sir, are no longer in the service of the United States Government."[6]

Lincoln liked the way Stanton got things done. His constant attitude toward him was one of patience and tolerance. He seemed willing to make any sacrifice of pride, if only Stanton's great energies might be ceaselessly applied to the prosecution of the war. The two great men came to work together day and night, and "there grew up between them an intimacy in which the mind and heart of each were given without reserve to the great work in which they bore such conspicuous parts."[7]

On one occasion, Owen Lovejoy, heading a delegation of Western men, came to Washington to urge upon the President the mingling of Western and Eastern troops in order to promote the spirit of national unity. Lincoln thought well of the plan and wrote a note to Stanton suggesting a transfer of certain regiments. When the committee presented it to Stanton, he not only said it was impractical, and refused to carry it out, but commented: "If Lincoln gave that order, he is a d--- fool." Returning to the White House, Lovejoy gave the President an exact report of the conversation.

"Did Stanton really say I was a d--- fool?" asked Lincoln. "He did," answered Lovejoy. "Then," said Lincoln, "I must be one, for Stanton is nearly always right."[8]

Lincoln understood the great problems with which the War Secretary had to contend, and said of him: "Stanton is the rock upon which are beating the waves of this conflict...He fights back the angry waters and prevents them from undermining and overwhelming the land. I do not see how he survives—why he is not crushed and torn to pieces. Without him I should be destroyed."[9]

If President Lincoln's search for the proper cabinet members was difficult, then his search for a Commander-in-chief of the combined armies was even more difficult. General Winfield Scott was too old and infirm to carry on longer. Robert E. Lee, the great Virginian, was the ablest military officer of the day, a man of refined characteristics, and a Christian gentleman who had long opposed slavery and favored the Union. The President, the Secretary of War, and the retiring General wanted him to take command of all the military forces. They sent for him, and on Thursday morning, April 18, he rode into Washington, where he was interviewed by General Scott and his close friend Francis P. Blair, Sr. They informed him of President Lincoln's anxious desire that he take command of the armies. Lee asked certain questions, and for a time seemed to show interest, but finally declined, and "rode silently and alone across the long bridge back to his stately home on Arlington Heights." Afterwards, he said, "I declined the offer

. . .stating as candidly and as courteously as I could that, though opposed to secession and depreciating in the defense of my native State, I never again desire to draw my sword." General Scott reckoned that Lincoln had lost a commander worth 50,000 men. [10]

The first battles of the war revealed just how sorely an expert field commander was needed. The North had great superiority in sea power, and the blockade was quite complete. But her first land battles were indecisive, or more often dismal defeats. The battle of *Bull Run,* on Sunday, July 21, 1861, looked favorable for a Union victory until a Confederate army of fresh reserves were thrown against them. The majority of the 30,000 tired, undisciplined Union lads threw aside canteens and haversacks and retreated in wild panic. By daylight the next morning, and during much of the day, steady streams of mud-covered and rain-soaked soldiers stumbled across the Long Bridge and up Pennsylvania Avenue to the Capitol and to private homes. Some 3,000 never returned. By Tuesday the survivors were reentrenched on Arlington Heights, but the public was aroused. General Scott apologized for allowing the poorly disciplined troops to fight, and Horace Greeley wrote Lincoln, "This is my seventh sleepless night. If it is best for the country and for mankind that we make peace with the rebels at once and on their terms, do not shrink even from that."

Greeley was not alone in being unable to sleep nights. Many a home over the land suffered from insomnia. Some spent the time in prayer. The heavier burden lay on the First Man of the United States, who occupied the Executive Mansion familiarly known as the White House. James F. Murdock, elocutionist and lecturer, who, as guest, spent three weeks in the White House with Mr. Lincoln, says:

> One night—it was just after the battle of Bull Run—I was restless and could not sleep. I was repeating the part which I was to take in a public performance. The hour was past midnight; indeed, it was getting near dawn, when I heard low tones proceeding from a private room near where the President slept. The door was partly open. I saw the President kneeling beside an open window. The light was turned low in the room, his back was toward me. For a moment I was silent, looking in amazement and wonder. Then he cried out in tones pleading and sorrowful: *'Oh, Thou God that heard Solomon in the night when he prayed for wisdom, hear me. I cannot lead this people. I cannot guide the affairs of this nation without*

139

Thy help. I am poor and weak and sinful. Oh, God, Who didst hear Solomon when he cried for wisdom, hear me and save this nation.' [11]

The President wrote out his Memoranda of Military Policy, set about the task of reorganizing and increasing the army, and strengthening the morale of officers and men in camps in the area. He assembled the soldiers and made a speech to them in which he spoke of "better days to come." As often as he could he went to the Arlington camps where he frequently left his carriage and walked up and down the lines shaking hands with the men, and repeating heartily as he did so, "God bless you, God bless you." He borrowed military manuals from the Library of Congress, and augmented his knowledge of military science which he had learned during the time he was captain in the Black Hawk War. [12]

A succession of battlefield defeats afflicted the Union, and a substantial body of Northern opinion demanded peace. Many were willing to fight to preserve the Union, but not to destroy slavery. Others urged the destruction of slavery as the war's supreme goal. Lincoln had to keep the antislavery extremist in check to prevent the secession of border states. Jealousies unsettled his cabinet, greed took its sad toll in supply, and friction among commanding officers ate deep into efficiency on battlefields.

The best military officers were leading Confederate armies. General Robert E. Lee had become Lieutenant Commander of the Southern forces, "Stonewall" Jackson, his "right arm," George Edward Pickett his dashing infantry officer, and J.E.B. ("Jeb") Stuart, the priceless cavalry officer, known as "the eyes of the army." Bereft of the services of so many of these able officers, President Lincoln had to experiment with leadership. He appointed and removed a succession of field commanders in the hope of securing a major military victory. In the meantime there were many reverses, and the President and the people were deeply concerned. In August of 1861, he issued an impressive proclamation for a National Day of Fasting and Prayer. [13]

Mr. Lincoln had a home life which, in many respects, was pleasant. Yet at times it, too, presented problems and sorrows. Mrs. Lincoln loved to spend money, and there were times when she might have been more congenial. Robert, their oldest son, was with considerable difficulty making grades in Harvard. The two younger boys played many pranks around the White House. Tad, who had a slight lisp in his speech, was over-mischievous, paid small attention to his lessons, and could scarcely read or write at twelve. Willie was a bright, lovable child, amazingly like his father. He studied faithfully, had a good memory, and at eight years of age did well at reading and writing. He was a good boy, found delight in memorizing long portions of the Bible in Sunday School, and told his mother and father he was going to be a preacher when he grew up. President and Mrs. Lincoln not only loved Willie deeply, but felt that he, above others, would be an honor to God and to the Lincoln name.[14]

In February of 1862, a deep sorrow came to the White House. The children, Tad and Willie, were constantly receiving presents. Willie was especially delighted with a little pony, which he and Tad insisted on riding every day. The weather was changeable, and exposure resulted in severe colds, which deepened into fever. Tad's case was not severe, and soon he was up and around, but Willie was so serious from the first day that Lincoln was alarmed and would slip away from callers and Cabinet at every opportunity.

At night he did little else but alternate with Mrs. Lincoln at Willie's bedside. Receptions at the White House were cancelled, and for days Willie was in delirium while both the father and mother shared with the nurse the nightly vigils at the bedside. Then, when Willie died at five o'clock in the afternoon of February 20, the President was so overcome with grief that he leaned his tall frame over his son's bed and said, *"My poor boy, he was too good for this earth. God has called him home. I know that he is better off in Heaven, but then we loved him so. It is hard, hard to have him die."*[15]

Standing with bowed head over his boy, the President said to the nurse, "This is the hardest trial of my life. Why is it? Why is it?" The nurse assured him that from her own experience she knew Christ could comfort him. He questioned her concerning her situation. She told him she was a widow; that her husband and two children were in Heaven; that she saw the hand of God in it all, and that she had never loved Him before as she had since her affliction.

"How was that brought about?" inquired Mr. Lincoln.

"Simply by trusting God and feeling that He does all things well," she replied.

"Did you submit fully to the first loss?" he asked.

"No," she answered, "not wholly, but as blow came upon blow and all was taken, I could and did submit, and was very happy."

He responded, "I am glad to hear you say that. Your experience will help me bear my affliction."

Thus God plowed Lincoln's soul with the iron share of sorrow. On being informed that the Christians were praying for him, he said, "I want them to pray for me. I need their prayers."[16]

On the way to the funeral, a good woman expressed her sympathy for him. He thanked her and said, "I will try to go to God with my sorrow." Later she spoke to him about faith, and asked him if he could trust God. He replied, "I think I can, and I will try. I wish I had the childlike faith you speak of, and I trust He will give it to me." Then he spoke of his mother who had held him upon her bosom and soothed his childish griefs. "I remember her prayers," said he, "and they have always followed me. They have clung to me all my life."[17] Some hours after the funeral Mr. Lincoln said:

I now see as never before the preciousness of God's love in Jesus Christ, and how we are brought near to God as our Father by Him.

The Rev. Dr. Francis Vinton, Rector of Trinity Church of New York, was in Washington and through Mrs. Lincoln he was invited to the White House. He spoke straight from the heart in pastoral consolation to the President: "Your Son is Alive."

"Alive?" exclaimed Mr. Lincoln, and threw his arms around Dr. Vinton's neck, laid his head upon his breast, and sobbed aloud, "Alive!" Then said Dr. Vinton, "God has called your son into His Upper Kingdom—a Kingdom and an existence as real, more real, than your own. It may be that he too, like Joseph, has gone, in God's good Providence, to be the salvation of *his* father's household. It is a part of the Lord's plan for the ultimate happiness of you and yours."

Dr. Vinton then told Lincoln that he had a sermon on the subject. Mr. Lincoln asked him to send a copy of it to him as early as possible, and thanked him repeatedly for his comforting words. When Lincoln received the sermon he read it over and over, and had a copy made for his own private use.

About this time he established an early morning hour of Bible reading and prayer. A new gravity settled in Mr. Lincoln's face, a deeper faith in God grew in his soul, and he came not only to have a greater interest in things pertaining to Christianity for himself, but desired to share them with the men in the army. He arranged special religious services for them, and later issued an order urging them to avoid swearing and to keep the Sabbath as far as it did not interfere with their duties in military service.[18]

One night during the darkest days of the war, when for a long time all news from the front had been most disturbing, the gracious Julia Ward Howe had a dream or vision of victory. Under the inspiration of that dream-vision she arose and wrote her famous song *Battle Hymn of the Republic* — which stirred President Lincoln "like a trumpet blast," and became his best loved marching song.

> Mine eyes have seen the glory of the coming of the Lord;
> He is trampling out the vintage where the grapes of wrath are stored;
> He hath loosed the fateful lightening of His terrible swift sword;
>   His truth is marching on.
>
> I have seen Him in the watch fires of a hundred circling camps;
> They have builded Him an altar in the evening dews and damps;
> I can read his righteous sentence by the dim and flaring lamps.
>   His day is marching on.
>
> In the beauty of the lillies Christ was born across the sea,
> With the glory in his bosom that transfigures you and me;
> As he died to make men holy, let us die to make men free,
>   While God is marching on.

While Lincoln mourned the loss of Willie, the Confederates raised the scuttled *Merrimac* from the Norfolk navy yard, and appointed a commission to draw plans for her conversion into the first ironclad war vessel in history. With it they would break out of the blockade.

Taking the cue, Lincoln and the Naval officials in Washington discussed the feasibility of their building an iron-clad vessel which would compete with the *Merrimac*. Finally, Captain John Ericsson won President Lincoln's hearty approval of his plans for a vessel which he said would resist the impact of any projectile which could be thrown by any gun then invented. The vessel was to be equipped with a revolving turret that housed two heavy guns invented by Admiral Dahlgren, and the vessel was to be called the *Monitor*. The Board of Construction became convinced also, and awarded the contract to Mr. Bushnell, and Messrs. Corning, Winslow, and Griswald of New York with the understanding that Captain Ericsson, under President Lincoln's influence, would have the oversight, and that the contractors would push the work to completion in the shortest time possible. Captain Worden volunterred to take command of the *Monitor* just as soon as it was completed.

On Saturday afternoon, March 8, 1862, the *Merrimac,* fitted with a cast-iron ram, and covered with three-inch iron plates, appeared in Hampton Roads where it shot and rammed the two Union War vessles, the *Congress* and the *Cumberland.* One was destroyed and the other left helpless. It had caused to run aground, another Union War vessel, the *Minnesota,* — ready for the next morning's sacrifice.

In great alarm the Naval officials in Washington met with President Lincoln. They forsaw the *Merrimac* sinking other Union ships on Sunday morning, then, as they said: "Who is to prevent her dropping her anchor in the Potomac where that steamer lies, and throwing her hundred-pound shells into this room, or battering down the walls of the Capitol?"

"The Almighty," answered the President, "The Almighty will prevent her. This is God's fight, and He will win it in his own good time. . . . You do not seem to take into account our little *Monitor* and her commander. The *Monitor* should be in Hampton Roads now. She left New York eight days ago. She may be the little stone in the sling of Almighty God that shall smite the *Merrimac* Philistine in the forehead."

After more conversation, the men took their leave, and walked in silence to the west entrance of the Treasury. Here the Assistant Secretary of the Navy said, "Is not our Lincoln the truest man, an example of the most genuine manhood, you have ever seen — of whom you have ever read? How sincere he is! He seems to have imparted some of his faith to me. I have avoided reliance upon the *Monitor.* Perhaps she may yet prove the good angel who will take us out of the Slough of Despond."

The *Monitor* was to justify the faith placed in her. On Saturday night she steamed up to Newport News and the next morning at two o'clock, she laid herself alongside the grounded *Minnesota.* This brought fresh courage to Captain Van Brunt who gave Captain Worden an account of Saturday's experience and notified him that he must be ready to receive the *Merrimac* the next morning. At daybreak the *Merrimac,* all unsuspecting, came out toward the *Minnesota* to finish her work. The *Monitor* made straight for her, "a David against a Goliath—two guns on the *Monitor* against ten on the *Merrimac*." [19]

The *Monitor* moved alongside the *Merrimac* and gave her a shot. The compliment was returned, and there followed a four hour battle of the juggernauts in which the *Monitor* moved in circles around the *Merrimac* and delivered her shots at vital points until some of the *Merrimac's* iron plates buckled under the *Monitor's* pounding. The *Merrimac* then drew off and steamed back to Norfolk giving no further trouble. The blockade of the Southern ports was ever afterwards effective. The battle had demonstrated the utility of ironclad ships, and thus determined the future direction of shipbuilding and naval warfare.

The question of slavery had been an issue of paramount interest leading up to the war—a burning issue with millions.

On coming to the presidency, Lincoln had been restricted by his electoral pledge to confine slavery to the states where it already existed, and to prevent it from expanding into territories. Yet ten states had unlawfully seceded and not only removed themselves from the protection of the United States Government, but had taken up arms against the Union. They were now making use of their three million slaves to do their labor, while they themselves entered military service and came to war against the Union. Thus slavery—a moral evil within itself—had come to be used as an indirect tool to defeat the Union which Lincoln had taken an oath to protect. As a war-time measure, the President had the power to emancipate the slaves in these rebel states.

Horace Greeley, Phillips Brooks and other Northern leaders made use of the news media, the platform, and the pulpit in urging the President to abolish slavery. Delegation after delegation marched to the White House to present urgent anti-slavery resolutions. The President tried to explain to each of them that he too detested slavery, but did not consider it "either wise or courageous" to make abolition of slavery the chief object of the war, especially when the Union was being supported by the border states of Kentucky, Missouri, Tennessee, Maryland and Delaware. His chief object, he said, was to save the Union.

As a measure toward effecting emancipation gradually and honorably, he held frequent conferences with representatives of the border states, earnestly urging them to join with him in some form of compensated emancipation. To these states he made the pathetic appeal:

> *I do not argue—I beseech you to make arguments for yourself. You cannot, if you would, be blind to the signs of the times. I beg of you a calm and enlarged consideration of them, ranging, if it may be, far above personal and partisan politics. This proposal makes common cause for a common object, casting no reproaches upon any. It acts not the Pharisee. The change it contemplates would come gently as the dews of heaven, not rending or wrecking anything. Will you not embrace it? So much good has not been done, by one effort, in all past time, as in the providence of God it is now your high privilege to do. May the vast future not have to lament that you have neglected it.* [20]

Meanwhile the tide of war continued to go against the Union armies. American ambassadors warned Lincoln that European recognition of the Confederacy could be averted only by a decisive military victory to impress European politicians or emancipation of slaves to gratify the millions of common people who desired it. Delegations and individuals kept urging some move in the direction of emancipation. At least one "Emancipation society" was organized in New York.

Finally, in Mid-1862—after days in meditation and prayer, Lincoln decided to drop his reserve. He wrote in his diary, "I promised my God I would do it," and went immediately to the War department. There, in a small office where he could be left alone, he began to write what he called "something special." The next day, and other days for weeks, he returned to write a few lines, or to revise what he had written.

Then, on July 22, the President called his Cabinet together and said, in substance, "I have considered everything that has been said to me about the expediency of emancipation, and have made up my mind to issue this proclamation, and I have invited you to come together, not to discuss what is to be done, but to have you hear what I have written, and to get your suggestions about form and style. *I have thought it all over, and have made a promise that this should be done to myself and to God.*"

The proclamation was read, and the matter was discussed at length, and upon the suggestion of Secretary Seward it was decided to withhold the proclamation until some encouraging military success was achieved. The President acquiesced, and while waiting he touched up and improved the form and content of the document. He hoped and prayed it might not sound dictatorial.

The President then turned toward efforts at prevailing upon the border states to free their slaves and thus both increase the extent of free territory and set a worthy example. He held frequent conferences with representatives of these states, in which he earnestly urged them to join with him in some form of compensated emancipation. [21]

Congress passed a bill, and the President signed it, to abolish slavery in the District of Columbia. The measure appropriated one million dollars to compensate the loyal slaveholders of the District, and set aside one hundred thousand dollars for the purpose of transporting those negroes who wished to go to Haiti or Liberia.

Again he made an earnest appeal to the border states to cooperate in some plan for purchasing and freeing their slaves.

On September 17, 1862, the long awaited victory came to the Union forces in the battle Antietam. Lee was repulsed and marched his army out of Maryland. Lincoln immediately finished work on his proclamation, and called the cabinet together to consider it on Monday, September 22nd.

Strangely enough, the President opened the meeting by reading a humorous selection from Artemus Ward, after which he laid aside the book and, taking a "graver tone," he said, "Gentlemen, I have, as you are aware, thought a great deal about the relation of this war to slavery. . . .I said nothing to any one, but I made the promise to myself and to my Maker. The rebel army is now driven out, and I am going to fulfill that promise. . . .I have got you together to hear what I have written down."

The proclamation was issued and appeared in the newspapers the following morning. It declared in substance that all persons held in slavery in all parts of the nation that should be in a state of rebellion on January 1, 1863, would be set at liberty and that the government would recognize and maintain their freedom. Slavery was not to be disturbed in the states which had remained in the Union. To a party of enthusiastic citizens who serenaded him the following night, he said: "I can only trust in God that I have made no mistake." [22]

In certain quarters, even in the North, there was noisy opposition to the proclamation. Some wondered if he would go through with it come January first. Lincoln's answer was, "I am a slow walker, but I never walk back."

In his message to Congress, which convened on December 1, he said:

"The dogmas of the quiet past are inadequate to the stormy present. The occasion is piled high with difficulty, and we must rise with the occasion. As our case is new, so we must think anew, and act anew. We must disenthrall ourselves, and then we shall save our country.

"Fellow-citizens, we cannot escape history. We of this Congress and this administration, will be remembered in spite of ourselves."

He then submitted the Proclamation, and suggested a plan of *compensated* emancipation. He argued that peaceful emancipation according to the plan would "end the struggle and save the Union forever. . .without slavery the rebellion could never have existed — with slavery it could not continue. Emancipation by this plan would cost no blood at all." He pleaded most earnestly for its adoption, climaxing with the words:

"We shall nobly save, or meanly lose, the last, best hope of earth. Other means may succeed, this cannot fail. The way is plain, peaceful, generous, just — a way which, if followed, the world will forever applaud, and God must forever bless." 23

But his plan for *compensated* emancipation did not prevail in Congress. There were 3,120,515 slaves in the Confederate states, and 832,000 in the border states. At $400 each, it would have cost $1,576,206,000 to compensate the owners for their slaves. It sounded like too much and too generous to commercially-minded Congressmen. But they would pay much, *much more* in the long run.

On New Years day, 1863, a splendid reception was held in the Executive Mansion. "Handsomely dressed ladies in their hoop skirts, men in frock coats, officers in blue and gold uniforms filed into the public rooms of the White House to be greeted by President and Mrs. Lincoln. For three hours he met and shook hands with hundreds of people. Meanwhile Secretary of State Seward and his son Frederick were waiting upstairs in the President's study with a final copy of the Proclamation. 24

When Mr. Lincoln had said good-by to the last of his guests, he walked upstairs to his office and went directly to his desk where the official Emancipation Proclamation awaited his signature. He picked up a pen and poised it above the document—his arm began to shake. Amazed, he put the pen back in its holder. After a moment he smiled as he recalled that he had just spent three hours shaking hands with several hundred people. To Seward he said, "If my name ever goes into history it will be for this act, and my whole soul is in it. If my hand trembles as I sign my name, all who examine the document will say, 'He hesitated.' " Once more he picked up the pen, and said, "I never in my life felt more certain that I am doing right than I do in signing this paper." Then slowly and firmly he wrote "Abraham Lincoln." After signing duplicate copies, he looked up, smiled, and said, "That will do."

At Tremont Temple in Boston where a crowd waited news of the signing, ex-slave Frederick Douglas tells of the final moments: "Eight, nine, ten o'clock came and went, and still no word. A visible shadow seemed falling on the expectant throng, which the confident utterances of the speakers sought in vain to dispel. At last, when patience was well-nigh exhausted and suspense was becoming agony, a man with hasty step advanced through the crowd, and with a face fairly illumined with the news he bore, exclaimed in tones that thrilled all hearts, 'It is coming, it is on the wires!' " As an immense excitement swept the crowd, a Negro preacher arose and led the people in singing:

Sound the loud timbrel o'er Egypt's dark sea,
Jehovah hath triumphed, his people are free.

The Emancipation Proclamation not only brought gladness and hope in many quarters, but it was "an immortal blow for human freedom." It changed the aims of the war in that it infused a new moral meaning into the conflict. It weakened the economy of the Southern states, caused England and France to definitely decide to throw all the weight of their influence in favor of the United States, and doomed the puppet French empire in Mexico which had been hastily set up under Archduke Maximilian.

Meanwhile the war went on, and Lincoln continued his search for a general who would fight. McClellan had been replaced by General Burnside. When Burnside was defeated with fearful loss at the battle of Fredericksburg, the President replaced him with General Joseph Hooker. Then on May 2-4, came Chancellorsville, one of the great battles of the Civil War. General Hooker commanded the Union forces of 130,000, against General Robert E. Lee with 60,000 Confederates.

Through General Hooker's inability to coordinate so large a force of men, the advantage at the end of the battle lay with the Confederates. However, while repulsing a flank movement by the 11th corps of the Union army, panic broke out among a section of the Confederates about nightfall, and "Stonewall" Jackson was wounded in the crossfire of his own men. That night, in a hospital tent, Jackson's left arm was amputated just below the shoulder. The next morning the wounded general was transported by ambulance to the farm home of his friend, Mr. Chandler. He was placed in quiet, comfortable quarters with his wife at his side. For several days his condition showed encouraging improvement, but pneumonia developed and on Sunday, May 10, the end came, when as though in benediction the great Christian general said: "...let us pass over the river, and rest under the shade of the trees."

Lee had lost the best of his subordinate generals. "I know not how to replace him," said Lee, "for he was my right arm." [25]

CHAPTER XIII
Lincoln and Gettysburg

All battles of the Civil War had been fought on slave soil until early in June, 1863, when General Lee marched his army northward and began his movements for the invasion of Pennsylvania. President Lincoln issued a call for 100,000 new troops to serve for six months.

Crossing the Potomac on the 24th and 25th, Lee reached Chambersburg, Pennsylvania on the 27th. He led an army of 73,000, the majority of which were seasoned soldiers who had been winning one battle after another until a measure of pride pervaded their ranks. One soldier called out a hope that they might find an opposing army whose soldiers could make fighting interesting for them. Fear and deep anxiety not only preceded the army, but the ominous news was flashed over the wires to the Northern states.

Then certain significant things happened: along the line of the Confederate march a brave woman swung open her window and shouted, "Look at Pharaoh's army going to the Red Sea." Another woman sang "The Star Spangled Banner." General Lee removed his hat. President Lincoln placed General Mead at the head of the army of the Potomac, consisting of 88,000 men and started him northward toward Gettysburg with orders to "fight."

Seeing the danger of his lines of communication being severed, Lee turned back toward Gettysburg when some of his forward marching divisions became entangled and traded shots with columns of the Union army. Scouts of the Union army reported that Gettysburg was the place to receive the Confederate attack, and Mead hurried his main force to strong positions on Cemetery Ridge. Other divisions took up positions on Culp's ,Hill and on Round Top Hill.

The line-up was impressive; the stakes startling. Both generals were good men, and great soldiers. Lee and his army had accustomed themselves to winning victories. Mead was a new commander. He saw the battle as one in which he and his men fought for their homes, wives, children, barns, cattle, and fields against invaders.

A deep concern, almost akin to frenzy, swept the country round about. Then when most everybody seemed panic-stricken and no one could tell what was going to happen, President Lincoln went to God about the matter. As he said:

> . . . *oppressed by the gravity of our affairs, I went to my room . . . and locked the door and got down on my knees before Almighty God and prayed to him mightily for victory at Gettysburg. I told Him that this war was His, and our cause His cause, but we could not stand another Fredericksburg or Chancellorsville. Then and there I made a solemn vow to Almighty God that if He would stand by our boys at Gettysburg, I would stand by Him. . . . And after that, I don't know how it was, and I cannot explain it, soon a sweet comfort crept into my soul. The feeling came that God had taken the whole business into His own hands, and that things would go right at Gettysburg. . . .* 1

Lee and his army reached Gettysburg on the early afternoon of July 1, and attacked Mead's left, inflicting heavy casualties, including the brave and able Major General John F. Reynolds, who died giving the command, "Forward! for God's sake forward." The fight was fierce and was definitely going against the Union cause. General Mead was tempted to discouragement, when a strange and irresistable impression moved him to order up his reserves.

On the second day, the Confederates delayed for reorganization which gave the Union forces time to reinforce—with the reserves, more men and artillery were put into position on Cemetery Ridge, Culp's Hill, and Little Round Top. When Lee did strike, it was in frontal attack and with deadly aim on all three fronts. Twice was Cemetery Ridge assaulted; Culp's Hill was taken but recaptured; and infantry and artillery were hurried into position just in time to save Little Round Top. Wave after wave of brave men went down on all fronts that second day, yet the Union lines held or were retaken so well that by evening Mead sent word to Lincoln that the enemy was "repulsed at all points."

That night a dreadful awe settled over the battlefield—a horror mingled with dark foreboding as to what unfinished tragedy might await tomorrow. General Mead yielded to a strong impression, and again ordered up more reserves.

On the third day, July 3, 1863, General Lee focused all his attention on an all-out attack on Cemetery Ridge, which was Mead's center. To command this all important drive, he and Longstreet chose Major General George Edward Pickett, a tall, daring and most successful infantry officer whose long ringlets of auburn hair floated in the air as he galloped his horse in directing the 15,000 men chosen to charge the Union center.

Before starting the charge, Pickett handed Longstreet a letter to a girl in Richmond he was to marry if he lived. It read: "If old Peter's (Longstreet's) nod means death, good-bye, and God bless you, little one." A fellow officer held out a flask of whiskey: "Take a drink with me; in an hour you'll be in hell or glory." Pickett replied, "No, I have promised the little girl I wouldn't."

In frontal assault, Pickett and his 15,000 men advanced over half a mile of broken ground as Union artillery plowed through them with a wild rain of rifle bullets, fired from Spencer repeater rifles—"the secret weapon" now in use by the Union army. For almost seven-eighths of a mile they marched in the open sunlight, every man a target for the Union marksmen behind stone fences and breastworks. When officers fell from horses, the horses were taken by others. When infantry ranks were broken, others closed in. About half who started the offense reached the Union lines surmounting Cemetery Ridge. Then came the bayonet and clubbed musket charge. For a brief time the Confederate battle flag waved over the defenses as the fighting over the walls became hand to hand, but more than half the Confederates having fallen, the column wavered and was practically annihilated, only a small portion escaping death or capture. [2]

Mead rode up white-faced to hear it was a repulse and cried, "Thank God." Lee said, "This has been a sad day for us, a sad day, but we cannot expect always to gain victories."

It had been a three-day battle the likes of which had never been suffered by Americans up to that time. One-hundred and sixty-one thousand soldiers had been locked in deadly combat, and there had been the most grimly appalling loss of lives on both sides that had ever occurred in the Western Hemisphere. Some 18,000 Confederates had been killed and wounded and 13,000 were missing, most of them prisoners. The Union loss had been 23,000, of whom 16,543 were killed or wounded. Such was the evil fruitage of war.

As a heavy rainfall came that night, Lee ordered a retreat southward. Mead issued a congratulatory order to his army thanking them for "driving the invaders from our soil."

In the meantime Vicksburg, located on a high bluff commanding a three-mile hairpin curve in the Mississippi River, sent up a flag of truce, and on July 4th a Confederate army of 31,600 surrendered to General Grant. Two weeks later, General Banks took Port Hudson, a little farther south on the Mississippi, and now the "Father of Waters" flowed free all the way to New Orleans, which was already occupied by the Union.

Lincoln's spirits, like those of other millions of Union-loving Americans, rejoiced with the victories of Gettysburg and Vicksburg. To his cabinet he said, "I knew it would come out all right, for God told me so." As the news spread to hundreds of cities in the North there were mass meetings, rejoicing, firing of guns, ringing of bells with torchlight processions, songs, speeches, and prayers of thanksgiving. The tide of war had definitely turned toward victory, and the people were glad. On July 15, a Presidential Proclamation of Thanksgiving went forth.

It has pleased Almighty God to hearken to the supplications and prayers of an afflicted people, and to vouchsafe to the army and the navy of the United States victories on land and on the sea so signal and so effective as to furnish reasonable grounds for augmented confidence that the Union of

these States will be maintained, their constitution preserved,
and their peace and prosperity permanently restored . . . It is
meet and right to recognize and confess the presence of the
Almighty Father and the power of His Hand equally in these
triumphs and in these sorrows . . .[3]

Scarcely had the smoke of battle cleared away when the Honorable David Wills, a citizen of Gettysburg, wrote to the Honorable Andrew G. Curtin, Governor of Pennsylvania, suggesting that a plot of ground in the midst of the battlefield be purchased and set apart as a soldiers' national cemetery. Governor Curtin not only approved the recommendation but corresponded with the governors of the loyal states whose troops had engaged in the battle of Gettysburg, asking them to co-operate in the movement. A Board of Commissioners was appointed, the grounds proposed by Mr. Wills were purchased, and arrangements made that a memorial dedication service be held to consecrate these grounds on the 23rd of October, 1863.

The Honorable Edward Everett, who had been U.S. Senator, Governor of Massachusetts, and President of Harvard, was invited to deliver the dedicatory oration. He replied that it was "wholly out of his power" to make the necessary preparations by the twenty-third of October. Therefore the dedication date was set forward to the nineteenth of November—nearly a month—to give him time to prepare. Formal invitations to be present were then sent to the President of the United States and his Cabinet; to Major General George G. Mead and his officers and soldiers who had gained the memorable victory at Gettysburg; and to Lieutenant Winfield Scott and to Admiral Charles Stewart, representatives of the army and navy; and to members of both houses of Congress.

A little more than two weeks before the dedication, the Board of Commissioners, through Mr. Wills their president, sent President Lincoln a belated invitation saying, "It is the desire that after the oration, you, as Chief Executive of the Nation, formally set apart these grounds to their sacred use by a few appropriate remarks."

Tardy as it was, the invitation to speak was promptly accepted by the President. He immediately set about preparing. He wrote to Edward Everett, secured a copy of the address that the orator was to deliver, and a day or two later, going to a photographer's

155

gallery to pose for his photograph, took Everett's manuscript with him and read it during the spare time he had at the studio. He thought over his talk for days, thought over it in the quiet hours of the night, thought of it while walking back and forth between the White House and the War office, thought of it while stretched out on a leather couch in the war office waiting for telegraphic reports. He wrote a rough draft of it and carried it about in the top of his tall silk hat. Ceaselessly he was brooding over it, and certainly it was taking shape. The Sunday before it was delivered he said to Noah Brooks: "It is not exactly written. It is not finished anyway. I have written it over two or three times, and I shall have to give it another lick before I am satisfied."

On November 18th, the President and his party proceeded from Washington to Gettysburg by special train. At sundown the train pulled into Gettysburg, and Lincoln was driven to the home of Mr. Wills where he was to be a guest.

At dinner that evening he met Edward Everett, Governor Curtin and others. Serenaders called on the President and heard him say a few words, then excuse himself from addressing them further. About eleven o'clock, he gathered the copy of his speech and went next door where he reviewed it with Secretary of State Seward, then returned to his room and retired for the night.

At ten o'clock the next morning Lincoln came out of the Wills' residence, mounted a beautiful chestnut horse, "the largest in the Cumberland Valley," and held a brief reception on horseback. At eleven the parade began with President Lincoln taking the lead. The Vice-President, governors, senators, representatives, military leaders and other dignitaries followed. The President sat "erect and looked majestic" as he rode on leading the procession; then when the cemetery, with its thousands of soldiers came in view, a strange, and powerful emotion swept over the President. "His body leaned forward, his arms hung limp, his head bowed." Clark E. Carr, and others, who rode just behind the President, noticed the change, but were left to wonder what strange power had possessed him. Later the President was to explain to his pastor.

Within a few minutes the march was over. The President, Edward Everett and his daughter, Secretary Seward, six governors and other distinguished citizens were escorted to the platform. A dirge was played. Then the U.S. House Chaplain, Reverend Thomas H. Stockton, offered prayer while the thousands stood with uncovered heads. Mr. Everett was introduced, and stood in silence for a brief time before a vast crowd that would test his voice; he then said: " . . . it is with hesitation that I raise my poor voice to break the eloquent silence of God and Nature. . . .As my eye ranges over the fields whose sods were so lately moistened by the blood of gallant and loyal men, I feel, as never before, how truly it was said of old that it is sweet and becoming to die for one's country." He then "gave the best in him, physically, intellectually and oratorically" as he held forth for two hours. His closing words were: "Down to the latest period of recorded time, in the glorious annals of our common country there will be no brighter page than that which relates *The Battles of Gettysburg.*"

The *Philadelphia Press* reporter described the orator's speech "like a bit of Greek sculpture—beautiful but cold as ice," but nonetheless "resonant, clear, splendid rhetoric."

The Baltimore Glee Club sang an ode written for the occasion. Ward Hill Lamon rose and by way of introduction spoke the words, "The President of the United States."

"The tall form of the President," wrote Ohio state legislator Robert Miller, "appeared on the stand, and never before have I seen a crowd so vast and restless, after standing so long, so soon stilled and quieted. Hats were removed and all stood motionless to catch the first words he should utter." Sensibly feeling the solemnity of the occasion, the President controlled his emotions by considerable effort as he drew from his pocket a paper, and "with more grace and splendor of eloquence than was his wont" read or spoke "in a firm, free way" the following words:

Four score and seven years ago our fathers brought forth on this continent, a new nation, conceived in Liberty, and dedicated to the proposition that all men are created equal.

Now we are engaged in a great civil war, testing whether that nation, or any nation so conceived and so dedicated, can long endure. We are met on a great battle-field of that war. We have come to dedicate a portion of that field, as a final resting place for those who here gave their lives that that nation might live. It is altogether fitting and proper that we should do this.

But, in a larger sense, we can not dedicate—we can not consecrate—we can not hallow—this ground. The brave men, living and dead, who struggled here, have consecrated it, far above our poor power to add or detract. The world will little note, nor long remember what we say here, but it can never forget what they did here.

It is for us the living, rather, to be dedicated here to the unfinished work which they who fought here have thus far so nobly advanced. It is rather for us to be here dedicated to the great task remaining before us — that from these honored dead we take increased devotion to that cause for which they gave the last full measure of devotion; that we here highly resolve that these dead shall not have died in vain; that this nation, under God, shall have a new birth of freedom; and that government of the people, by the people, for the people, shall not perish from the earth. [4]

Lincoln's enemies, as usual, made light of the two minute speech. But everywhere men of depth of character and intellect found difficulty in coining words sufficient to praise so great a speech. The special committee in charge of the burial of soldiers at Gettysburg said in its report: "Perhaps nothing in the whole proceedings made so deep an impression on the vast assemblage . . . as the remarks of the President. Their simplicity and force made them worthy of a prominence among the utterances from high places."

When Stanton read the speech the next day, he told Dana, his assistant secretary, "The people will be delighted with those Gettysburg speeches. Everett's speech is the speech of a scholar: It is elegant and learned. But, Lincoln's will be read by a thousand people for every one who reads Everett's, and will be remembered as long as anybody's speeches are remembered."

The *Providence Journal* said, "We know not where to look for a more admirable speech than the brief one which the President made at the close of Mr. Everett's oration."

The *Chicago Tribune* said, "The dedicatory remarks of President Lincoln will live among the annals of man."

The *Springfield* (Massachusetts) *Republican* commended it as "a perfect gem; deep in feeling, compact in thought and expression, and tasteful and elegant in every word and comma. It has the merit of unexpectedness in its verbal perfection and beauty . . . It will repay study as a model speech." The *Harper's Weekly* said, "The few words of the President were from the heart to the heart. They cannot be read, even, without kindling emotion . . . It was as simple and felicitous and earnest a word as was ever spoken."

Everett, whose two-hour address had been prepared with considerable thought, wrote to Lincoln:

> Permit me also to express my great admiration of the thoughts expressed by you with such eloquent simplicity and appropriateness at the consecration of the cemetery. I should be glad if I could flatter myself that I came as near to the central idea of the occasion in two hours as you did in two minutes.

The sheer genius and beauty of Lincoln's mind and soul are clearly revealed in his immediate reply:

> *In our respective parts yesterday, you could not have been excused to make a short address, nor I a long one. I am pleased to know that, in your judgment, the little I did say was not entirely a failure.*

Aye, President Lincoln your address was one of the most beautiful ever spoken by mortal man. It has been cast in imperishable bronze and placed in the library at Oxford University as an example of what can be done with the English language.

CHAPTER XIV
Abraham Lincoln
The Imponderable

Following the Gettysburg dedication, large minded men almost everywhere began to inquire inwardly, "What imponderable is this—what mighty force at Washington which we have inaccurately weighed?"

From boyhood Abe Lincoln had been "most unusual" wherever he had gone—a strangely strong and different character. This they knew, faintly, and because of it, he was President Lincoln. But he had grown, and at Gettysburg the place and occasion had come, when, for two minutes, he stood out before the world, and by the strength and inspiration of God, stood tall and strong and straight —taller and straighter perhaps than any man had ever stood as a Statesman. In simple, easy-to-be-understood language he had defined democracy, narrowed the distance between the people and government, and had plainly, yet profoundly, stated the most worthy goal to which every true American should be dedicated.

Good men in the western world, as well as America, were, through him, being helped in their efforts to sense the possible dignity of the common man and common things—a government under God "of the people, by the people, and for the people." These memorable utterances they would quote more often than any other in American history, and they would exert a determining influence upon the thoughts and lives of men everywhere.

Seven days after the memorable Gettysburg Address, Lincoln nationalized the New England observance of Thanksgiving Day. By his proclamation that day was set aside as *National* Thanksgiving—the first ever to be observed by presidential proclamation, but followed yearly by every president since.

During the months following, the President issued a proclamation of amnesty to Confederates who would take the oath of allegiance; he placed Ulysses S. Grant in command of the Army of the West. He continued to devote himself to a multitude of duties incident to the war, and welfare of the Union.

The construction of railroads was sponsored, agriculture expanded, long lines of homesteaders were encouraged to emigrate to the west, factories were enlarged, inventions patented, and foreign trade established so that the North actually was enjoying more prosperity than when the war began.

There was now a bright prospect of winning the war, and that prospect, said Lowell, "was mainly due to the good sense, the good humor, the sagacity, the large-mindedness, and the unselfish honesty of the unknown man whom a blind fortune, as it seemed, had lifted from the crowd to the most dangerous and difficult eminence of modern times."[1]

A more careful analysis of those factors which made Lincoln uniquely great involve (1) the "guidelines" which he set for himself and the people; (2) his profound reverence for law; (3) his religious faith; and (4) his philosophy.

Lincoln's profound insight as shown in his *"Ten Guidelines"* not only went far in guiding him in administrative affairs, but also helped to stimulate the country's economic and social wellbeing. Note the depth of wisdom couched in those ten lines:

You cannot bring about prosperity by discouraging thrift.

You cannot help small men by tearing down big men.

You cannot strengthen the weak by weakening the strong.

You cannot lift the wage earner by pulling down the wage payer.

You cannot help the poor man by destroying the rich.

You cannot keep out of trouble by spending more than your income.

You cannot further brotherhood of men by inciting class hatred.

You cannot establish security on borrowed money.

You cannot build character and courage by taking away man's initiative and independence.

You cannot help men permanently by doing for them what they could and should do for themselves.

One of the most significant forces which made for order and tranquility was Lincoln's reverence for the *law*. Twenty years of his life had been given to the study and practice of law at its highest level. He was known for his gentleness, but this gentleness was combined with a "terrific toughness" which caused him to agree heartily with the words inscribed in the dome of the nearby Library of Congress: "Law is the harmony of the universe."

As President he urged respect for the law by publicizing his admonition in the form of this beautiful ode:

Let reverence for the laws be breathed by every American mother to the lisping babe that prattles on her lap; let it be taught in schools, in seminaries, and in colleges; let it be written in primers, spelling books, and in almanacs; let it be preached from the pulpit, proclaimed in legislative halls, and enforced in courts of justice. And, in short, let it become the political religion of the nation; and let the old and the young, the rich and the poor, the grave and the gay of all sexes and tongues and colors and conditions, sacrifice unceasingly upon its altars.

Lincoln's religious life was a factor which was definitely for the good of the Country. In the early formative years of life — from age two to nine — he saw God in the life of his mother, heard those sublime Bible stories, received her godly teachings, and heard her going-away words, "I am going away from you, Abraham, and I shall not return. I know you will be a good boy . . . I want you to live as I have taught you, to love your Heavenly Father and keep His commandments." He promised!

All through life God to him was not the god of the philosophers, but the God of Nancy Hanks Lincoln and of the Bible. Religion

162

to him was not a philosophy which he was to formulate, but a personal experience into which he was to enter, whereby he was to "confess his sins and transgressions in humble sorrow," and trust in the mercy and grace of a Merciful God to forgive his sin and grant him a change of heart so he would become a child of God, and love God with all his heart. This his mother told him was the way by which she had come into the Kingdom of God at the camp meeting, and in this spirit her life had been lived before him. It had accompanied him as a pillar of cloud by day and a fire by night; and had always produced a powerful effect upon him. He had read his Bible, gone to church, and refrained from swearing, from drinking, and from tobacco in all of its forms. Many a time, he said, he had found the courage to decline some tempting bribe, or resist some particularly insidious suggestion, because at that critical hour he heard his mother's voice repeating once more "I am the Lord thy God; thou shalt have no other gods before me." Yet, all this was not enough. He longed for complete acceptance with God so that he could know his sins all forgiven and that he was God's son.

He had sought God for this conversion experience night by night in the inquiry room during the revival meetings at the First Presbyterian Church at Springfield; in the parsonage of the First Methodist Church, also at Springfield, after Pastor Jacquess had preached on the text "Ye must be born again'" and, under the nurse's directions following Willie's passing. In appointing a National Fast Day, the President had stated plainly, *"It is the duty of nations as well as of men, to own their dependence upon the overruling power of God, to confess their sins and transgressions, in humble sorrow, yet with assured hope that genuine repentance will lead to mercy and pardon."* Yet seemingly, his faith had not been sufficient in attaining an entirely satisfactory conversion experience.

The time came, however, when he told friends how the peace of heaven stole in his heart. Said he:

"When I left Springfield, I asked the people to pray for me; I was not a Christian. When I buried my son — the severest trial of my life — I was not a Christian. But when I went to Gettysburg, and saw the graves of thousands of our soldiers, I then and there consecrated myself to Christ."

With tears in his eyes he told his friends that he had at last found the faith that he had longed for. He realized, he said, that his heart was changed, and that he loved the Saviour supremely. [2]

Thereafter, he talked of his inmost feelings to those who were spiritually minded. Carpenter reports the President's statement to the Christian Commission, "that it has been my intention for some time at a suitable opportunity to make a public religious profession." This matter he had also discussed with his pastor, Dr. Gurley, and with Noah Brooks. [3] To his friend, Joshua Speed, he wrote: "I am profitably engaged in reading the Bible. Take all this Book upon reason that you can and the balance by faith, and you will live and die a better man."

Lincoln's *philosophy* was summed up in the terse phrase: *RIGHT IS MIGHT.* It all grew out of his teaching, his reading, and his whole life—just as it had been lived. And, too, it was all tied up with his firm belief in God—not only as the Creator of the physical universe, but also as the Creator and *Governor of the moral universe.* He said:

> *God did not place good and evil before man, telling him to make his choice. On the contrary, He did tell them there was one tree of the fruit of which he should* not *eat, upon pain of certain death.* [4]

In accepting a case in law, he had asked, "Is this right? In this case am I to plead for the right?" On the underlying principles of truth and justice, observed Billy Herndon, "Lincoln's will was firm as steel and tenacious as iron . . . He scorned to support or adopt an untrue position . . . on moral and ethical principles he was immovable as a rock . . . " [4a]

In considering the question of slavery, he asked, "Is it right, or wrong?" Then answered:

> *It is the eternal struggle between these two principles— right and wrong—throughout the world. They are the two principles that have stood face to face from the beginning of time; and will ever continue to struggle. The one is the common right of humanity and the other the divine right of kings. It is the same principle in whatever shape it develops itself. That eternal world-wide struggle between right and wrong that runs through all human history.* [5]

In all the changing vicissitudes of life, and in the affairs of the government, he was ever deeply concerned about being on the side of right. *"Let us have faith that right makes might, and in that*

164

faith, let us, to the end, dare to do our duty as we understand it."

The unprejudiced have seen a strange heavenly unction firing his words, and at times lifting him out above the mundane sphere. Men in all walks of life have asked, "From whence came this transparency, this strange wisdom, this power to choose the correct words and deliver them in just the right emotional tempo?" The only known answer is God, and the Bible, whom he regarded as the ultimate in *right,* and who was with him in the most memorable utterances of men.

If we sum up the pageantry and beauty of his memorable oration on the battle-field of Gettysburg, we find that there vibrates through it "the deep organ notes of Biblical words and phrases" — "fourscore," "conceived," "brought forth," "new birth," "dedicated," "consecrated," "gave their lives that that nation might live," "hallow," "increased devotion," "last full measure," "resting place," "unfinished work," "long endure," "resolve," and "shall not perish from the earth." His second inaugural address contains fourteen references to God and four direct quotations from Genesis, Psalms and Matthew. What an ongoing sense of moral and spiritual responsibility he bequeathed to all men as he reached that grand climax.

Fondly do we hope, fervently do we pray, that this mighty scourge of war may speedily pass away. Yet, if God wills that it continue . . . it must be said that the judgments of the Lord are true and righteous altogether.

With malice toward none, with charity for all, with firmness in the right as God gives us to see the right, let us strive on to finish the work we are in. . . .

CHAPTER XV
The President's "Open Door" Policy

As President of the United States, Mr. Lincoln not only had a war to prosecute—a war of which he was Commander in Chief—but he also had the affairs of the nation to administer. Either would have been an enormous job; the two together constituted a commitment beyond mere mortal power.

His great humility caused him to own his dependence on God, to seek advice from the normal sources such as his Cabinet and Congress, and to maintain an "open door" policy regarding the public. That is, he had a calendar for special appointments, and certain hours during the week when anyone who cared to come might see him personally. These contacts he felt would keep him directly in touch with the people, and would give him information which would help him understand the needs of the country.

With unbounded confidence, committees, representatives of commissions, and individuals came to visit the President. Their errands, problems, questions, and requests, were as varied as human wants and needs, and the answers were accompanied by his unusual insight and common sense. Often a word fitly spoken had good results, yet the interviews took physical and nervous energy from the President. When those around him attempted to stop the people from coming, he replied, with a smile, "They don't want much; they get but little. I must see them."

Blondine Across The Niagara

An excited delegation from the west came with a complaint regarding the conduct of certain aspects of the war. The President heard them patiently, then said:

> *Gentlemen, suppose all the property you were worth was in gold and you had put it in the hands of Blondine, to carry across the Niagara River on a rope. Would you shake the cable or keep shouting at him, 'Blondine, stand up a little straighter—Blondine, stoop a little more—go a little faster—lean a little more to the north—lean a little more to the south?' No, you would hold your breath as well as your tongue, and keep your hands off until he was safe over. The Government is carrying an enormous weight. Untold treasures are in their hands; they are doing the very best they can. Don't badger them. Keep silence, and we will get you safe across.* 1

Shadrach, Meshach, and Abednego

One day, Senator Henderson of Missouri came to the President's office and advised him of certain radicals in Congress who always opposed measures which the President initiated. Lincoln intimated that he understood, then told a story of his Hoosier school days. Said he:

> *Our reading was done from the Scriptures, and we stood up in a long line and read in turn from the Bible. Our lesson one day was the story of the faithful Israelites who were thrown into the fiery furnace and delivered by the hand of the Lord without so much as the smell of fire upon their garments. It fell to one little fellow to read the verse in which occurred, for the first time, the names of Shadrach, Meshach, and Abednego.*
>
> *Little Bud stumbled on Shadrach, floundered on Meshach, and went all to pieces on Abednego. Instantly the hand of the master dealt him a cuff on the side of the head and left him,*

wailing and blubbering, as the next boy in line took up the reading. But before the girl at the end of the line had done reading, he had subsided into sniffles and finally became quiet. His blunder and disgrace were forgotten by the class until his turn was approaching to read again. Then, like a thunderclap out of a clear sky, he sat up a wail that alarmed the master, who with rather unusual gentleness inquired, 'What's the matter now?'

The little boy pointed with shaking finger to the verse which in a few moments he would be expected to read, and to the three proper names which it contained.

"Look, master," he cried, "there comes them same three fellers again!"

"As Lincoln finished the story, he stepped to the window overlooking Pennsylvania Avenue, and pointed his finger at three men who were then crossing the street to the White House—Charles Summer, Thaddeus Stevens and Henry Wilson." [2]

A Presumptuous Blockhead?

To Noah Brooks, who expressed empathy for the President's grave responsibilities, he replied:

"I should be the most presumptuous blockhead upon this footstool, if I for one day thought that I could discharge the duties which have come upon me since I came into this place, without the aid and enlightenment of One Who is stronger and wiser than all others." [3]

God Bless All The Churches

The various churches sent delegations to thank him, and assure him of their loyalty and support. To the Society of Friends (Quakers) on September 28, 1862, he said:

"I am glad to know I have your sympathy and prayers. In the very responsible position in which I happen to be placed, being a humble instrument in the hands of our Heavenly Father, as I am and as we all are to work out His great purposes, I have desired that all my works and acts may be according to His will and that it might be so, I have sought His aid." [4]

In a letter of reply to a deputation of ministers who presented to him resolutions adopted by the General Conference of the Methodist Episcopal Church, May 18, 1864, he said:

"God bless the Methodist church, bless all the Churches — and blessed be God who in this our great trial, giveth us the Churches."[5]

The More Churches The Better

One man came lamenting the divided condition of Protestantism and the number of churches. The President patiently heard his lament, then replied:

"My good brother, you are all wrong. The more sects we have, the better. They are all getting somebody in that the others could not; and even with the numerous divisions, we are all doing tolerably well....What we need is not fewer sects or parties, but more freedom and independence for those we have. The sects are all right . . . and should hammer away until they reach the best that is attainable. Think of what the sects drilling so many of us have passed through, mostly to our advantage as responsible beings.

Our people came from the good old Quaker stock, through Pennsylvania, Virginia, and Kentucky. Circumstances took us into the Baptist sect in Indiana, in which several of our people have remained. While there, a good Methodist elder rode forty miles through winter storm out of his way to preach my mother's funeral sermon at Spencer Creek. In Illinois, we were with the Presbyterians, where the Methodists were as thick as bees all about us."[6]

Bible Is God's Best Gift

The colored people of Baltimore, to show their appreciation of the "distinguished services of President Lincoln in the cause of human freedom," contributed $580.75 to have a copy of the Bible bound in purple velvet, mounted in gold, engraved with a representation of Lincoln striking the shackles from a slave, and enclosed in a walnut case lined with white silk.

When they presented this to the President at the White House in September, 1864, he said to them, in part:

"In regard to this Great Book, I have only to say that it is

*the best gift which God has given to man. All the good from
the Saviour of the world is communicated to us through this
Book. But for this Book we could not know right from
wrong."* [7]

What Constitutes A True Religious Experience?

A lady, who was a member of the "Christian Commission," in
discharging her duties—had several interviews with Mr. Lincoln.
The President, being much impressed with her devotion and earnestness, said to her:

*"Mrs. — I have formed a high opinion of your Christian
character, and now, as we are alone, I have a mind to ask you
to give me, in brief, your idea of what constitutes a true religious experience."* The lady replied that, in her judgment, it
consisted of a conviction of one's own sinfulness and weakness, and personal need of the Saviour for strength and support, that views of mere doctrine might and would differ, but
when one was really brought to feel his need of Divine help
and to seek the aid of the Holy Spirit for strength and guidance, it was satisfactory evidence of his having been born
again.

When she had concluded, President Lincoln was very
thoughtful for a few moments. He at length said, very earnestly, *"If what you have told me is really a correct view of this
great subject, I think I can say with sincerity, that I hope I
am a Christian. I had lived until my boy Willie died, without
realizing fully these things. That blow overwhelmed me. It
showed me my weakness as I had never felt it before, and if I
can take what you have stated as a test, I think I can safely
say that I know something of that change of which you
speak; and I will further add, that it has been my intention
for some time, at a suitable opportunity, to make a public
religious profession."* [8]

God Has Hewn You Out Of A Rock

Caroline Johnson, an active colored nurse in the hospitals of
Philadelphia, as an expression of reverence and affection for
President Lincoln, prepared a superb collection of wax fruits,
together with a stem-table, appropriately ornamented, which she

and her minister presented to the President. When asked to speak, she said, "Mr. President, I believe God has hewn you out of a rock, for this great and mighty purpose. Many have been led away by bribes of gold, of silver, of presents; but you have stood firm, because God was with you, and if you are faithful to the end, he will be with you." With tear-filled eyes, the President examined the present, pronounced it beautiful, and thanked Mrs. Johnson very kindly, then said: *"You must not give me the praise — it belongs to God."*[9]

But For Those Prayers I Should Have Failed

A clergyman from New York, during a call at the White House said: "I have not come to ask any favours of you, Mr. President; I have only come to say that the loyal people of the North are sustaining you and will continue to do so. We are giving you all that we have, the lives of our sons as well as our confidence and our prayers. You must know that no boy's father or mother ever kneels in prayer these days without asking God to give you strength and wisdom."

His eyes brimming with tears, Mr. Lincoln replied:

"But for those prayers, I should have faltered and perhaps failed long ago. Tell every father and mother you know to keep on praying, and I will keep on fighting, for I know God is on our side."

As the clergyman started to leave the room, Mr. Lincoln held him by the hands and said: "I suppose I may consider this as a sort of pastoral call?" "Yes," replied the clergyman. *"Out in our country,"* continued Lincoln, *"when a parson makes a pastoral call, it was always the custom for the folks to ask him to lead in prayer, and I should like to ask you to pray with me today. Pray that I may have the strength and wisdom."*

The two men knelt side by side, and the clergyman offered the most fervent plea to Almighty God that ever fell from his lips. As they arose, the President clasped his visitor's hand and remarked in a satisfied sort of way: "I feel better."[10]

You Are On The Right Track

A portly, well dressed gentleman, carrying a gold headed cane, was ushered into Lincoln's office one day. He gave the President the impression, "I'm in for it now." Yet, he visited only briefly, then, rising to go, he said, "Mr. President, I have no business with you, none whatever. I was at the Chicago convention as a friend of Mr. Seward. I have watched you narrowly ever since your inauguration, and I called merely to pay my respects. What I want to say is this: I think you are doing everything for the good of the country that is in the power of man to do. You are on the right track. As one of your constituents I now say to you, do in the future as you d--- please, and I will support you!" Lincoln almost collapsed with laughter. He took the visitor's hand: "I thought you came here to tell me how to take Richmond." They looked into each other's faces. "Sit down, my friend," said the President. "Sit down, I am delighted to see you. Lunch with us today. I have not seen enough of you yet."[11]

Tom Thumb

One evening President Lincoln gave a private reception to "General" Tom Thumb, the midget, and his tiny bride who were traveling under P. T. Barnum's management. Other guests, including government officials and their families, were present.

The "General" wore his wedding suit, and Mrs. Thumb appeared in white satin with a train, orange blossoms and pearls. The couple entered by the East room, and advanced toward the President looking up into his kindly face with profoundest respect. He, as their tall host, bent—and bent, to take their small hands in his great palm, "holding the Madam's hand with special care as though it were a robin's egg, and he afraid of breaking it." With grave courtesy he presented them to Mrs. Lincoln, and treated them as normal people. Tad was delighted with the tiny guests, and was most solicitous of their comfort. When they were leaving, Lincoln told the "General" that during the reception that evening he had been the center of attraction, rather than the President.

Fourteen Indian Chiefs

The Executive Mansion was the scene of a very interesting ceremony on March 27, 1863, when fourteen fine looking Indian Chiefs, from six tribes (Cheyennes, Kiowais, Arapahoes, Comanches, Apache, Caddo) came to Washington to meet with the President. The Indians were all seated on the floor in a circle in the East Room.

172

At half-past eleven President Lincoln entered the circle, and was introduced by Mr. Commissioner Dole. Each one of the chiefs came forward and shook him by the hand. Mr. Lincoln then told them he was very glad to see them, and if they had anything to say, it would afford him great pleasure to hear them. Speeches were made by Lean Bear of the Cheyennes and Spotted Wolf of the Arapahoe tribe, through an interpreter. The President then spoke:

> You have all spoken of the strange sights you see here, among your pale-faced brethren; the very great number of people that you see; the big wigwams; the difference between our people and your own. But you have seen but a very small part of the pale-faced people. You may wonder when I tell you that there are people here in this wigwam, now looking at you, who have come from other countries a great deal farther off than you have come.

> We pale-faced people think that this world is a great round ball, and we have people here of the pale-faced family who have come almost from the other side of it to represent us, as you now come from your part of the round ball.

Here a globe was introduced, and ... Professor Henry showed them the position of Washington and that of their own country, from which they had come.

The President then said:

> ... There is a great difference between this pale-faced people and their red brethren, both as to numbers and the way in which they live. We know not whether your own situation is best for your race, but this is what has made the difference in our way of living.

> The pale-faced people are numerous and prosperous because they cultivate the earth, produce bread, and depend upon the products of the earth rather than wild game for a subsistence.

> This is the chief reason of the difference; but there is another. Although we are now engaged in a great war between one another, we are not, as a race, so much disposed to fight and kill one another as our red brethren.

> You have asked for my advice. I really am not capable of advising you whether, in the providence of the Great Spirit,

173

who is the great Father of us all, it is best for you to maintain the habits and customs of your race, or adopt a new mode of life.

I can only say that I can see no way in which your race is to become as numerous and prosperous as the white race except by living as they do, by the cultivation of the earth.

It is the object of this Government to be on terms of peace with you, and with all our red brethren. We constantly endeavor to be so. We make treaties with you, and will try to observe them; and if our children should sometimes behave badly, and violate these treaties, it is against our wish.

You know it is not always possible for any father to have his children do precisely as he wishes them to do. . . .

The President's remarks were received with frequent marks of applause and approbation. "Ugh," "Aha" sounded along the line as the interpreter proceeded, and their countenances gave evident tokens of satisfaction. [12]

Many of the President's interviews had to do, in one way or another, with the men in the army. Of the 2,500,000 men who served in the army and navy, only 170,000 had to be drafted, and of these only 43,343 were actually conscripted, the remainder served as paid substitutes or as volunteers.

The majority of these men in uniform had come at Lincoln's call, and they bore a peculiar attachment to him. They often talked of him, spoke of his goodness of heart, of his deep concern for the Union, and of their sure confidence that he would champion their cause when justice was involved. Such confidence was well placed. This was shown in the fact that amid the many duties and weighty cares of office, he found time to listen to them, or to their mothers, fathers, wives, sweethearts, or friends who came to him in their behalf. And as a result of these simple interviews, during four war-torn years, he commuted many overly drastic sentences, saved literally hundreds of sincere soldiers from being executed, and righted the wrongs of vast numbers of others. Even captured Confederates received consideration or were pardoned when such seemed justified. Some army officers complained that the leniency of the President interfered with army discipline, but those capable of judging these matters were wholehearted in saying that President Lincoln "was well aware of what he was doing."

You Want To Be A Captain?

One day a boy in army uniform took the reception chair, and handed his papers to the President, who read them and said,

"And you want to be a captain?" "Yes, sir," "And what do you want to be captain of? Have you got a company?" "No, sir, but my officers told me that I could get a captain's commission if I were to present my case to you." "My Boy — excuse me calling you a boy — how old are you?" "Sixteen." "Yes, you are a boy, and from what your officers say of you, a worthy boy and a good soldier, but commissions as captains are generally given by the governors of the States." "My officers said you could give me a commission." "And so I could, but to be a captain you should have a company or something to be captain of. You know a man is not a husband until he gets a wife — neither is a woman a wife until she gets a husband. I might give you a commission as captain and send you back to the Army of the Potomac, where you would have nothing to be captain of, and you would be like a loose horse down there with nothing to do and no one having any use for you."

The boy began breaking, tears in his eyes. The President, put a hand on the boy's shoulder, patting while he spoke:

"My son, go back to the army, continue to do your duty as you find it to do, and with the zeal you have hitherto shown, you will not have to ask for promotion, it will seek you. I may say that had we more like you in the army, my hopes of the successful outcome of this war would be far stronger than they are at present. Shake hands with me and go back the little man and brave soldier that you came."

The boy stepped away as if he had been home to see a wise and kindly father. [13]

I Thought It Was To Be A Pardon

A weeping old father told the President his son who was serving with Butler's army had been convicted of a crime and sentenced by court martial to be shot. The President read him a telegram from General Butler protesting executive interference with cases of army court-martial. The dazed old father shook with desperate grief. While Lincoln made further examination of the papers, he observed the old man's grief. Then, after a time, he said, *"By jings,*

Butler or no Butler, here goes," and he wrote an order that the son was *"not to be shot until further orders from me."*

When it was shown to the old gentleman, he continued to weep, saying, "I thought it was to be a pardon. But you say 'not to be shot till further orders,' and you may order him shot next week." Lincoln smiled. *"Well, my old friend, I see you are not very well acquainted with me. If your son never looks on death till further orders come from me to shoot him, he will live to be a great deal older than Methuselah."*

"Scott's Life Is Valuable."

Perhaps the best known case ever brought to the President was that of William Scott, the soldier from Vermont, who slept at his post when on sentry duty. He had taken the place of a sick comrade one night, and the very next night was detailed for picket duty himself. He said frankly he was afraid he couldn't keep awake two nights in succession, but if it was his duty he would do his best. The next morning his relief found him sound asleep on his post. For this offence he had been tried by a court-martial, found guilty, and sentenced to be shot in twenty-four hours. Scott's comrades, including his captain, had set about saving him. They were told that there was only one man on earth who could save their comrade's life, and that was President Lincoln.

The group went to the White House, and in dramatic earnestness the captain presented a graphic account of Scott's case to the President, ending by saying, "He is as brave a boy as there is in your whole army, sir. Scott is no coward. Our mountains breed no cowards. They will not be able to see that the best thing to be done with William Scott will be to shoot him like a traitor and bury him like a dog! Oh, Mr. Lincoln, can you?"

"No, I can't!" exclaimed the President, "I do not think an honest, brave soldier, conscious of no crime, but sleeping when he was weary, ought to be shot or hung. The country has better use for them. . . .I will have to attend to this matter myself. I have for some time intended to go up to the Chain Bridge. I will do so to-day."

When the officer apologized for imposing on the President in behalf of a private soldier, Mr. Lincoln said: "Scott's life is as valuable to him as that of any person in the land. You remember the remark of a Scotchman about the head of a nobleman who

176

was decapitated. 'It was a small matter of a head, but it was valuable to him, poor fellow, for it was the only one he had.' "

During the day Lincoln went out to the camp, and called for the condemned soldier. Scott afterwards told the story of his interview with the President. Said he:

"*The President was the kindest man I had ever seen; I knew him at once, by a Lincoln medal I had long worn. I was scared at first, for I had never before talked with a great man. But Mr. Lincoln was so easy with me, so gentle, that I soon forgot my fright. He asked me all about the people at home, the neighbors, the farm, and where I went to school, and who my schoolmates were. Then he asked me about mother, and how she looked, and I was glad I could take her photograph from my bosom and show it to him. He said how thankful I ought to be that my mother still lived, and how, if he was in my place, he would try to make her a proud mother, and never cause her a sorrow or a tear. I cannot remember it all, but every word was so kind.*

"*He had said nothing yet about that dreadful next morning. I thought it must be that he was so kind-hearted that he didn't like to speak of it. But why did he say so much about my mother, and my not causing her a sorrow or a tear when I knew that I must die the next morning? But I supposed that was something that would have to go unexplained, and so I determined to brace up, and tell him that I did not feel a bit guilty, and ask him wouldn't he fix it so that the firing-party would not be from our regiment! That was going to be the hardest of all—to die by the hands of my comrades. Just as I was going to ask him this favor, he stood up, and he says to me, 'My boy, stand up here and look me in the face.' I did as he bade me. 'My boy,' he said, 'you are not going to be shot tomorrow. I believe you when you tell me that you could not keep awake. I am going to trust you, and send you back to your regiment. But I have been put to a good deal of trouble on your account. I have had to come up here from Washington when I have got a great deal to do; and what I want to know is, how you are going to pay my bill?' There was a big lump in my throat; I could scarcely speak. I had expected to die, you see, and had kind of got used to thinking that way. To have it all changed in a minute! But I got it crowded down, and managed to say, I am grateful, Mr. Lincoln! I hope I am as grateful as ever a man can be to you for saving my life. But it comes upon me sudden and unexpected like. I didn't lay out for it at all. There is the bounty in the savings-bank. I guess we could borrow some money on the mortgage of the farm. There was my pay which was something, and if he would wait until pay-day I was sure the boys would help, so I*

*thought we could make it up, if it wasn't more than five or six hund-
red dollars. 'But it is a great deal more than that,' he said, Then I
said I didn't just see how, but I was sure I would find some way—if
I lived.*

*"Then Mr. Lincoln put his hands on my shoulders and looked into
my face as if he was sorry, and said, 'My boy, my bill is a very large
one. Your friends cannot pay it, nor your bounty, nor the farm, nor
all your comrades! There is only one man in all the world who can
pay it, and his name is William Scott! If from this day William Scott
does his duty, so that, if I was there when he comes to die, he can
look me in the face as he does now, and say, "I have kept my promise, and I have done my duty as a soldier," then my debt will be
paid. Will you make that promise and try to keep it?'*

*"I said I would make the promise, and, with God's help, I would
keep it. I could not say any more. I wanted to tell him how hard I
would try to do all he wanted; but the words would not come, so I
had to let it all go unsaid. He went away, out of my sight forever. I
know I shall never see him again; but may God forget me if I ever
forget his kind words or my promise."* [14]

William Scott was released for duty with his regiment, and in
two engagements performed the most exposed service with singular bravery. Seven months later, with his company, he charged at
Lee's Mill. Near the last of the battle he was carrying his wounded
comrades across the river, when six enemy bullets entered his
body, and he was carried out of the line of fire, and laid on the
grass to die. Later he was placed on a cot in a tent. Just at daylight, the next morning, the word was passed that Scott wanted to
see his comrades.

When they gathered about his cot, he said, "Boys, I shall never
see another battle. . . .I have tried to do the right thing! You can
tell them at home about me." Then while his strength was failing,
his life ebbing away, and they looked to see his voice sink into a
whisper, his face lighted up and his voice came out natural and
clear as he said: "If any of you ever have a chance, I wish you
would tell President Lincoln that I have never forgotten the kind
words he said to me at the Chain Bridge—that I have tried to be a
good soldier and true to the flag. . . .I think of his kind face and
thank him again, because he gave me the chance to fall like a
soldier in battle, and not like a coward by the hands of my comrades. . . .Good bye boys," he said cheerily, then closed his eyes,
crossed his hands on his breast, and was gone. The boys wept like
children. Only one spoke, as if to himself, "Thank God, I know
now how a brave man dies."

CHAPTER XVI
Lincoln Saves
The Union

Abraham Lincoln's mission was made plain by the time he was elected President. The South wanted slavery. It felt that it could not exist without it, and was determined to stick to it under all circumstances. Its attitude was one of belligerent defensiveness. In the North there was a group known as Abolitionists who hated slavery and were dedicated to its destruction. Others in the North did not believe in slavery, but were willing for the South to have its way. For years leading statesmen, newspaper editors, ministers, and writers heatedly discussed the subject, but when no way to satisfy both North and South was found, the South grew tired of being condemned, and threatened to leave the Union unless it was left alone. Being aware of all this, and more, Lincoln said, "A house divided against itself cannot stand."

On leaving Springfield he suggested that a "task" lay before him "greater than that which rested upon Washington." Both he, and the people knew, of course, that Washington had *made* the country. Lincoln knew that his job was to *save* the country. For two years he had worked faithfully, heroically, and had learned much and accomplished many things.

Now that Gettysburg and Vicksburg were past, he thanked the army and navy and the people for assignments "well done," then went on to say, "Peace does not appear so distant as it did. I hope it will come soon." Yet, it had become clearer than ever that the issue dividing the nation would be settled, in the main, by decisive victories on the battlefield.

To win victories, Lincoln needed generals. He had liked the ultimatum given by Ulysses S. Grant, at Ft. Donelson. "No terms except unconditional and immediate surrender. I propose to move immediately upon your works." As a result of this, and other victories, Lincoln had given him command of the Army of the West. Yet, serious complaints had been lodged against him—he was a heavy drinker, and had been known to go on drunken sprees. The President had investigated, and found it all true. Grant thought of quitting the Army. Lincoln recognized his fighting qualities, and said "I can't spare this man . . . he fights." Grant thought highly of Lincoln's compliment, loved his family, and his country. He reformed. After Vicksburg, Lincoln wrote Grant to thank him for "the almost inestimable service" he had done the country.

Now came the storming of Missionary Ridge—"one of the greatest miracles in military history." Grant's men had overrun the first line of entrenchments at the base of the cliff, then forced the Confederates up the mountainside, captured the batteries on the crest and turned them on the enemy, which had fled in panic. East Tennessee was now fairly secure for the Union.

The President induced Congress to revive the rank of lieutenant general, a rank previously held by George Washington in Revolutionary days. He then sent for Grant, and at one o'clock in the afternoon of March 9, in the presence of the Cabinet, General Halleck, and Grant's staff, the President presented him with the commission constituting him Lieutenant General and Commander-in-Chief of all the armies of the United States.

"As the country herein trusts you, so, under God, it will sustain you," Lincoln said. "With what I speak here for the nation goes my own hearty concurrence."

Grant responded: "Mr. President: I accept this commission with gratitude for the high honor conferred. With the aid of the noble armies that have fought in so many fields for our country, it will be my earnest endeavor not to disappoint your expectations. I feel the full weight of the responsibilities now devolving on me and know that if they are met it will be due to those armies, and above all to the favor of that Providence which leads nations and men."

After pouring over maps and considering strategies together, it was decided that the western army under Sherman should clear out any remaining enemy regiments in Tennessee, enter Georgia to capture Atlanta, then march through Georgia to capture and occupy the seaport of Savannah. Grant was to lead the Army of the Potomac with a hundred thousand men. General Philip H. Sheridan was to command his cavalry, and they were to conquer Lee, seize the Confederate capitol of Richmond, and conclude the war.

Two months later Grant had reorganized the Army of the Potomac and started marching southward toward Richmond. To the President's good wishes, Grant replied: "Should my success be less than I desire, and expect, the least I can say is, the fault is not with you."

The two armies met north of Richmond in a dense, marshy, tangled forest known as "the Wilderness." General Lee had only 60,000 men, but he was a military genius. He had placed his troops behind strong breastworks, and he knew the terrain. Grant had twice as many men, but he was not acquainted with the country, and his artillery was difficult to operate in the marshy forest. The toll of death was tremendous on both sides, the jungle woods caught on fire and hundreds of the wounded were consumed by the flames. The Union lost some 14,000 men, killed, wounded or missing in the first 48 hours of fighting. The Confederates lost more than they could spare.

Normally armies should rest after prolonged and desperate fighting, but Grant gave the order "Advance! Advance!" He, therefore, moved his forces on to the left and fought the Confederates at Spotsylvania Court House, and at Cold Harbor, then crossed the James River and attacked the Petersburg defenses which at the time was defended by only 2,000 men under Beauregard. The Confederates held him off, however, until Lee arrived with reinforcements. On his failure to make a breakthrough, Grant dug in on the ramparts east of Petersburg, and settled down for a siege which was to last for nine months. His spring campaign had lost near 55,000 men, which in the eyes of many was not worth the appalling cost. Grant and Lincoln understood, however, that the strategy of eroding Lee's irreplaceable army was the objective. Lincoln wired him: "Hold on with a bulldog grip, and chew and choke as much as possible."

Carpenter, who was then staying at the White House, says that during the darkest of these days and nights, Lincoln scarcely slept at all, but in the late hours of the night, walked the floor, praying and crying, "My God! My God!" On June 15, however, he wired Grant, "I begin to see it. You will succeed. God bless you all." Grant wired back: "I purpose to fight it out on this line if it takes all summer."

The end of President Lincoln's first term was now only months away. Therefore politics claimed a large share of public interest in the spring and summer of 1864. The course of the administration had been most difficult at times. The Emancipation Proclamation had been issued, there had been military reverses, and other irregularities of which designing politicians were making the most. The nation, they said, would be obliged to have a new leader for the next four years. Certain newspapers engaged in bitter belittlement of the administration. Nevertheless the governor of Illinois made a speech in which he said, "Let the politicians say what they will, yet when election time comes the people will reelect 'Old Abe' as their President."

When the National Union Convention met at Baltimore on June 7, the clerk read a resolution demanding the renomination of Abraham Lincoln, of Illinois, and Hannibal Hamlin of Maine. No sooner had the clerk finished reading the resolution than pandemonium reigned—every delegate was on his feet demanding to be heard. When quiet had been restored Henry J. Raymond, Chairman of the Republican Committee, moved that nominations be made by a call of states. Before the applause which followed the adoption of Raymond's resolution had entirely subsided, B. C. Cook, of Illinois, mounted a settee and shouted: "Illinois once more presents to the nation the name of Abraham Lincoln—God bless him!"

When the clerk of the convention announced the results of the roll call, it was found that Abraham Lincoln had 507 votes and U. S. Grant 22 votes. Then the chairman of the Missouri delegation, who had cast the 22 votes, immediately moved that the nomination be declared unanimous. The motion passed and immediately enthusiasm burst forth in a scene of wildest confusion. Men hurrahed, threw up their hats, embraced each other, danced in the aisles, waved flags, and the big brass band played "Hail Columbia."

When the news of the renomination was officially carried to Lincoln, he said: *"I am reminded of a story of an old Dutch farmer, who remarked to a companion once that 'it was not best to swap horses when crossing streams.'"* This homely figure of swapping horses in the middle of the stream appealed to the people's humor and common sense. It was taken up as a slogan and repeated in all the newspapers of the country, and was of inestimable value in helping the people to see the wisdom of keeping Lincoln as their President during the great crisis then facing the country.

The Convention which renominated Lincoln was not, strictly speaking, a Republican Convention. In an effort to attract War Democrats, the party had taken the name of Union Party and thought it advisable to select Andrew Johnson, a Democrat and former Senator from Tennessee, to be Lincoln's running mate.

A splinter party of dissatisfied Republicans met in Cleveland and nominated John C. Fremont for president. Lincoln seemed amused. When a friend told him that, instead of the thousands who had been expected at the Convention, only about four hundred persons had been present, he was struck by the number. Reaching for the Bible that lay handy on his desk, he turned to I Samuel 22:2 and read: *"And every one that was in distress, and everyone that was in debt, and every one that was discontented, gathered themselves unto him, and he became a captain over them: and there were with him about four hundred men."* [1] Sensing its weakness this party later withdrew from the race.

The Democrats met in a new Wigwam in Chicago, like the one where Lincoln had been so spectacularly elected in 1860. After declaring, "the administration cannot save the Union. . . .We think the blood of our people more precious than edicts of the President," they nominated General George B. McClellan as their candidate for the presidency.

At a mass meeting in Philadelphia soon after his renomination, the President said, "If I shall discover that General Grant . . . can be greatly facilitated in his work by a sudden pouring forward of men and assistance, will you give them to me? (Cries of "Yes") Then stand ready."

183

The President not only sent fresh supplies, but on June 20, rode a steamer down to Grant's headquarters at City Point for a conference with Grant, Sherman, and Sheridan. While he was there, the soldiers passed the word along that "Uncle Abe" had joined them. Cheers and shouts broke forth, and familiar greetings met him on all sides. At the 18th corps camp, Lincoln met throngs of black soldiers who circled roundabout him. Tears ran down their faces as they cheered, laughed, and sang. They waved their hands and shouted: "God bless Massa Linkum!" "De Laud save Fader Abraham!" The President rode with bowed head; tears in his eyes, and his voice broken with emotion. 2

During that same summer, there were two victories which gave further encouragement to the Union cause. On a Sunday morning in June, two ships met outside the international line near Cherbourg, France, and fought to a finish. The pirate ship *Alabama,* while flying the Confederate flag, had mercilessly captured 62 merchantmen and robbed or burned most of them at sea. The *Kearsarge,* an ironplated Union vessel, had long trailed the *Alabama* and at last penned her in Cherbourg Harbor. The 370 shells fired by the *Alabama* only tore away the smokestack of the other, while 173 projectiles fired from the *Kearsarge* tore open the sides and sank the *Alabama,* killing forty men. The losses on the *Kearsarge* were one man killed and two wounded.

On August 5, Admiral Farragut achieved a brilliant victory when he led his fleet into Mobile Bay (Alabama) with a prayer on his lips, "O God, who created man and gave him reason, direct me what I shall do. Shall I go on?" He did go on "full speed ahead" and not only captured the *Tennessee,* one of the most powerful vessels afloat, but his auxiliary forces reduced the three Confederate forts guarding Mobile Bay. This was indeed a significant victory since only the port at Wilmington, North Carolina remained to the Confederates. And on January 15, after three days of bombardment by a formidable Union armada of sixty war vessels, Wilmington, along with Fort Fisher, fell. The Confederate States were now virtually landlocked. Only a very few ships ever got through by running the blockade at night.

Nevertheless, July and August of '64 were difficult months for the President and the Union. Grant was settled in siege before Petersburg, and Sherman hesitated before Atlanta. In July General Lee sent a Confederate force under General Jubal Early

184

up the Shenandoah Valley to make a diversionary attack on Washington. Early crossed the Potomac and was on his way through Maryland toward Washington, when Major General Lew Wallace (the author of *Ben Hur*) hastily gathered an army of sorts — raw recruits, clerks, and semi-invalids — and went out to halt the Confederates. But after a day's fighting Early easily pushed Wallace out of the way, and two days later was within sight of the Capitol Dome itself.

In the meanwhile, Lincoln had sent an urgent plea to Grant for help. The General replied by sending a corps of his best troops by steamboat. When they arrived, Early saw that he was now outnumbered and calling off the attack, marched southward by way of the Shenandoah Valley.

Major General Philip H. Sheridan, with a new army of 30,000 men, received orders from Grant to dispose of General Jubal Early's forces and devastate the Shenandoah's fertile farmland, the Confederate's bountiful "bread basket." On September 19, Sheridan's cavalry forces defeated Early's army at Winchester. Two days after he whipped him the second time at Fisher's Hill, then proceeded to lay waste the Valley. Lincoln wired him: "Have just heard of your great victory. God bless you all, officers and men. Strongly inclined to come up to see you."

Three weeks later, with an army augmented by fresh troops, Early returned and attacked the Union forces in the Commander's absence. They were retreating in terror when Sheridan rushed to the battlefield, rallied his men and defeated Early so thoroughly that he retired from the Valley. Lincoln wired Sheridan a word of appreciation.

Lincoln saw clearly that the army must be re-enforced by a fresh ingathering of men. A draft of some kind seemed necessary, yet his counselors advised that a new draft would give a new weapon to the Radicals and the Democrats, and make his re-election uncertain. Lincoln said: "We must lose nothing even if I am defeated . . . I am quite willing the people should understand the issue. My re-election will mean that the rebellion is to be crushed by force of arms." Therefore, on July 18, he called for 500,000 volunteers for one, two, and three years.

All the discontent that had been prophesied broke forth with this call. All kinds of complaints, old and new, were urged against Lincoln by radical Republicans, Democrats, and dissidents of every sort. Much of the news media boldly displayed the horrors of war, gave loud voice to those who abused the President as a military dictator, and spoke of the call for more soldiers as the arbitrary call of a tyrant. They criticized his treatment of supposed peace overtures, and demanded that he withdraw from the presidential race, and that General Grant, or some other leader's name be presented for the coming election. The clamor was so loud and insistent that for a time Lincoln himself was made to wonder if he could be elected.

Then Lincoln made this significant statement:

"I desire to so conduct the affairs of this administration that if, at the end, when I come to lay down the reins of power, I have lost every other friend on earth, I shall at least have one friend left, and that friend shall be deep down inside me. . . .I am not bound to win, but I am bound to be true. I am not bound to succeed, but I am bound to live up to the light I have."

Colonel Eaton was sent to ask Grant if he could be induced to run against Lincoln, "not as a partisan, but as a citizen's candidate, to save the Union." Grant brought his hand down emphatically on the strap arm of his camp-chair, and said: "They can't do it! They can't compel me to do it!" "Have you said this to the President?" asked Colonel Eaton. "No," said Grant, "I have not thought it worth while to assure the President of my opinion. I consider it as important for the cause that he should be elected as that the army should be successful in the field."

During the months of September and October, conditions improved in favor of the Union. On September 3, Sherman wired Lincoln, "Atlanta is ours and fairly won." The news was spread that these "strategic crossroads, the supply depot and transportation center of a pivotal cotton state in the Deep South had been taken. The "dull ache of defeat and failure" in many hearts changed to one of faith. Bells rang, guns boomed, and the President requested Thanksgiving to be offered in all places of worship the following Sunday.

The overwhelming majority of the common people shared Grant's conviction that Lincoln should be re-elected. They had confidence that "Old Abe" was leading them in the right direction. Loyal party members, along with Chase, Seward, and others of position and influence, went on lecture tours, and laid the record straight before the public. Thus when election day came, on November 8, most of the country knew for whom they were voting. Out of 233 electoral votes, President Lincoln received 212, and General McClellan 21.

Ralph Waldo Emerson supposed that "never in history was so much staked on a popular vote." The common people had given Lincoln a second term—a mandate to "finish his Union-saving task." They felt him to be ordained of God, and frequently likened him to Abraham of Biblical fame. The night following his re-election, a clergyman of Middletown, Connecticut, at a torch-light display, exhibited a transparency over his door, with a quotation from Genesis 22:15, "The angel of the Lord called unto Abraham out of heaven the second time."

With his prestige and power of patronage stabilized the President wore his mantle of authority even more becomingly. In response to a crowd who serenaded him the night of the election returns, he said:

> *I am thankful to God, for this approval of the people; but while grateful for this mark of their confidence in me, if I know my heart, my gratitude is free from any taint of personal triumph. I do not impugn the motives of any one opposed to me. It is no pleasure to me to triumph over any one, but I give thanks to the Almighty for this evidence of the people's resolution to stand by free government and the rights of humanity.*

Later in November, in response to a letter from Governor Andrew of Massachusetts, he wrote a letter to Mrs. Bixby of Boston, who had five sons in the army, all of whom had been killed in battle. The letter was sent through the War Department to Adjutant General Schouler of Massachusetts. On Thanksgiving day the General took a holiday dinner, some money, and President Lincoln's letter and delivered them to Mrs. Bixby at her home at 15 Dover Street. On opening the letter she read:

> *Dear Madam—I have been shown in the files of the War Department a statement of the Adjutant General of Massachusetts, that you are the mother of five sons who have died gloriously on the field of battle.*
>
> *I feel how weak and fruitless must be any words of mine which should attempt to beguile you from the grief of a loss so overwhelming. But I can not refrain from tendering to you*

the consolation that may be found in the thanks of the Republic they died to save.

I pray that our Heavenly Father may assuage the anguish of your bereavement, and leave you only the cherished memory of the loved and lost, and the solemn pride that must be yours, to have laid so costly a sacrifice upon the altar of Freedom.

Yours, very sincerely and respectfully, A. Lincoln. [3]

The letter had woven in it the "awful implication that human freedom so often was paid for with agony." It was not only read, and reread by Mrs. Bixby, but publicized in the papers, and a copy hung up in the halls of Oxford University. There was in it "the love of its words" and a harmony that arose over the country in so many homes where parents had "mournfully but willingly sent their boys to take a chance with death on the field of battle."[4] It drew the President and the people more closely together, for Mr. and Mrs. Lincoln, too, had lost a son during those years of trouble.

On November 15, Sherman divested Atlanta and on the 16th set out with sixty thousand men on his famous "March through Georgia." Striking a path sixty miles wide and two hundred fifty miles long, the army gathered their provisions from the country-side as they went—corn, meat, poultry, sweet potatoes, etc.—and arrived at Savannah the week before Christmas. After taking the city, Sherman sent Lincoln a message which was received on December 25: "I beg to present you as a Christmas gift the city of Savannah, with 150 heavy guns and plenty of ammunition; also about 25,000 bales of cotton." Lincoln answered:

My Dear General Sherman: Many, many thanks for your Christmas gift, the capture of Savannah. When you were about leaving Atlanta for the Atlantic coast I was anxious, if not fearful; but feeling that you were the better judge, and remembering that 'nothing risked, nothing gained,' I did not interfere.

Now, the undertaking being a success, the honor is all yours, for I believe none of us went farther than to acquiesce . . . —it brings to those who sat in darkness to see a great light. But what next? I suppose it will be safe if I leave General Grant and yourself to decide. Please make my grateful acknowledgements to your whole army, officers and men. [5]

188

In his Annual Message to Congress on December 6, 1864, Lincoln had recommended favorable action on the proposed Thirteenth Amendment to the Federal Constitution which would forever abolish slavery when ratified by the people. In January, when it seemed the Amendment needed more support, the President used the weight of his personal influence with various Congressmen, and when the Amendment finally passed by an uncomfortably close margin of only three more House votes than the necessary two-thirds majority, William Lloyd Garrison said: "And to whom is the country indebted more immediately for this vital and saving amendment to the Constitution than, perhaps, to any other man? I believe I may confidently answer — to the humble railsplitter of Illinois, to the Presidential chain-breaker for millions of the oppressed — to Abraham Lincoln."[6]

At various times pressure had been brought to bear on President Lincoln to make peace with the Confederate States. Some even going so far as to insist on "Peace at any cost." Lincoln always kept the door open for negotiations, yet at the same time held tenaciously to his one main objective — to save the Union, unimpaired. Very pointedly he stated, *"There is no line, straight or crooked, suitable for a national boundary upon which to divide the Northern and Southern States."*[7]

However, with the North quite sick of war, and the South foreseeing defeat even more clearly, men's thoughts turned increasingly toward the possibility of peace. With Lincoln's consent, Horace Greeley went to Canada for the purpose of meeting supposed Confederate emissaries, only to learn that the reputed diplomats had no authority. Soon afterwards, Lincoln's two friends — James F. Jaquess and J. R. Gilmore — felt sure that they could obtain peace overtures by dealing personally with Jefferson Davis. Armed with Lincoln's blessings, they went to Richmond for a conference with the Confederate President, but found him "still insistent upon full Southern independence."

With Union victories at Franklin and Nashville, Tennessee, and Sherman's devastating "March through Georgia," there seemed more reason for peace by negotiations. Therefore Francis P. Blair sought Lincoln's permission to visit Davis in Richmond. On December 28, Lincoln handed him a pass: "Allow the bearer, F. P. Blair, Senr. to pass our lines, go South and return." After a lengthy conversation, Jefferson Davis signed a letter saying if

President Lincoln would receive peace commissioners, Davis would appoint such to negotiate with a view to bringing peace to "the two countries."

Lincoln caught the significance of the last phrase, but wishing to overlook no chance for peace, he permitted Blair return to Richmond with a letter from Lincoln saying, *"I have constantly been, am now, and shall continue, ready to receive any agent whom he, or any other influential person now resisting the national authority, may informally send me with the view of securing peace to the people of our one common country."* [8]

Jefferson Davis appointed three peace commissioners: Alexander H. Stephens of Georgia, Vice President of the Confederacy, for whom Lincoln had possessed a genuine fondness and admiration since their days in Congress; Judge John A. Campbell of Alabama; and R. M. T. Hunter of Virginia. On February 3, 1865, President Lincoln and Secretary Seward sat down with the three in the cabin of the *River Queen* in Hampton Roads. Greetings were cordial between those who had met before, then they launched into the conference; beginning with Stephens query, "Mr. President, is there no way of putting an end to the present trouble existing between the different states and sections of the country?" Lincoln replied to the Confederate Vice President that he knew of only one way and that was for those who were resisting the laws of the Union to cease that resistance.

For four hours there was "a swift interplay of acute minds across the council table." The talk ranged around States Rights, slavery, and possible terms of settlement. All the while Lincoln held to the one thought of a preserved Union—any other discussion was ruled out on the basis that there could be no bargaining with an enemy at arms against his government. When Hunter suggested that Charles I of England had bargained with people in arms against his government, Lincoln replied that he was not posted on history; all that he distinctly remembered about the matter was that Charles had lost his head. After a few moments of silence, Hunter said: "Mr. President, if we understand you correctly, you look upon the leaders of the Confederacy as traitors to your government; that we have forfeited our rights, and are proper subjects for the hangman. Is not that about what your words imply?" Lincoln replied, "Yes, that is about the size of it." Then Hunter smiled, "Well, Mr. Lincoln, we have about concluded that we shall not be hanged as long as you are President—if we behave ourselves."[9]

At one point Stephens in effect asked, "Why not stop fighting among ourselves and take on a war together against Mexico?" Lincoln answered that we would consider taking on another war only after the question of the Union was settled, and the Southern people were again under the Constitution "with all their rights secured thereby."

Lincoln suggested that he favored compensation to the owners of emancipated slaves. He believed that the people of the North and South were responsible for slavery, and if hostilities should cease and the states would voluntarily abolish slavery, he thought the government should indemnify the owners—to the extent, possibly, of $400,000,000. [10]

When it became apparent that nothing more might be said, there came the friendly handshakings of saying good-by, and the ending of the Hampton Roads conference. Then President Lincoln said to the Vice-President of the Confederacy, "Well, Stephens, there has been nothing we could do for our country. Is there anything I can do for you personally?" "Nothing," said Stephens. Then his face brightened, "Unless you can send me my nephew who has been for twenty months a prisoner on Johnson's Island." Lincoln's face brightened. "I shall be glad to do it. Let me have his name." And he wrote it down in his notebook. Later the release was affected, and the young man returned to the Confederate Vice-President who was then virtually retired on his farm in Georgia.

With the coming of spring in 1865, the capital city of Washington had been grooming itself for one of its grandest Inaugural pageants. On the morning of March 4, the official parade moved along Pennsylvania Avenue from the White House to the Capitol. This time a battalion of Negro troops dressed in Union Army blue formed a part of the President's escort.

Once more the inaugural platform was erected on the Capitol's East wing, and the great crowds assembled on the lawn and in the street while the weather fell in feather-like drizzles. The usual procedures of swearing the Vice President and the newly elected Senators took place in the Senate Chamber, then the dignitaries formed a line and filed onto the inaugural platform.

The waiting crowds filled the air with thunderous applause, the drizzle of rain ceased, and suddenly the sunshine flooded the scene as Abraham Lincoln, the mightiest living advocate of freedom, stepped forward and stood before the people. In silence almost profound, the audience listened as the President read or spoke his carefully and deliberately prepared address:

(Fellow Countrymen:) At this second appearing to take the oath of the presidential office, there is less occasion for an extended address than there was at the first. Then a statement, somewhat in detail, of a course to be pursued, seemed fitting and proper. Now, at the expiration of four years, during which public declarations have been constantly called forth on every point and phase of the great contest which still absorbs the attention, and engrosses the energies of the nation, little that is new could be presented. The progress of our arms, upon which all else chiefly depends, is as well known to the public as to myself; and it is, I trust, reasonably satisfactory and encouraging to all. With high hope for the future, no prediction in regard to it is ventured.

On the occasion corresponding to this four years ago, all thoughts were anxiously directed to an impending civil-war. All dreaded it — all sought to avert it. While the inaugural address was being delivered from this place, devoted altogether to saving the Union without war, insurgent agents were in the city seeking to destroy it without war — seeking to dissolve the Union, and divide effects, by negotiations. Both parties deprecated war; but one of them would make war rather than let the nation survive; and the other would accept war rather than let it perish. And the war came.

One eighth of the whole population were colored slaves, not distributed generally over the Union, but localized in the Southern part of it. These slaves constituted a peculiar and powerful interest. All knew that this interest was, somehow, the cause of the war. To strengthen, perpetuate, and extend this interest was the object for which the insurgents would rend the Union, even by war; while the government claimed no right to do more than to restrict the territorial enlargement of it. Neither party expected for the war, the magnitude, or the duration, which it has already attained. Neither anticipated that the cause of the conflict might cease with, or even before, the conflict itself should cease. Each looked for an

192

*easier triumph, and a result less fundamental and astounding.
Both read the same Bible, and pray to the same God; and
each invokes His aid against the other. It may seem strange
that any men should dare to ask a just God's assistance in
wringing their bread from the sweat of other men's faces; but
let us judge not that we be not judged. The prayers of both
could not be answered; that of neither has been answered
fully. The Almighty has His own purposes. 'Woe unto the
world because of offences! For it must needs be that offences
come; but woe to that man by whom the offence cometh!' If
we shall suppose that American Slavery is one of those offences which, in the providence of God, must needs come, but
which, having continued through His appointed time, He now
wills to remove, and that He gives to both North and South,
this terrible war, as the woe due to those by whom the offence
came, shall we discern therein any departure from those divine attributes which the believers in a Living God always
ascribe to Him? Fondly do we hope—fervently do we pray—
that this mighty scourge of war may speedily pass away. Yet,
if God wills that it continue, until all the wealth piled by the
bond-man's two hundred and fifty years of unrequited toil
shall be sunk, and until every drop of blood drawn with the
lash shall be paid by another drawn with the sword, as was
said three thousand years ago, so still it must be said 'the
judgments of the Lord, are true and righteous altogether.'*

*With malice toward none; with charity for all; with firm-
ness in the right, as God gives us to see the right, let us strive
on to finish the work we are in; to bind up the nation's
wounds; to care for him who shall have borne the battle, and
for his widow, and his orphan—to do all which may achieve
and cherish a just, and a lasting peace, among ourselves, and
with all nations.* [11]

Reporters observed that at the reading of the final paragraph
there were "many moist eyes and here and there tears coursing
down faces unashamed." [12]

The Clerk of the Supreme Court brought the Bible. Lincoln
laid his right hand on the Book, and repeated the oath of office
after Chief Justice Chase, then bent forward and kissed the pencil-
marked verses of Isaiah 5:27, 28:

None shall be weary nor stumble among them; none shall slumber

193

nor sleep; neither shall the girdle of their loins be loosed, nor the latchet of their shoes be broken:
Whose arrows are sharp, and all their bows bent, their horses hoofs shall be counted like flint, their wheels like a whirlwind.

This Second Inaugural was immediately pronounced "a mighty and inspiring message, so free from tawdry partisanship and lack of vindictiveness." After reading and reflecting competent men described it in their choicest phrases.

Said the editor of the *Spectator* of London: "No statesman ever uttered words stamped at once with the seal of so deep a wisdom and so true a simplicity."

The Earl of Curzon, Chancellor of Oxford University, declared that this speech ending was "Among the glories and treasures of mankind . . . the purest gold of human eloquence, nay, of eloquence almost divine."

The French minister said: "No such document as that ever before came to the French court."

"Noble as was the Gettysburg address," says William E. Barton in his *Life of Abraham Lincoln,* "this rises to a still higher level of nobility. . . .It is the greatest of the Addresses of Abraham Lincoln and registers his intellectual and spiritual power at their highest altitude."

Carl Schurz who had known Lincoln most all his political career, and heard the Second Inaugural, said: "This was like a sacred poem. . . .No American President had ever spoken words like these to the American people. America had never had a president who had found such words in the depths of his heart."

Dale Carnegie pronounced it "the most beautiful speech ending ever delivered by the lips of mortal man."

Later in March, General Grant who had been besieging the Confederate capitol for several months wrote asking the President to visit his headquarters, as he would like to talk with him, and besides, "the rest will do you good." Lincoln boarded the *River Queen,* and with Mrs. Lincoln and Tad, arrived at City Point and was greeted by Grant.

General Sherman arrived from North Carolina, and on the evening of the 27th the President met with Grant, Sherman and Admiral Porter in the cabin of his boat for an extended conference. Richmond was tottering toward its fall. They talked mostly about the terms of surrender, the rights of citizenship to be restored to the Confederate soldiers, and the future of the South.

"Was there a chance of ending the war without another battle, without further bloodshed?" the President asked. Grant thought not. Yet when Lincoln returned to Washington, Grant said to an aid, "I think we can send him some good news in a day or two."

At 5 o'clock on Sunday morning, April 2, hundreds of Union guns opened fire on Petersburg defences. Point after point gave way, as Lee's resistance crumbled. That morning President Jefferson Davis sat in his pew at St. Paul's church in Richmond, devout as usual, but as the clergyman was delivering the sermon, an official messenger came down the aisle and handed him a message. After reading the message from General Lee saying the armies were evacuating Pettersburg and Richmond, Davis hurriedly followed the messenger out of the church, met with his cabinet, gave last minute orders, and before eventide the President and nearly all high-ranking officials of the Confederacy were in flight. [13]

That day Lee's army set fire to the cotton and tobacco warehouses, scuttled gunboats along the water front, burned factories, mills, and arsenals, and that night slipped off toward the southwest while towering flames roared high in the darkness. The next morning at the City Hall, General Godfrey Weitzel received the surrender of Richmond, and by midafternoon order was restored. That same day, Lincoln boarded the *River Queen* and returned to City Point. "Thank God," said he, "that I have lived to see this! It seems to me that I have been dreaming a horrible dream for four years, and now the nightmare is gone. I want to see Richmond."

Admiral Porter, with an escort of ten seamen, took the President up the river and into Richmond. He says that on landing they saw some twelve negroes digging with spades. The leader of them was an old man sixty years of age. He raised himself to an upright position, put his hands up to his eyes, then dropped his spade and sprang forward. "Bress de Lord," he said, "dere is de great Messiah! I knowed him as soon as I seed him. He's been in my heart fo' long yeahs, an' he cum at las' to free his chillun from deir bondage! Glory, Hallelujah!" And he fell upon his knees before the President and kissed his feet. The others followed his example, and in a minute Mr. Lincoln was surrounded by these people, who had treasured up the recollection of him caught from a photograph, and had looked to him for four years as one who was to lead them out of captivity.

195

Mr. Lincoln looked down at the poor creatures at his feet, and being embarrassed, said: *"Don't kneel to me. That is not right. You must kneel to God only, and thank Him for the liberty you will hereafter enjoy. I am but God's humble instrument; but you must rest assured that as long as I live no one shall put a shackle to your limbs, and you shall have all the rights which God has given to every other free citizen of this Republic."* 14

Admiral Porter asked the Negroes to withdraw and let the President pass on. "Yess, Massa," said the old man, "'Scuse us, sir; we means no disrespec' to Mass' Lincoln: we means all love and gratitude." And there, joining hands together in a ring, the negroes sang with melodious voices:

Oh, all ye people clap your hands,
And with triumphant voices sing;
No force the mighty power withstands
Of God, the universal King.

While the hymn went forth from the Negroes' lips, the streets seemed suddenly to come alive with the colored race. They came tumbling and shouting from every direction. Some rushed forward trying to "touch the man they had talked of and dreamed of for four long years, others stood off a little way and looked on in awe and wonder. Others turned somersaults, and many yelled for joy." At length, when Lincoln could not move for the mass of people, he spoke:

"My poor friends you are free—free as air. You can cast off the name of slave and trample upon it; it will come to you no more. Liberty is your birthright. God gave it to you as He gave it to others, and it is a sin that you have been deprived of it for so many years.

But you must try to deserve this priceless boon. Let the world see that you merit it, and are able to maintain it by your good works. Don't let your joy carry you into excesses. Learn the laws and obey them; obey God's commandments and thank Him for giving you liberty, for to Him you owe all things. There, now, let me pass on; I have but little time to spare. I want to see the capital, and must return at once to Washington to secure to you that liberty which you seem to prize so highly. . . ." 15

As the news of the President's arrival spread, the whites crowded the sidewalks, and gazed from every window. All were pleased

196

to see this large man, with soft eyes, a kind benevolent face, and a grace that could not be excelled—so different to the one who had been held up to them as "the incarnation of evil, the destroyer of the South." From the crowd one man cried out, "Abraham Lincoln, God bless you! You are the poor man's friend." A beautiful young woman struggled through the crowd and gracefully presented her bouquet to the President.

When they arrived at the home of President Jefferson Davis, Lincoln sat for a time in Mr. Davis' official chair, then inspected the modest mansion. After lunch the Presidential party entered a carriage and visited the State House, Libby Prison and other Confederate Military prisons. Evidence of how Union prisoners suffered moved an officer to exclaim that Jefferson Davis should be hanged. Lincoln answered softly: *"Judge not, that ye be not judged."*

When General Weitzel questioned him about the treatment of Richmond's conquered people, Lincoln said: *"If I were in your place, I'd let 'em up easy, let 'em up easy."* Lincoln returned from Richmond to City Point, visited some of the hospitals in that area, then prepared to return to Washington to visit Secretary Seward who had been injured in a carriage accident. [16]

On retreating from Petersburg and Richmond, General Lee marched his army southwest hoping to reach the railroad at Danville, and eventually join forces with General Johnston, but Sheridan's cavalry outdistanced him and siezed the Danville railroad. Lee then marched westward hoping to reach Lynchburg but Sheridan's troopers and Mead's infantry captured a train of wagons, and several thousand prisoners, including Curtis Lee, the son of General Lee, and five of his generals. Sheridan wired Grant of Lee's desperate situation, and added: "If the thing is pressed, I think Lee will surrender." Grant relayed the message on to Lincoln, and received back the reply: *"Let the thing be pressed!"* It was pressed, and after a running fight of eight miles, Grant and Sheridan trapped the Confederate troops and hemmed them in on all sides. On Friday night, Lee realized that further fighting was futile, and said to his staff officers, "There is nothing left for me to do, but go and see General Grant, and I would rather die a thousand deaths."

In the meantime Grant had fallen behind his army, and halted at a farmhouse where he spent the night "bathing his feet in hot water and mustard and putting mustard plasters on his wrists and the back of his neck," in an attempt to relieve a violent sick headache.

The next morning a horseman galloped down the road with a letter from Lee asking for terms of surrender. Grant replied, and the next day, Palm Sunday, April the ninth, the two generals met at the small village of Appomattox Courthouse, in the home of Major Wilmer McClain. Lee was dressed in a full uniform beaded with gauntlets, and a sword studded with jewels. Grant, in his rough battle uniform of a private with shoulder straps of a lieutenant-general, and no sword, explained, apologetically, that he had not had time to change after hurrying from the field. They soon fell into conversation about old army times.

"I met you once before, General Lee, while we were serving in Mexico. . . .I have always remembered your appearance, and I think I should have recognized you anywhere." Lee replied, "Yes, I know I met you on that occasion, and I have often thought of it and tried to recollect how you looked, but have never been able to recall a single feature."

Thus they talked on, reminiscing about the winter the "regulars" spent on the border "when the wolves howled on the prairies . . . and the sunlight danced on the waves . . . and wild horses could be bought for three dollars apiece."

"Our conversation grew so pleasant," said Grant, "that I almost forgot the object of our meeting." Finally, Lee brought him to the point. "I suppose, General Grant, that the object of our present meeting is fully understood. I asked to see you to ascertain upon what terms you would receive the surrender of my army."

"The terms I propose are those stated substantially in my letter of yesterday—that is, the officers and men surrendered to be paroled and disqualified from taking up arms again until properly exchanged, and all arms, ammunition and supplies to be delivered up as captured property." "Those," said Lee, "are about the conditions I expected would be proposed."

Grant sat at a table and put in writing the terms of surrender, which President Lincoln had previously advised, then stepped over to Lee and handed him the paper. Lee wiped his glasses and after a careful reading of the terms, looked up and in a pleasant tone said, "This will have a very happy effect on my army."

When Grant inquired if the General had "any further suggestions," Lee explained that in his army the cavalrymen and artillerists owned their horses, and would like them to be permitted to have them on their farms for spring plowing. "I take it that most of the men in the ranks are small farmers," Grant said, and without changing the written terms, agreed to "let all the men who claim to own a horse or mule take the animals home with them to work their little farms." Lee was visibly relieved. "This will have the best possible effect upon the men. It will be very gratifying and will do much toward conciliating our people." [17]

Lee wrote an acceptance of Grant's terms, signed it, then as the staff officers copied the letters of surrender and the terms, Lee gravely shook hands with Grant, and bent toward him, as in confidence, and whispered that his men hadn't had anything but parched corn to eat in several days. It was like one brother confiding in another. Grant turned to his staff officers and ordered twenty-five thousand rations to be dispatched to them. [18]

After his interview with General Grant, General Lee again appeared, and a shout of welcome instinctively went up from his army. But remembering the sad occasion that brought him before them, their shouts sank into silence, every hat was raised, and thousands of grim warriors broke into tears as their general slowly rode along the lines.

"Hundreds of his noble veterans pressed around their chief, trying to take his hand, touch his person, or even lay hands upon his horse, thus exhibiting for him their great affection." The General then removed his hat, and with tears flowing freely down his manly cheeks, bade adieu: "Men, we have fought through the war together. I have done the best I could for you. By the terms of the agreement officers and men can return to their homes. . . . You will take with you the satisfaction that proceeds from the consciousness of duty faithfully performed; and I earnestly pray that a merciful God will extend to you his blessing and protection. . . . My heart is too full to say more. I bid you an affectionate farewell." [19]

After Lee and his party had left, General Grant wired President Lincoln: "General Lee surrendered the army of Northern Virginia this morning on terms proposed by myself." And the two men understood very well, for the "generous and gentle terms" granted Lee were the ones President Lincoln had advised some twelve days before at the conference with his generals in the cabin of the *River Queen,* at City Point. [20]

That same Palm Sunday, April ninth, Lincoln arrived back in Washington, and rushed to the bedside of Secretary Seward, who had been injured in a carriage accident. To him he conveyed the good news and the bright prospects from the Richmond scene, then added, "We must proclaim a thanksgiving day soon." That evening he received Grant's telegram telling of Lee's surrender.

An account of the long hoped for surrender was put on the wires, and the morning papers blazoned it abroad in the land.

Cannon salutes were bloomed, bells rang, and flags were hung out on homes, and public buildings. Business houses closed, Government departments gave their clerks the day off, and the people gave themselves to rejoicing as they danced and ran happily through the streets.

In New York City 20,000 businessmen uncovered their heads and sang the psalm "Praise God." That evening a great crowd gathered about the White House, singing, cheering and calling for the President. He appeared briefly at a window, addressed them in a few words, and promised to make a speech the following evening. "I see you have a band of music with you. I always thought 'Dixie' one of the best tunes I ever heard. Since yesterday, I insist that we have fairly captured it. I now request the band to favor me with its performance." The band played "Dixie" and the crowd dispersed for the night.

The next evening an immense crowd overflowed the White House lawn and blocked traffic on the sidewalks along Pennsylvania Avenue. There was band music and banners of freedom. As Lincoln stepped to the window and looked out upon a sea of faces, cheers surged and broke, and surged again. The crowd was vibrating with emotion, but became silent as the President began his prepared message:

> We meet this evening not in sorrow, but in gladness of heart. The evacuation of Petersburg and Richmond and the surrender of the principal insurgent army, give hope of a righteous and speedy peace, whose joyous expression cannot be restrained. In the midst of this, however, He from whom all blessings flow must not be forgotten. A call for a national thanksgiving is being prepared, and will be duly promulgated. . . . To General Grant, his skillful officers, and brave

200

men, all belongs. The gallant Navy stood ready, but was not in reach to take part.

The President then directed his hearer's attention to *reconstruction*, the subject, he said, which from the first had pressed closely upon his attention. He made it clear that there was no vindictiveness, no triumph or revenge over a fallen foe, but a "binding up the nation's wounds." He wanted the seceding states to be treated as returning brothers—the prodigal who, being back home, was to have a robe, a ring of authority, and a feast.

There was an awareness that the President spoke, not merely to those who thronged the White House lawns, but to all America and the European world. He would *save the Union.* Therefore, he appealed to the people to act with mercy and forgiveness. Said he:

"We all agree that the seceded states, so called, are out of their proper practical relation with the Union; and that the sole object of the government, civil and military, in regard to those states is to again get them into that proper practical relation. I believe it is not only possible, but in fact, easier to do this, without deciding, or even considering, whether these states have ever been out of the Union, that with it. Finding themselves safely at home, it would be utterly immaterial whether they had ever been abroad. Let us all join in doing the acts necessary to restoring the proper practical relations between these states and the Union, and each forever after, innocently indulge his own opinion whether, in doing the acts, he brought the states from without into the Union, or only gave them proper assistance, they never having been out of it." [21]

It was a noble speech—the last for America's great liberator statesman. And right well did it reflect the Master's teaching, "If ye forgive men their trespasses. . . ."

One evening during this Holy Week, Ward Hill Laymon visited Mr. and Mrs. Lincoln in the White House. The President was in a melancholy, meditative mood, and had been silent for some time when Mrs. Lincoln inquired as to his want of spirit. In slow and serious tones he said:

"It seems strange how much there is in the Bible about dreams. There are, I think, some sixteen chapters in the Old Testament and four in the New in which dreams are men-

tioned; and there are many other passages scattered through-
out the Book which refer to visions. If we believe the Bible,
we must accept the fact that in the old days God and His
angels came to men in their sleep and made themselves known
in dreams." 22

Mrs. Lincoln remarked, "Why, you look dreadfully solemn; do
you believe in dreams?"

"I can't say that I do," returned Mr. Lincoln, "but I had one the
other night which has haunted me ever since. After it occurred I
opened the Bible, strange as it may appear, it was at the twenty-
eighth chapter of Genesis, which relates the wonderful dream
Jacob had. I turned to other passages, and seem to encounter a
dream or a vision wherever I looked. I kept on turning the leaves
of the old Book, and everywhere my eyes fell upon passages recording matters strangely in keeping with my own thoughts—super-
natural visitations, dreams, visions, etc."

He looked so serious and disturbed that Mrs. Lincoln exclaimed:
"You frighten me! What is the matter?"

"I am afraid," said Mr. Lincoln, observing the effect his words
had upon his wife, "that I have done wrong to mention the subject
at all; but somehow the thing has got possession of me, and like
Banquo's ghost, it will not down." Mrs. Lincoln strongly urged
him to tell the dream which seemed to have such a hold upon him.
At length he commenced very deliberately:

"About ten days ago, I retired very late. I had been up wait-
ing for important dispatches from the front. I could not have
been long in bed when I fell into a slumber, for I was weary.
I soon began to dream. There seemed to be a death-like still-
ness about me. Then I heard subdued sobs, as if a number of
people were weeping. I thought I left my bed and wandered
downstairs. There the silence was broken by the same pitiful
sobbing, but the mourners were invisible. I went from room to
room; no living person was in sight, but the same mournful
sounds of distress met me as I passed along. It was light in all
the rooms; every object was familiar to me; but where were all
the people who were grieving as if their hearts would break. I
was puzzled and alarmed. What could be the meaning of
this. . . .I kept on until I arrived at the East Room, which I
entered. There I met with a sickening surprise. Before me was
a catafalque, on which rested a corpse wrapped in funeral

vestments. Around it were stationed soldiers who were acting as guards; and there was a throng of people, some gazing mournfully upon the corpse, whose face was covered, others weeping pitifully. 'Who is dead in the White House.' I demanded of one of the soldiers. 'The President,' was his answer; 'he was killed by an assassin!' Then came a loud burst of grief from the crowd, which awoke me from my dream, I slept no more that night; and although it was only a dream, I have been strangely annoyed by it ever since. [23]

Later, when he and Laymon had briefly discussed the dream and its possible implications, Lincoln said, *"Well, let it go. I think the Lord in His own good time and way will work this out all right. God knows what is best."* [24]

CHAPTER XVII
The Cruelest Shot Ever Fired

"The war is over" was the jubilant cry with which people greeted each other throughout the North on Palm Sunday morning of April 14, 1865.

Such a day of rejoicing as followed our nation has rarely seen. Cities and towns, hamlets and country roadsides were decorated with flags and buntings. Bells rang and people came together in gladness. Even those who mourned their dead came exultant that their loved and lost had saved the Union and freed a people. A subtle joy, mingled with triumph, resignation and hope, swept over the North.

James Russell Lowell wrote: "The news is from Heaven. I felt a strange and tender exaltation. I wanted to laugh and I wanted to cry, and ended up by holding my peace and feeling devoutly thankful." [1]

In Washington the flowers bloomed, the birds sang, and the capital was awake with thanksgiving and celebration. President Lincoln received a new spring in his step, his shoulders were uplifted, and his face became all aglow with serene joy and happiness. To a serenading party that evening he said: "So long as I have been here, I have not willingly planted a thorn in any man's bosom."

At the Cabinet meeting next morning he talked of reconstruction — of how the southern states should be brought back into their old relations with no feelings of hate and vindicativeness being shown them. Of him, Secretary Stanton said: "He was more cheerful and happy than I had ever seen him, rejoiced at the near prospects of firm and durable peace at home and abroad, manifested in marked degree the kindness and humanity of his disposition, and the tender and forgiving spirit that so eminently distinguished him."

After lunch, he and Mrs. Lincoln went for a carriage ride in the country. They planned for far into the future. "Mary," he said, "We have had a hard time of it since we came to Washington; but the war is over, and with God's blessings we may hope for four years of peace and happiness, and then we will go back to Illinois, and spend the rest of our lives in quiet. . . .I will take you and the boys to Europe, and after our return we will cross the Rocky Mountains and go to California where the soldiers will be digging out gold to pay the national debt."

President and Mrs. Lincoln returned from their carriage ride soon after five o'clock. Waiting for him was Governor Richard J. Oglesby of Illinois and Isham N. Haynie, Illinois Adjutant General. He read Petroleum V. Nashby's recently published book to them, then at six went to dinner with his family. Afterwards he made another quick trip to the War Department to learn of the latest news and have a brief talk with his Secretary of War. Before leaving they again exchanged congratulations on the success of the armies, and at their parting "Lincoln from his greater height, dropped his long arm upon Stanton's shoulder, and a hearty embrace terminated their rejoicing over the close of the mighty struggle." They both went home happy.[2]

A theater party had been made up by Mrs. Lincoln for that evening — General and Mrs. Grant being their guests — to see Laura Keen's "Our American Cousin" at the Ford's theater. The box had been ordered in the morning and unusual preparations had been made to receive the presidential party. Word was received that General and Mrs. Grant had decided to go north that night. Miss

Clara Harris and Major Henry R. Rathbone were invited to go in their place. Lincoln did not want to go, and suggested that the party be given up, but Mrs. Lincoln insisted, arguing that he could not disappoint the people.

Being detained by visitors, the play had begun when the Presidential party arrived and was escorted to their box. The orchestra broke into "Hail to the Chief," and the people rising in their seats waved handkerchiefs and cheered. The President bowed in acknowledgement, and the play went on.

A few minutes before ten o'clock, John Wilkes Booth left his horse at the rear entrance of the theater in charge of a callboy, went into a neighboring saloon, took a drink of brandy, and entering the theater, passed rapidly into the hallway leading to the President's box. Showing his card to the servant in attendance, he was allowed to enter.

Mrs. Lincoln said the President had shown little interest in the play. He was thinking and speaking of the better days to come—of going home and settling down in peace for a time, then, as soon as circumstances would permit, taking the trip to Europe, and continuing on to Palestine. A yearning had come over him, he said, "*to tread those holy fields over whose acres walked those blessed feet . . . nailed for our advantage on the bitter cross.*"

No place, he said to Mrs. Lincoln, he wished so much to see as Jerusalem. The word was but half finished on his lips—"Jeru--!" when Booth, who had slipped into the back of the box, raised at arm's length a small one-shot Derringer pistol and shot Lincoln in the back of the head.

A woman screamed, and all eyes turned toward the presidential box. The bullet plowed into the lower brain and Lincoln toppled sideways into the arms of Mrs. Lincoln. His blood spattered her dress as she struggled to hold him upright. Major Rathbone sprang to grapple with Booth, and received a savage knife wound in the arm. Then, rushing forward, the assassin placed his hand on the railing of the box and jumped to the stage—a long leap, but Booth was an athlete. He would have gotten safely away but the spur on his riding boot caught in the silk flag that draped the front of the box. He fell on the stage, the torn flag trailing on his spur; though the fall had broken his leg, he rose instantly, and brandishing his knife he shouted, "Sic semper tyrannis" (so be it always to tyrants). "Stop that man," someone shouted as Booth hurried off the stage,

206

and by a rear exit gained the alley, mounted his horse, and swiftly disappeared in the night.[3]

Pandemonium broke out among the confused and terrified people. Finally the audience was quieted and the theater vacated — never to be opened again for public performances.* Three physicians from the audience made a preliminary examination of the wounded President, then ordered that he be moved to the nearest bed. He was carried across the street to the house of William Peterson and laid, still unconscious, on a bed in a small downstairs room. Mrs. Lincoln followed, tenderly cared for by Miss Harris. Messengers went for the Cabinet, for the Surgeon General, and for Dr. Stone, the family physician. News came that Secretary Seward had been critically stabbed, and that his son Frederick had been wounded. Soon Robert Lincoln arrived and was met at the door by Dr. Stone, who tenderly informed him that there was no hope. Secretary Wills and Secretary Stanton arrived and Stanton took over the direction of affairs.

Throughout the night his pastor, and the doctors at the bedside maintained their hopeless vigil. From time to time they gave the President stimulants and removed blood clots to relieve pressure on the brain. There was that moan of labored breathing as the President clung tenaciously to life. Then about dawn the tortured breathing became faint, and his pulse began to fail. A little later "a look of unspeakable peace came over his worn features," and at 7:22 in the morning of April 15, 1865, Abraham Lincoln, the "true American," gained release and passed to his eternal reward.

Secretary Stanton broke the "tomb-like stillness" by asking Reverend Gurley: "Doctor, will you say something?"

The minister answered quietly, "I will speak to God." As he prayed, all in the room bowed their heads. When he had finished, they spontaneously said, "Amen." Surgeon-General Barns tenderly drew a sheet over the dead President's face. Then in solemn tones Stanton uttered that immortal phrase: "Now he belongs to the ages."

Two hours later the body of the President, wrapped in an American flag, was taken from the house on Tenth Street, and borne through the hushed, black-draped streets to an upper room in the private apartments of the White House, where in its embalmed state it lay for three days.

*The theater was reopened as a museum and for public performances in 1968.

207

News of the sad tragedy went out over the wires to all America, indeed to all the world—a great Friend of Man had suddenly gone away. The slow tolling of bells began in Washington, then in New York, Chicago, Springfield, and a thousand other centers and crossroads villages. Flags at halfmast, and crepe of any shade of black was hung up on front doorways.

Gideon Wells, Secretary of the Navy, went on the morning of Lincoln's death to the White House and saw outside it "several hundred colored people, mostly women and children, weeping and wailing their loss," and the sight affected him more than anything else. Yet, to more than the colored people, for all Americans there was never a more untimely death.

In pointing to the universal sense of dismay, indignation and deep emotion, the *New York Times* said, "That a man so gentle, so kind, so free from every particle of malice, and whose every act has been marked by benevolence and goodwill, should become the victim of cold-blooded killing has shocked the people beyond expression."

In the *New York Tribune,* Horace Greeley said, "If ever a man made war in the Christian spirit, that man was Abraham Lincoln."

Newsboys cried no headlines, but merely handed the fresh sheets from the press to the buyers. Thousands of merchants closed their stores for the day. To the father, or the children coming home unexpectedly, the mother asked what was wrong, and heard, "They have killed our President." On the streets, in railway cars and street cars, and in public places men tried to talk about it, but words failed them. Lincoln had died—a good, and great and irreplaceable friend was gone.

In Charleston, South Carolina, an elderly black woman walked the street looking straight ahead, wringing her hands and crying: "O, Lawd! O, Lawd! Marse Sam's dead! O, Lawd! Uncle Sam's dead!" In Boston "a thousand or more men found themselves on the Commons marching in a silent procession, two by two, not a word spoken, just walking, just seeing each other's faces, marching for an hour or so and then slowly scattering, having reached some form of consolation in being together, seeing each other in mute grief."[4] In Huntington Long Island, Walt Whitman and his mother heard the news as they sat at breakfast, and ate nothing and said little all the rest of the day. Walt decided that as long as he lived he would have sprigs of lilacs in his room on April 14, and keep it as a holy day for the man he later characterized as "the grandest figure on the crowded canvas of the drama of the nineteenth century."

Out in what was then "the Iowa frontier," a farmer rode a fast horse and shouted, as he passed from one farm to the next, "Lincoln is shot!" or "Lincoln is dead—shot in a theater!" As the rider passed on the people were amazed, many saying, "What will the country do now?"5

On Easter morning, in churches both large and small, in cities and at country crossroads, there were sermons memorializing the President "who being dead yet speaketh."

Over and over again the parallels were drawn of Lincoln and Christ in atonement dying for mankind. "The last and costliest offering which God demanded has been taken," said the Rev. C.B. Crane of the South Baptist Church of Hartford, Connecticut. "Jesus Christ died for the world, Abraham Lincoln died for his country." A New York pastor said, "The country does not go wild over him; it silently weeps for him; it does not celebrate him as a demigod—it mourns for him as a friend." The Reverend Edward Everett Hale of Boston said: "I dare not trust myself to speak a word regarding this simple, godly, good, great man....To speak of him I must seek some other hour....Fear not little flock, it is your Father's good pleasure to give you the Kingdom."

In his eloquence, Henry Ward Beecher said: "Four years ago, oh Illinois, we took from your midst an untried man, and from among the people. We return him to you a mighty conqueror. Not thine anymore, but the nation's; not ours, but the world's."

In his Easter message Dr. Phillips Brooks of Boston praised Lincoln's submission to God's will and said of him that "....he was the man most distinctly and in the truest sense an American....I believe from my heart that if there be a man who has left on record that he was a Christian man, a servant and follower of Jesus Christ, it is he who lies in the coffin today."

As the spokesman for world sentiment, Tolstoy said: "Of all great national heroes and statesmen of history, Lincoln is the only real giant....Lincoln was....a Christ in miniature, a saint of humanity whose name will live thousands of years in the legends of future generations."

On Tuesday morning, his mahogany casket, lined with lead, covered with black broadcloth, and ornamented with massive silver handles, was placed on a platform under a canopy of black silk and crepe in the center of the great East Room. At the head of the casket was a cross formed of fresh, fragrant lilies. Strewn over, and banked about it were early magnolias, balmy lilies, and fragrant roses. On top of the casket was a shield and a silver plate on which was inscribed:

ABRAHAM LINCOLN

Sixteenth President of the United States

Born Feb. 12, 1809
Died April 15, 1865

Early in the morning the gates were thrown open. All day long, in two columns, the mourning throngs filed through the East Room, and at night when the gates were closed, some twenty-five thousand had looked on the face of the President. Yet, Lafayette Park and the adjoining streets were still packed with people waiting for admission. Among those who came to view the President were people of all ranks and classes. Conspicuous in the great company of mourners were soldiers, sailors, and negroes. To some he had been a father, to others a liberator, and to the people in general the greatest and best man they had known.

On Wednesday, April 19, at the appointed hour for the official funeral ceremony, there arrived sixty clergymen, the new President Andrew Johnson, the Cabinet members, the Supreme Court Justices, Senators, Congressmen, important officials from coast to coast, foreign diplomats, representatives of the churches, of the courts, of commerce, General Grant, and Admiral Farragut — six hundred dignitaries in all-who crowded in the East Room. Only Robert Lincoln represented the family. Mrs. Lincoln was not able to endure the emotion of the scene, and Tad could not be induced to be present, but said, "Father is happy in that world where he has gone." 6

"Hear my prayer, O Lord. . . .I am a stranger with Thee, and a sojourner, as all my fathers were," intoned the Reverend Dr. C.H. Hall, rector of the Church of the Epiphany. "For a thousand years in Thy sight are but as yesterday. . . .Man is cut down as a flower. He fleeth as a shadow. Yet death may be swallowed up in victory. . . .Thou knowest, Lord, the secrets of our hearts; shut not thy merciful ears to our prayers."

210

Bishop Matthew Simpson of the Methodist Episcopal Church offered prayer, that smitten hearts might endure, might not be called upon for further sacrifices, that the widow and children be comforted, and he concluded with the Lord's prayer, emphasizing those words: "Thy will be done on earth, as it is in Heaven. . . . "

The Reverend Dr. Phineas D. Gurley, President Lincoln's pastor, in giving the funeral address from the text, "His way is in the sea, and his path in the great waters; and His footsteps are not known," commented on his personal relationship with the President and said he never could forget the time in this very room when Lincoln received a company of clergymen who had called upon him to pay their respects during the darkest days of the war and he told them: "Gentlemen, my hope of success in this great and terrible struggle rests on that immutable foundation, the justice and goodness of God." Said Dr. Gurley:

> "This abiding confidence in God and the final triumph of truth and righteousness, was his noblest virtue, the secret alike of his strength, his patience, and his success. . . .God be praised that our fallen chief lived long enough to see the day dawn and the star of joy and peace arise upon the nation. He saw it and was glad. . . .Abraham Lincoln's life will enter the register of the ages, triumph over the injustices of time, and survive busts and statues."[7]

The Reverend E. H. Gray, Baptist clergyman and Chaplin of the United States Senate, pronounced the benediction. And the service was over.

CHAPTER XVIII
Going Home
To Springfield

At two o'clock in the afternoon, the booming of cannons and the tolling of bells announced that the official funeral services were completed. A few minutes later, the twelve Veteran Reserve Corps sergeants who were to be the only ones to lift the casket until it reached Springfield took hold of the eight silver handles of Lincoln's casket and bore it out of the great front door of the White House—his home for more than four years—and placed it in a large specially built funeral hearse, surmounted by a gilt eagle, covered with crepe.

Six white horses drew the hearse as the procession moved down Pennsylvania Avenue, and just behind the hearse came Mr. Lincoln's favorite horse, branded U.S., bearing his master's boots reversed in the stirrups. Robert Lincoln and Tad rode in a carriage together, and Tom Pendel, the doorkeeper of the White House, rode up in front with the coachman. President Johnson, and all the high officials of church and state, the army, navy, and marines, and people of every sort—a hundred thousand, it was estimated—marched in that "solemn, impressive, and unforgettable procession" while bands played and drums beat their funeral dirges. The most impressive of all the scenes that day were the negro citizens who walked in lines of forty, straight across the avenue from curb to curb—four thousand of them—wearing high silk hats and white gloves and marched holding hands.[1]

At the east front of the Capitol the procession halted, and the body of Abraham Lincoln was borne across the protico, from which six weeks before he had given his second inaugural: *"With malice toward none; with charity for all; with firmness in the right, as God gives us to see the right, let us strive on to finish the work we are in, to bind up the nation's wounds; to care for him who shall have born the battle, and for his widow and his orphan—to do all which may achieve and cherish a just and lasting peace among ourselves, and with all nations."*

The casket was then carried into the rotunda of the Capitol, and placed under the dome on a great catafalque, where it was left alone, save for the soldiers who kept guard.

On the following day, the Capitol was opened, and all day long people entered in a double line from the west, silently formed an ellipse around the casket, and joined lines again as they marched out at the east portal.

At six o'clock on Friday morning, April 21, there gathered in the rotunda of the Capitol the many officials of the Government and other dignitaries. After Dr. Gurley prayed, beseeching God to "watch over this sleeping dust of our fallen Chief Magistrate as it passes from our view and is born to its resting place in the soil of that state which was his abiding and chosen home," the party followed the casket to the railway station, where stood the funeral train of nine cars, the engine and pilot engine, which was to convey the remains of Abraham Lincoln from Washington to Springfield.

A great company of people waited in silence while the casket was placed on the "Pioneer," a special railway sleeping car just completed by George M. Pullman. The car was second from the rear. At the foot of Lincoln's casket was placed a smaller one, that of little Willie Lincoln, who had passed away more than three years before. At Mrs. Lincoln's request, Willie's little metallic coffin had been disinterred from his vault, and enclosed in a new black walnut one, and taken to the depot ready for the departure.

Father and son were to make together this last earthly journey. [2]

The engine was highly polished and heavily draped in black. Flags were here and there, and a large, black framed photograph of Lincoln was attached just above the cowcatcher. Three hundred people were to accompany the earthly remains of the President on the seventeen hundred mile trip which had been carefully planned by a committee of Illinois citizens. Judge David, Ward Hill Lamon, Ninan Edwards, and other close friends and relatives were among the notables selected to make the journey. Even Tom Pendell, the faithful doorkeeper at the White House, made the trip.

The itenerary was to include Baltimore, Harrisburg, Philadelphia, New York, Albany, Buffalo, Columbus, Indianapolis, Chicago, and Springfield—each of the cities—except Cincinnati—at which Lincoln as President-elect had stopped on his trip to Washington for the inauguration. A delegation from Cincinnati was to come to the Columbus funeral.

All heads were uncovered as the bells tolled and the Baltimore and Ohio engine slowly moved out of the station at eight o'clock. Lining the track, on either side, was a grief stricken Negro regiment who called after the train, "Good-by, Father Abraham."

The first stop was in Baltimore where guns boomed and bells tolled, and the Veteran Sergeants transferred the casket to what Baltimore newspapers described as "the most beautiful hearse ever constructed"—a genuine rosewood, with back and sides of French plate glass three quarters of an inch thick—drawn by *four black* horses. The procession was so long and congestion so great that it took three hours to get to the Merchants Exchange where the casket was opened for viewing. When it was closed at two o'clock only ten thousand had looked on Lincoln's face. The long lines of school children and many thousands more were disappointed, but the train was on schedule. [3]

Governor Andrew Curtiss of Pennsylvania and his staff boarded the train at the state line, and thus set a precedent for other governors to ride the train through their states. At York six ladies of that city entered the funeral car and placed a three-foot-wide cartwheel of red, white, and blue flowers on Lincoln's casket.

At Harrisburg *four white* horses drew the gorgeously constructed hearse to the House of Representatives where Lincoln had spoken four years previously. The viewing was by double lines, as usual, and went on during the evening hours and the next morning until eleven o'clock, when forty thousand people saw the casket to the train and on its way.

All along the way shops closed, farm work ceased, and the people stood with bowed heads, or knelt as the funeral train passed. Enormous crowds were at Lancaster — ex-President Buchanan's home city.

At Philadelphia, *eight black* horses harnessed in silver and led by grooms, drew the hearse in an impressive procession to Independence Square. The casket was placed in the East Wing of Independence Hall where the Declaration of Independence had been signed, and only a few yards away from the Liberty Bell, and near the very spot where Lincoln had made his great speech in that Hall, on Washington's Birthday in 1861, when he said he had "rather be assassinated on the spot than surrender the promise of equal chance for all men" as stated in the Declaration of Independence.

Saturday evening, and all day Sunday the viewers, in double lines, passed by the casket. At midnight, when it was all over, three ladies entered and deposited on the casket a cross of huge white flowers. Philadelphia claimed that more than three hundred thousand people had looked on Lincoln, the war President, who Judge Kelley said had "lived in full consciousness of his mortality judgments of a just God. . . .and with a deep sense of dependence on God."[4]

In New York City *sixteen gray* horses drew the large and elaborately decorated hearse in a procession which took three hours and forty-eight minutes to pass each point. Single positions in windows along Broadway rented for from fifty to one hundred dollars for the afternoon. All along the march the chimes of Trinity Church rang out *"Praise God from whom all blessings flow."* Ceremonies in Union Square were rather awkwardly arranged, yet a half million people gathered to see the President's face.

A brawny backwoodsman, who looked as though he could cut a few cords of wood a day and still have plenty of time left over, pushed his way through the spectators. "Don't walk on my feet!" cried an irate individual. "Excuse me, sir," apologized the weather-beaten woodsman, "but I must see the coffin." "Why must you?" "Two of my brothers died in the same cause he did," replied the big fellow sadly. "Besides, he's one of my craft. I could never go back to the woods again until I see and bless his coffin."[5]

The interest was so great that after the casket was closed at four o'clock, and returned to the train, a huge crowd remained, and that evening in the Square, Dr. George Bancroft, the historian, delivered such a mighty oration on Lincoln and the goals for which he worked that William Cullen Bryant caught inspiration and wrote his "Ode for the Burial of Abraham Lincoln" which began:

Oh slow to smite and swift to spare,
Gentle and merciful and just;
Who in the fear of God did'st bear
The sword of power, a nation's trust.

So sincere was the affectionate reverence which the people held for the President that at West Point the uniformed cadets had come across the river to Garrison with their band and silently walked through the funeral car. And as the train passed through town after town, on the way to Albany, bells rang, bands played, and cannons boomed. At Poughkeepsie the train made a stop and "the whole hillside was black with people."

"As the train sped the rails at night," says Chauncy Depew, "the scene was the most pathetic ever witnessed. At every cross-road the glare of innumerable torches illuminated the whole population, from age to infancy, kneeling on the ground and their clergymen leading in prayers and hymns....other groups stood about the roadway with bowed heads, weeping." Great bonfires were built in lonely country-sides, around which the farmers waited patiently to salute as the train passed bearing the President's remains.

And thus it was from Washington to Springfield, "the funeral train entered scarcely a town that the bells were not tolling, the minute guns firing, the stations draped, and all the space beside the track crowded with people with uncovered heads." The country-sides showing equal respect in their way. It was "a veritable mass pageant of exaltation to the dead" as untold hundreds of thousands—estimated at more than two million—thronged the tracks over which the train slowly traveled on its 1,700 mile trip to Springfield.

Indianapolis honored her one-time Indiana farm boy whose mother lay buried in her soil. *Eight white* horses drew the hearse to the State House where the casket was banked with flowered crosses, wreaths, harps and anchors. Five thousand Sabbath School children led the viewing procession, and the last to pass in review were Colored Masons and hundreds of Colored citizens who carried copies of the Emancipation Proclamation. [6]

Chicago, which had long known and respected Lincoln, spent $15,000 for decorations alone, and met his body at the station, from whence *eight black* horses bore him under a magnificent Gothic three section arch on which was inscribed: "We honor him dead who honored us while living. Rest in Peace Noble Soul, Patriot. Faithful to Right, A Martyr to Justice." Over the door of the Courthouse, where some 170,000 people viewed Lincoln's remains, was inscribed "The beauty of Israel is slain upon her high places." [7]

As the train advanced from Chicago toward Springfield and home, the character of the mourning grew more personal and intimate. The journey was made at night, yet most of the population of the country lined the route. Nearly every one of the towns passed — indeed, many of the farms passed — had been visited personally by Lincoln on legal or political errands, and a vast number of those who thus in the dead of night watched the flying train, he had at some time in his life taken by the hand." [8]

There was much about this home-coming that touched the people of Illinois very deeply, and caused them to weep. Their newspapers spoke for them. One tribute read:

He who writes this is weeping, he who reads it is weeping; all are weeping who knew him, loved him, trusted him, confided in him, believed in him, leaned upon him — this foremost man, this honest soul, this upright ruler, this Washington of his people, this Moses of us all; for here he comes back to us — dead! O, they have slain the beauty of our Israel! [9]

At nine o'clock on the morning of May 3 the funeral train arrived in Springfield. Some seventy-five thousand people had poured into town from seemingly everywhere in Illinois, and outside the state. The most of these were at the station where the twelve Veteran Sergeants transferred Lincoln's body from the funeral car to the glittering gold, silver, and black hearse. Drawn by *six* beautiful *black* horses, a long procession made up of Illinois Infantry, Wisconsin troops, a guard of honor, and thousands of sorrowing citizens followed Lincoln's remains to the Hall of the House of Representatives in the state Capitol where eight years

217

before Lincoln had given his famous "house divided against itself" speech. For twenty-four hours the body lay in state, while a silent procession of fellow citizens came to say farewell to Abraham Lincoln. Many of these thought of him not only as a great national and world leader, but as a father, a friend, a neighbor, and a counsellor. All the rest of their lives they would think and talk of Abe Lincoln as they knew him—of his unusual ways, of what he did, and said, and of the many meaningful human interest stories. They recalled his farewell in 1861, and especially his phrase "I now leave not knowing when or whether ever I may return. . . ."

"Billy Herndon, Lincoln's former law partner, looked for the last time upon the face of his illustrious partner, and observed that among the mourners were his former colleagues of bench and bar, Old New Salem neighbors, crippled soldiers from battlefields, and little children who would live to tell their children the sad story of Lincoln's death."[10] In a letter to a friend, he wrote:

My good friend—is gone—yet with us in Spirit. The news of his going struck me dumb. . . . It is . . . grievously sad to think of one so good, so kind, so loving, so honest, so manly, and so great, taken off by the murderous hand of an assassin.

In the long lines of people who bade Lincoln farewell that day, none felt the significance of the occasion quite so much as the hundreds of Negroes who had benefited so much from Lincoln's life and labors. One mother, a former slave, held up her little child to see the flag-draped casket containing the great Emancipator's body, and said to her child: "Take a long look, honey! That's the man who set us free."

Either before or after the viewing, five thousand people walked slowly to Lincoln's old home at Eighth and Jackson, where they were shown through room after room, and manifested deep interest in everything with which the great man had once had to do. Two of the special attractions at the home were Lincoln's horse, Old Bob; and Lincoln's dog, Fido. Both of them had been brought back especially for the return of their master. Lincoln's law office, the Globe Tavern, and other places in the city with which Lincoln had been associated were visited with deep interest.[11]

CHAPTER XIX
The March To
The Tomb

At noon on Thursday, May 4, Lincoln's casket was sealed—nineteen days after he died. The Veteran Sargeants carried the casket out to the hearse surmounted by flowers and evergreens. As the funeral procession formed and moved out on its two mile journey to Oak Ridge Cemetary, a choir of 250 voices solemnly sang:

Children of the Heavenly King,
As we journey let us sing,
Sing our Saviour's worthy praise,
Glorious in his works and ways.

Lord, obediently we'll go,
Gladly leaving all below:
Only thou our leader be,
And we still will follow thee.

At the head of the procession rode Major General Joseph Hooker. Behind him came a thousand soldiers—the entire 146th Illinois Infantry. Then the hearse, drawn by *six black* horses, with six pallbearers on either side. Immediately after the hearse came Old Bob,

Lincoln's horse of many years, led by his handyman, the Rev. Henry Brown. Then came the guard of honor, followed by relatives (including Robert Lincoln), and family friends. After these came the congressional delegation, foreign ministers, governors, "citizens at large," and "colored persons," among whom was Billy the Barber, who had been invited to march with Lincoln's important associates, but had chosen to walk with "those who cared most."[1]

On the way, from time to time the bands played funeral dirges, four of which had been newly composed as "Lincoln's Funeral Marches." In between was heard the roll of muffled drums. The final journey went by Lincoln's home at Eighth and Jackson Streets, out to the city limits, then north past the Governor's Mansion to Fourth Street and out Fourth to Oak Ridge Cemetery.[2]

At the entrance of the cemetery the procession marched under an evergreen arch, and on to the iron-gated receiving tomb set in the hillside, some 220 yards from the entrance. Two platforms were near, one for the 300 singers, the other for the clergy and other officials. As their last service the twelve Veteran Sergeants tenderly lifted the casket from the hearse and bore it through the open iron gates and placed it on the marble slab inside the vault.

"As soon as the hearse and horses moved away and let the people come in close, it was seen that there were two coffins on the slab—'The littlest one for me, the biggest one for father,' as Willie had so touchingly written in Three Bear style of beds and washbowls and towels in his letter about his Chicago trip with his father a few years before. Willie had been brought to the vault first and had been waiting."[3]

Robert Lincoln, Judge David Davis, friends and relatives stood near the tomb, while according to estimates some 75 thousand people covered the hillsides. The large choir sang two hymns, then prayer was offered by Rev. Albert Hale; a portion of the first chapter of John's Gospel was read by Reverend N.W. Miner, then Rev. A.C. Hubbard read those simple, yet profound words of Lincoln's Second Inaugural: "With malice toward none; with charity for all; with firmness in the right, as God gives us to see the right—let us strive on to finish the work we are in: to bind up the nation's wounds; to care for him who shall have borne the battle, and for his widow and his orphan; to do all which may achieve a just and lasting peace among ourselves, and with all nations."

Bishop Matthew Simpson of the Methodist Church—one of

President Lincoln's closest friends and esteemed counsellors—gave a moving funeral oration, in which he said:

> There are moments which involve in themselves eternities. There are instants which seem to contain germs which shall develop and bloom forever. Such a moment came in the tide of time to our land when a question must be settled, affecting all the powers of the earth. The contest was for human freedom. Not for this republic merely, not for the Union simply, but to decide whether the people, as a people, in their entire majesty, were destined to be the Governments or whether they were to be subject to tyrants or aristocrats, or to class rule of any kind. This is the great question for which we have been fighting, and its decision is at hand, and the result of this contest will affect the ages to come. If successful, republics will spread in spite of monarchs all over this earth. [4]

Then directing his attention to the immediate present he continued:

> More people have gazed on the face of the departed than ever looked upon the face of any other departed man. More have looked upon the procession for 1,600 miles or more—by night and by day—by sunlight, dawn, twilight and by torchlight than ever before watched the progress of a procession. . . .The cause of this mourning is to be found in the man himself. Mr. Lincoln was no ordinary man. . . .In his domestic life he was exceedingly kind and affectionate. . . .He made all men feel a sense of himself—a recognition of individuality—a self-relying power. They saw in him a man who they believed would do what is right, regardless of all consequences. It was his moral feeling that gave him the greatest hold on the people, and made his utterances almost oracular. . . .
>
> Chieftain, farewell! The nations mourn thee. Mothers shall teach thy name to their lisping children. The youth of our land shall emulate thy virtues. Statesmen shall study thy record, and from it learn the lessons of wisdom. . . .We crown thee as our Martyr, and humanity enthrones thee as her triumphant son. Hero, Martyr, Friend, farewell.

The funeral service closed with the choir singing the familiar "Praise God from whom all Blessings Flow," and Reverend Gurley raising his hand and pronouncing the final benediction with every head bowed. While the choir sang "Rest, Noble Martyr! Rest in Peace!" the heavy doors of the tomb, and the iron gates were closed and locked, and the key handed to Robert Lincoln, who confided them to Hon. John Stuart, Lincoln's first law partner and later his cousin by marriage. [5]

At last Abraham Lincoln was "at rest. . . in a quiet place," a citizen of that far country where there is neither war nor strife, nor suffering, but peace forevermore.   He had kept the faith.

REFERENCE NOTES

Chapter I

1. Hill, *Abraham Lincoln, Man of God*, p. 10.
   This information was supposed to come from eye-witnesses who remembered the incident, and wrote it in a letter to Herndon in 1865. This is but one version of the story, yet it is in harmony with the spirit of the campmeetings of those days.
2. Tarbell, *The Life of Abraham Lincoln*, Vol. I, p. 10; also see
   Tarbell, *In the Footsteps of the Lincolns*, p. 89.
3. Warren, *Lincoln's Youth, Indiana Years*.
   Tarbell, *In the Footsteps of the Lincolns*, p. 89.
4. *Ibid.*, 92, 93.
5. Tarbell, *The Life of Abraham Lincoln*, Vol. I, p. 17.
6. Barton, *The Soul of Abraham Lincoln*, p. 30.
7. *Ibid.*, p. 31.
8. Boreham, *A Temple of Topaz*, p. 27.
   Arnold, *Life of Lincoln*, p. 27.
   Hill, *Abraham Lincoln, Man of God*, p. 14.
9. *Ibid.*, p. 15.
10. *Ibid.*, p. 15, 16.
11. *Ibid.*, p. 16, 17.
12. Boreham, *A Temple of Topaz*, p. 26, 27.

Chapter II

1. Rankin, *Personal Recollections of Abraham Lincoln*, p. 12.
2. Trueblood, *Abraham Lincoln*, p. 96.
3. Sandburg, *Abraham Lincoln*, p. 18.
4. Beveridge, *Abraham Lincoln*, Vol. I, p. 72.
   Lockridge, *A. Lincoln*, p. 122.
5. Thompson, *Abraham Lincoln, the First American*, p. 16, 17.
6. Lockridge, *A. Lincoln*, p. 34, 35.
7. Hill, *Abraham Lincoln, Man of God*, p. 34.

Chapter III

1. Hill, *Abraham Lincoln, Man of God*, p. 35, 36.
2. Thomas, *Lincoln's New Salem*, p. 44-45.
3. *Ibid.*, p. 46, 47.
4. Tarbell, *Life of Abraham Lincoln*, p. 65.
5. Thomas, *Lincoln's New Salem*, p. 47.
6. *Ibid.*, p. 49.
7. Lockridge, *A. Lincoln*, p. 93.
8. *Ibid.*, p. 94.
9. *Ibid.*, p. 95.
10. Thomas, *Lincoln's New Salem*, p. 53.
11. Sandburg, *Abraham Lincoln*, p. 28, 29.
12. Thomas *Lincoln's New Salem*, p. 55.
    Lockridge, *A. Lincoln*, p. 101.

223

13. *Ibid.*
14. Thomas, *Lincoln's New Salem*, p. 58.
15. *Ibid.*, p. 60.
16. Lockridge, *A. Lincoln*, p. 110.
17. Sandburg, *Abraham Lincoln*, p. 33.
18. Lockridge, *A. Lincoln*, p. 111.
19. Thomas, *Lincoln's New Salem*, p. 68-69.
20. Thomas, *Ibid.*, p. 74-75.
21. Woldman, *Lawyer Lincoln*, p. 19.
22. Whitney, *Life on the Circuit with Lincoln*, p. 169.
23. Lockridge, *A. Lincoln*, p. 160.
24. Hill, *Abraham Lincoln*, Man of God, p. 58.

Chapter IV
1. When Bowling Green died, Lincoln was asked to speak over his grave. For once in his life he broke down completely; "the tears ran down his yellow shrivelled cheeks. . . After repeated efforts he found it impossible to speak and strode away sobbing."
2. Hill, *Abraham Lincoln, Man of God*, p. 29.
3. Sandburg, *Abraham Lincoln*, p. 59.
4. Basler, *Collected Works of Abraham Lincoln*, Vol. I, pg. 78.
5. *Ibid*, Vol. I, pg. 94
6. Hill, *Abraham Lincoln, Man of God*, p. 51, 52, 53.
   Tarbell, *Life of Lincoln*, Vol. I, p. 237.
   Bishop C. H. Fowler's *Patriotic Orations*.
7. Tarbell, *Life of Abraham Lincoln*, Vol. I, p. 238, 239.

Chapter V
1. Sandburg, *Abraham Lincoln*, p. 69.
2. *Ibid.*, p. 69, 70.
3. Angle, *The Lincoln Reader*, p. 125.
4. Sandburg, *Abraham Lincoln*, p. 70.
5. Lockridge, *A. Lincoln*, p. 132.
6. Angle, *The Lincoln Reader*, p. 127.

Chapter VI
1. Newman, *Lincoln for the Ages*, p. 120.
2. *Ibid.*, p. 121.
3. Luthin, *The Real Abraham Lincoln*, p. 67, 68.
4. *Ibid.*, p. 68, 69.
5. Woldman, *Lawyer Lincoln*, p. 43, 44.
6. *Ibid.*, p. 54.
7. Sandburg, *Abraham Lincoln*, p. 83, 84.
8. Lockridge, *A. Lincoln*, p. 153.
9. Woldman, *Lawyer Lincoln*, p. 58, 59.
10. Luthin, *The Real Abraham Lincoln*, p. 101.
11. Sandburg, *Abraham Lincoln*, p. 93.
12. *Ibid.*, p. 93.

224

Chapter VII

1. Thomas, *Abraham Lincoln*, p. 117.
2. Sandburg, *Abraham Lincoln*, p. 97.
3. Woldman, *Lawyer Lincoln*, p. 73, 74.
4. Sandburg, *Abraham Lincoln*, p. 107.
5. Barton, *The Soul of Abraham Lincoln*, p. 311-313; and see Baltimore, Maryland Methodist Christian Advocate, Nov. 11, 1909.
   During the war this same Rev. Jacquess became a Colonel in the army. Lincoln regarded him as "wise, sagacious, and God-fearing" and approved of his going along with James R. Gilmore, on a peace mission to Jefferson Davis.
6. Hill, *Abraham Lincoln, Man of God*, p. 238.
7. Sandburg, *Abraham Lincoln*, p. 107.
8. Bevridge, *Abraham Lincoln*, p. 541-543.
9. Lockridge, *A. Lincoln*, p. 174.
10. Herndon: Weik, *Lincoln*, II, p. 340-42.
    Woldman, *Lawyer Lincoln*, p. 106-108.
11. Beveridge, *Abraham Lincoln*, p. 558.
12. *Ibid.*, p. 578-580.
13. Lockridge, *A. Lincoln*, p. 182.
14. *Ibid.*, o. 177, 78.
15. Luthin, *The Real Abraham Lincoln*, p. 169.
16. Beveridge, *Abraham Lincoln*, Vol. I, p. 560, 567.
17. *Ibid.*, p. 568.
18. *Ibid.*, p. 590-93.

Chapter VIII

1. Tarbell, *Life of Abraham Lincoln*, Vol. I, p. 281.
2. Nicolay, *Abraham Lincoln*, p. 97, 98.
3. Tarbell, *Life of Abraham Lincoln*, Vol. I, p. 294.
4. *Ibid.*
5. Luthin, *The Real Abraham Lincoln*, p. 184.
6. Tarbell, *Life of Lincoln*, Vol. I, p. 302.
7. Lockridge, *A. Lincoln*, p. 193.
8. Sandburg, *Abraham Lincoln*, p. 138, 39.
9. Luthin, *The Real Abraham Lincoln*, p. 195.
10. Lockridge, *A. Lincoln*, p. 195.
11. *Ibid.*, p. 196-97.
12. Thomas, *Abraham Lincoln*, p. 186.
13. Lockridge, *A. Lincoln*, p. 201-203.
14. *Ibid.*, p. 200.
15. Tarbell, *Life of Lincoln*, Vol. I, p. 322.
16. Lockridge, *A. Lincoln*, p. 207.
17. *Ibid.*, p. 208.
18. Tarbell, *Life of Lincoln*, Vol. I, p. 325-7.

Chapter IX

1. Sandburg, *Abraham Lincoln*, p. 167.
2. *Ibid.*, p. 165.
3. Thomas, *Abraham Lincoln*, p. 204, 5.
4. *Ibid.*, p. 205.
5. Thomas, *Abraham Lincoln*, p. 206, 7.
6. Sandburg, *Abraham Lincoln*, p. 174.
7. Luthin, *The Real Abraham Lincoln*, p. 228.
8. Sandburg, *Abraham Lincoln*, p. 183.
9. Luthin, *The Real Abraham Lincoln*, p. 456.

Chapter X

1. Sandburg, *Abraham Lincoln*, p. 185.
2. Luthin, *The Real Abraham Lincoln*, p. 242.
3. Lockridge, *A. Lincoln*, p. 219.
4. Sandburg, *Abraham Lincoln*, p. 194.
5. Tarbell, *Abraham Lincoln*, Vol. I, p. 409.
6. Hill, *Abraham Lincoln, Man of God*, p. 169, 70.
   Tarbell, *Life of Lincoln*, Vol I, p. 410.
7. *Ibid.*, p. 411.
8. Hill, *Abraham Lincoln, Man of God*, p. 171.
9. Tarbell, *Life of Lincoln*, Vol I, p. 411-12.
10. Sandburg, *Abraham Lincoln*, p. 198, 99.
11. Hill, *Abraham Lincoln, Man of God*, p. 173.
12. Tarbell, *Life of Abraham Lincoln*, Vol. I, p. 421, 422.
13. *Ibid.*, p. 423.
14. Luthin, *The Real Abraham Lincoln*, p. 259.

Chapter XI

1. Angle, *The Lincoln Reader*, p. 332, 33.
2. Basier, *Collected Works of Abraham Lincoln*, Vol. IV, p. 271.

Chapter XII

1. Luthin, *The Real Abraham Lincoln*, p. 266, 67
2. Sandburg, *Abraham Lincoln*, p. 229.
3. *Ibid.*, p. 229.
4. *Ibid.*, p. 230.
5. Sumner, *Abraham Lincoln as a Man Among Men*, p. 21.
6. Thomas, *Abraham Lincoln*, p. 296.
7. *Ibid.*, p. 297.
8. Sumner, *Abraham Lincoln as a Man Among Men*, p. 23.
9. *Ibid.*, p. 25.
10. Sandburg, *Abraham Lincoln*, p. 234.
11. Hill, *Abraham Lincoln, Man of God*, p. 283.
12. Thomas, *Abraham Lincoln*, p. 264.
13. Tarbell, *Life of Lincoln*, Vol. III, p. 91.
14. Kunhardt, *Twenty Days*, p. 135.

15. Angle, *The Lincoln Reader*, p. 428-30.
16. Hill, *Abraham Lincoln, Man of God*, p. 321.
    Carpenter, *Six Months at the White House*, p. 117-19.
17. Hill, *Abraham Lincoln, Man of God*, p. 321-22.
18. *Ibid.*, p. 324-5.
    Carpenter, *Six Months at the White House*, p. 117-19.
19. Angle, *The Lincoln Reader*, p. 380-82.
20. Lockridge, *A. Lincoln*, p. 250.
21. *Ibid.*, p. 249.
22. *Ibid.*, p. 254-55.
23. Basler, *The Colected Works of Abraham Lincoln*, Vol. V, p. 537.
24. Newman, *Lincoln for the Ages*, p. 234.
25. Luthin, *The Real Abraham Lincoln*, p. 426.

Chapter XIII

1. Hill, *Abraham Lincoln, Man of God*, p. 284-5.
2. For the first time the Spencer repeating rifle had been in the hands of many Union soldiers in this battle, and it had proven superior to the arms of the Confederates.
3. Basler, *The Collected Works of Abraham Lincoln*, Vol. VI, p. 332.
4. *Ibid.*, Vol. VII, p. 23.

Chapter XIV

1. James Russell Lowell, *The North American Review*, Jan., 1864.
2. Oldroyd, *Lincoln's Memorial Album*, p. 366.
   Boreham, *A Temple of Topaz*, p. 31.
   Hill, *Abraham Lincoln, Man of God*, pp. 240, 261, 2.
3. Carpenter, *Six Months at the White House*, p. 187.
   Hill, *Abraham Lincoln, Man of God*, p. 264.
4. Sandburg, *The Living Words of Abraham Lincoln*, p. 34.
5. *Ibid.*, p. 21-22.

Chapter XV

1. Lockridge, *A. Lincoln*, p. 290.
2. *Ibid.*
3. Carpenter, *Six Months at the White House*, p. 188, 89.
4. Nicolay and Hay, *Completed Works*.
5. Basler, *Collected Works of Abraham Lincoln*, Vol. VII, p. 350.
6. Henry J. Clyde, *The Making of a Minister*.
7. Randall, *Lincoln the President*, p. 320.
8. Carpenter, *Six Months at the White House*.
9. *Ibid.*
10. Luthin, *The Real Abraham Lincoln*, p. 383-4.
11. Sandburg, *Abraham Lincoln*, p. 391.
12. Basler, *Collected Works of A. Lincoln*, Vol. VII, p. 151-53.
13. Sandburg, *A. Lincoln*, pg. 390.
14. Chittenden, *Recollections of President Lincoln and His administration*, p. 275-77.

Chapter XVI

1. Thomas, *A. Lincoln*, p. 426.
2. Sandburg, *Abraham Lincoln*, p. 513.
3. Basler, *Collected Works*, Vol. VIII, pg. 116-7.
4. Sandburg, *Abraham Lincoln*, p. 640.
5. Angle, *The Lincoln Reader*, p. 475.
6. Luthin, *The Real Abraham Lincoln*, p. 574.
7. Lewis, *Living Words of Abraham Lincoln*, p. 36.
8. Thomas, *Abraham Lincoln*, p. 501.
9. Angle, *The Lincoln Reader*, p. 498-501.
10. Thomas, *A. Lincoln*, p. 501.
11. Basler, Vol. VIII, p. 332-33.
12. Sandburg, *Abraham Lincoln*, p. 664.
13. Luthin, *The Real Abraham Lincoln*, p. 599.
14. Angle, *The Lincoln Reader*, p. 588 — as told by Admiral Porter.
15. *Ibid.*, p. 510.
16. Thomas, *Abraham Lincoln*, p. 511-512.
17. Angle, *The Lincoln Reader*, p. 513-15.
18. Plowden, *Lincoln and His America*, p. 318.
19. Stark, *A House Divided*, p. 58.
20. Thomas, *Abraham Lincoln*, p. 514.
21. *Ibid.*, p. 515.
22. Angle, *The Lincoln Reader*, p. 520.
23. *Ibid.*, p. 521.
24. *Ibid.*, p. 521-23.

Chapter XVII

1. Tarbell, *The Life of Lincoln*, Vol. 111, p. 27.
2. Luthin, *The Real Abraham Lincoln*, p. 630.
3. Booth raced away through the night, talked his way across the Anacostia bridge. At a given rendezvous was joined by David Herold, an accomplice. About daylight the next morning (Saturday), they reined up their horses in front of the home of a country physician named Dr. Samuel A. Mudd, who lived twenty miles southeast of Washington. Dr. Mudd set and splinted the fractured bone, and let Booth sleep until early Sunday morning, when he and Herold rode away into a nearby swamp. On a dark night later an agent for the Confederate Government helped them ferry or row across the Potomac into Virginia. They made their way to the Garrett farm near Port Royal, Virginia, where Booth gave his name as Boyd, saying he had been wounded in Lee's army near Richmond. Two nights later, while sleeping in a nearby tobacco barn, they were surrounded by Union soldiers. The barn was set on fire, Herold surrendered, Booth was shot, and died on the porch of the Garrett farm, 'ust before sunrise, eleven days after Lincoln had passed away.

Eight Conspirators who aided Booth were tried by the Federal Courts and sentenced. Four were to be executed by hanging — Mrs. Mary Surratt, George Atzerodt, David Herold, and Lewis Paine; and four were to serve federal prison terms — Samuel Arnold, Edmond Spangler, Michael O'laughlin, and Dr. Samuel Mudd.

The four were quickly executed, and the others sent to prison.

4. Sandburg, *Abraham Lincoln*, p. 727
5. *Ibid.*, p. 729-33.
   Mingled with the sorrow was a note of regret in some pastor's messages that "our lamented President fell in a theater . . . one of the last places to which a good man should go." Pastor Justin D. Fulton of Tremont Temple, Boston, added, "If ever any man had an excuse to attend a theater he had. The cares of office were heavy upon him, his brain reeled. His frame grew weak. . . He said, 'I love to be alone, and yet be with people. A hearty laugh relieves me; and I seem better able to bear my cross.' This was his excuse. Upon it we will not pronounce judgment. This we will say: we are all sorry our best loved died there."
6. Angle, *The Lincoln Reader*, p. 534.
7. *The Washington Chronicle*, April 20, 1865. Quoted by Searcher.
   The Farewell To Lincoln, p. 76, 77.

Chapter XVIII

1. Kunhardt, *Twenty Days*, p. 131.
2. Tarbell, *Abraham Lincoln*, Vol. III, p. 49.
   Luthin, *The Real Abraham Lincoln* 668.
3. Kunhardt, *Twenty Days*, p. 141.
4. Searcher, *The Farewell To Lincoln*, p. 120.
5. Searcher, *Ibid.*, p. 127.
6. Kunhardt, *Twenty Days*, p. 143, 144.
7. Searcher, *The Farewell To Lincoln*, p. 237-38.
8. Tarbell, *Abraham Lincoln*, Vol. III, p. 55.
9. Kundardt, *Twenty Days*, p. 240.
10. Searcher, *The Farewell To Lincoln*, p. 243.
11. Searcher, *Ibid.*, p. 244-45.

Chapter XIX

1. Kunhardt, *Twenty Days*, p. 284.
2. Searcher, *The Farewell To Lincoln*, p. 245-46.
3. Kunhardt, p. 286-87.
4. Sandburg, *Abraham Lincoln*, p. 742.
5. Searcher, *The Farewell To Lincoln*, p. 247-48.

BIBLIOGRAPHY

Angle, Paul M. *The Lincoln Reader.* Rand McNally & Co., N.Y., 1964.

Banks, Louis Albert. *Capital Stories About Famous Americans.* Christian Herald. N.Y., 1905.

Basler, Roy P. *The Collected Works of Abraham Lincoln.* 8 vols. & index. Rutgers University Press. New Brunswick, N.J. 1953.

Beardslee, C.S. *Abraham Lincoln's Cardinal Traits.* Goreham Press, Boston. 1914.

Beveridge, Albert J. *Abraham Lincoln.* 2 vols. Houghton Mifflin Co. Boston. 1928.

Boreham. F.W. *A Temple of Topaz.* Judson Press. Philadelphia. 1928.

Brogan, D.W. *Abraham Lincoln.* Schocken Books. New York. 1963.

Carnegie, Dale. *Lincoln The Unknown.* Dale Carnegie & Associates, Inc. Garden City, N.Y. 1959.

Carpenter, F.B. *Six Months at the White House.* Hurd & Houghton. N.Y. 1866.

Charnwood, Lord. *Abraham Lincoln.* Henry Holt & Co., N.Y., 1917.

Chittenden, L.E. *Recollections of President Lincoln And His Administration.* Harper & Bros. Pub. New York. 1891.

Cody, Sherwin. *An Evening with Lincoln.* Sherwin Cody School of English. Rochester, New York. 1927.

Depew, Chauncey M. *The Library of Oratory.* Vol. 15. The New Werner Company, Akron, Ohio. 1902.

Draper, Andrew Sloan. *What Makes Lincoln Great.* The Torch Press. Cedar Rapids, Iowa. 1940.

Duncan, Kunigunde & Nichols, D.G. *Mentor Graham, The Man Who Taught Lincoln.* University of Chicago Press. Chicago. 1944.

Hayman, Leroy. *The Death of Lincoln.* Scholastic Book Svcs. N.Y., 1968.

Hill, John Wesley. *Abraham Lincoln—Man of God.* G.P. Putnam's. N.Y. 1922.

Hubbard, Elbert. *Abe Lincoln & Nancy Hanks.* The Roycrofters. East Aurora, Erie County. N.Y. 1920.

Kempf, Edward J. *Abraham Lincoln's Philosophy of Common Sense; an Analytical Biography of a Great Mind.* Special Publications of the New York Academy of Sciences. N.Y. Vol. 6. 1965.

Kunhardt, Dorothy Meserve & Philip B. Jr. *Twenty Days.* Harper & Row. N.Y. 1965.

Lang, H. Jack. *The Wit & Wisdom of Abraham Lincoln.* World Pub. Co. Cleveland, Ohio. 1941.

Lewis, Edward & Bleck, Jack. *The Living Words of Abraham Lincoln.* Hallmark Cards, Inc. 1967.

Lincoln, Abraham. *Lincoln's Devotional.* Channel Press Inc., Great Neck N.Y. 1957.

Lockridge, Ross F. *A. Lincoln.* World Book Co. N.Y. 1930.

Lorant, Stefan. *The Life of Abraham Lincoln*. New American Library. N.Y. 1954.

Luthin, Reinhard H. *The Real Abraham Lincoln*. Prentice-Hall Inc., N.J. 1960.

Miers, Earl Schench. *Abraham Lincoln in Peace & War*. American Heritage Pub. Co. Inc., New York. 1964.

Miller, Walter. *The Standard American Encyclopedia*. Vol. 8, Standard American Corp. Chicago. 1937.

Newman, Ralph G. *Lincoln For The Ages*. Doubleday & Co., Inc., Garden City, N.Y. 1960.

Nolan, Jeanette Covert. *Abraham Lincoln*. Julian Messner Inc., N.Y. 1953.

Plowden, David. *Lincoln & His America—1809-1865*. Viking Press. N.Y. 1970.

Randall, J.G. & Current, Richard N. *Lincoln The President; Last Full Measure*. Dodd, Mead & Co., N.Y. 1955.

Rankin, Henry B. *Personal Recollections of Abraham Lincoln*. N.Y. 1916.

Sandburg, Carl. *Abraham Lincoln—The Prairie Years & The War Years*. Harcourt, Brace & World, Inc., New York. 1954.

Searcher, Victor. *The Farewell to Lincoln*. Abingdon Press. Nashville. 1965.

Stackpole, Edward K. *Chancellorsville: Lee's Greatest Battle*. Stackpole Co., Harrisburg Pa. 1958.

Stark, David & Seymour, Peter. *A House Divided*. Hallmark Cards. Kansas City, Missouri. 1968.

Stephenson, Mathaniel Wright. *Lincoln*. Bobbs-Merrill Co. Indianapolis. 1922.

Stern, Philip Van Doren. *The Life & Writings of Abraham Lincoln*. Random House, Inc. New York. 1940.

Sumner, G. Lynn. *Abraham Lincoln—As A Man Among Men*. Harper Bros. Pub. N.Y. 1922.

Tarbell, Ida M. *In the Footsteps of the Lincolns*. Harper Bros. N.Y. 1924.

_____*The Life of Abraham Lincoln*. in four vols. Lincoln Historical Society. New York. 1897.

_____ *The Life of Abraham Lincoln*. in two vols. Lincoln Memorial Association. New York. 1900.

_____ *The Life of Abraham Lincoln*, in two vols. McClure Phillips & Co. New York. 1900.

Thomas, Benjamin P. *Abraham Lincoln*. Alfred A. Knopf. New York. 1952.

_____ Lincoln's New Salem. The Abraham Lincoln Association, Springfield, Illinois. 1934.

Thompson, D.D. *Abraham Lincoln, the First American.* Jennings & Pye. Cincinnati, 1894.

Trueblood, Elton. *Abraham Lincoln — Theologian of American Anguish.* Harper & Row Pub. New York. 1973.

Van Doren, Carl. *The Literary Works of Abraham Lincoln.* The Press of the Readers Club. New York. 1942.

Warren, Louis A. *Lincoln's Youth, Indiana Years Seven to Twenty-One, 1816-1830.* Appleton-Century-Crofts, Inc. New York. 1959.

Whitney, Henry Clay. *Life on the Circuit with Lincoln.* Caxton Printers Ltd. Caldwell, Idaho. 1940.

Wolf, William J. *The Almost Chosen People.* (A Study of the Religion of Abraham Lincoln.) Doubleday & Co., Inc., Garden City, New York, 1959.